SPANISH POETRY SINCE 1939

By

CHARLES DAVID LEY
Professor and Lecturer

THE CATHOLIC UNIVERSITY OF AMERICA PRESS
WASHINGTON 17, D. C.
1 9 6 2

With deep gratitude is this volume

dedicated to

PROFESSOR E. M. WILSON

CONTENTS

Introduction

Twentieth-century poetry can be distinguished from that of earlier ages because it habitually associates images in new ways. Adjectives previously only applied to sounds may be used about objects of sight, for instance, or a spiritual struggle may be described in terms of feeling or taste. Or again, words or phrases apparently quite irrelevant to the matter in hand may be introduced because the poet sees a personal and probably irrational likeness between two disparate things.

The first of these two new poetic expedients—the mixture of different sense-impressions to complement and, as it were, explain one another—was used by Baudelaire in the middle of the last century, and described by him as *Correspondances*. Towards the end of the nineteenth century, several other French poets had imitated him, but the device only became general in the literature of countries other than France in the present century.

Baudelaire is one of the first poets who makes us conscious that he lives in a large town, Paris. He often finds his city grey and ugly and contrasts it with tropical lands he visited in youth, yet Paris is as essential a part of his artistic material as it is to the novelist Balzac. Possibly a poet living in the country would not have turned to *Correspondances*. In any case, the civilization of the twentieth century, being increasingly more urban and mechanized, has, just for that reason, found that sense-impressions merge into each other easily. A poet living in the country might feel this less acutely.

The second expedient—introducing what appear to be irrelevances —quite possibly developed out of the first. It is bound up with what is an almost exclusively twentieth-century characteristic—the claim of authors and artists to use a purely personal imagery and oblige the reader to follow them. This is part of the crisis in the individual sensibility which has taken place in this century. In previous centuries even obscure or rebellious writers drew on the same sources as plainer or more traditional ones. Anyone trained in Latin poetry

ix

and prepared to read very slowly can follow what Góngora says, however intricate his syntax may become. A Catholic theologian can follow everything Milton or Blake says, however heterodox it may be. And this would be true even if a fragment of their poetry was chosen for examination on its own.

With many twentieth-century writers, however, our only chance of achieving even a partial understanding of what they say is to study the whole of the poet's work and to accustom ourselves to the eccentric workings of his mind. Representative writers like Valéry and Eliot have attended lectures in which the lecturer has interpreted their work in a new light. The poets admitted the right of the critic to see a meaning in their poetry of which they themselves were not previously aware. Those who wish to read James Joyce or Ezra Pound are recommended to use commentaries by writers who have studied them exhaustively, or they may well find many pages of these authors quite impossible to understand. While these are extreme cases, the authors mentioned have also a great international reputation as representative figures.

The breakdown of classical Greek and Latin education in favor of a more scientific training is, no doubt, partly responsible. Classical mythology has lost the appeal it had for so many centuries. More serious still is the decline of Christian religious imagery. Even the greatest religious poets of the age mingle their personal imagery closely with their theology.

All this is to explain the presence of what we are going to call "allusive" imagery in modern poetry. Thus we find Dame Edith Sitwell, explaining her own poetry in this way: "By 'decoy-duck dust' I mean very thick dust. A duck's quacking is, to me, one of the driest of sounds, and it has a peculiar deadness."[1] Incidentally, Dame Edith's sentence shows us how *correspondances* can easily have led up to and been the cause of "allusive" images.

The increasing use of machines in daily life everywhere, as this century progresses, does not seem to have had such an obvious effect on poetry as might have been expected. Possibly the decline of traditional verse-forms may have corresponded to the more hectic, less tidy rhythm of modern life, with the noise of motors instead of horses' hooves as the background of our lives. Nevertheless, few poets have written either entirely in free verse or entirely in traditional forms; the latter are still often used.

Technical inventions may, therefore, have affected poetry relatively little. But another branch of science has had more disturbing effects. This is psychology, with its special branch known as psychoanalysis, above all of the Freudian variety. This effect has little to do with the validity or mistakenness of Freud's conclusions or the practice of his followers. What is important is the suggestive appeal his theory of the unconscious and of sleeping and waking dreams has had for a number of writers and artists in the present century. Because of psychoanalysis, dreams have assumed an importance which perhaps they never had before. Thus some people have come to consider sleeping thoughts better than waking thoughts because they reveal something deeper and more important. The conscious mind seeks to hide even to itself what the wiser unconscious mind knows. This is the theory which was responsible for the Surrealist movement, in France and elsewhere.

The Surrealists held that the more directly writers put down what came into their mind, without directing or correcting the flow of images, the more genuine the result would be. Art would become the naked expression of what a man was. If the taking of drugs aided this spontaneity in an artist, it was to be recommended. Moral licentiousness would also help him to be a truer artist.

This extreme form of Surrealism was only practiced by a small group in France, but many poets all over the world felt encouraged to introduce their dream-world into their writing as a result of these theories. Accordingly, their imagery became still more personal and therefore difficult for others to follow. This kind of dream-writing has perhaps been rarer in Spain than in most other countries, but even there it has been practiced by some writers. They did not, however, become drug-addicts in order to help their writing, nor did they practice what is called "automatic writing," putting down the first thing that came into their head, as bona fide Surrealists are supposed to do.

These are some of the general features of twentieth-century poetry. They all apply fully to Spanish poetry. Yet, in many ways, that poetry has developed differently from poetry in other countries. The beginning of the century saw the arrival in Spain of a movement known as *modernismo*. The first *modernistas* were three Spanish-American poets strongly influenced by French poetry. These were the Mexican Manuel Gutiérrez Nájera (1859-1895),[2] the Colombian José Asunción Silva (1865-1896) and the Cuban Julián del Casal (1863-1893). Greater than these was the Nicaraguan Rubén Darío, whose best work comes after them in time. Perhaps no writer in Spanish has ever had a stronger musical sense, which by itself sets his works above comparison with his predecessors. Still, his constant debt to nineteenth-century French poetry is obvious from frequent references to this literature in his poems. He lived in Spain from 1898 to 1900 and visited it several times after that. His personal contact with Spanish writers was significant to them, apart from his being the most powerful and vital poet of his generation in the Spanish language. Without Darío, there might have been no *modernista* movement in Spain. As it was, the movement was an important one, with Manuel Machado, Francisco Villaespesa (1877-1935) and the early Juan Ramón Jiménez as three of its principal figures.

The poetry of the *modernistas* is very different from that of the present day. In it remains something of the late Romanticism of the end of the last century. It is eloquent and rhetorical and loves to manipulate verse-forms which it is a triumph to use well in Spanish, such as rhyming alexandrines. It delights to picture the exotic, either in history or scenery. It represents a reaction from the poetry of an older generation, the prophetic thunderings of Gaspar Núñez de Arce (1834-1903), the lively legendary narratives of José Zorrilla (1817-1893), the high-sounding praise of country life and the peasantry in Gabriel y Galán (1870-1905), or even the simple, direct, realistic, almost homely poetry of Ramón de Campoamor (1817-1901).

The mature work of Antonio Machado and Juan Ramón Jiménez brings us far closer to contemporary Spanish poetry. We therefore begin with a reference to their work, though it comes before the end of the Spanish Civil War in 1939, which is our true starting-point. We have also had to deal briefly with some of the exiled poets, because they too are an essential part of modern Spanish poetry. Yet this is all in the first chapter. After that, all the poets discussed have lived in Spain and written in Spanish (not in other Iberian languages) since 1939.

A period of more than twenty years is covered, since some of the poems commented on were published as early as 1939 itself and some as late as 1961. Nevertheless, owing to the enormous number of writers who have published poetry—of some value—in present-day Spain, the account obviously cannot be exhaustive. We are not attempting to write an encyclopedia, but a selective account of the course of Spanish poetry in these years. We have taken a few of the most representative poets to show what their work stands for. Much similar, and often equally good, poetry has been written by others. A poet's not receiving a special mention does not imply criticism.

The poets chosen for examination are treated in a number of ways, according to the poetic tendency they represent. Some require a more biographical approach than others, others call for the quotation of critical comments on their work, others excite comparison with poets like themselves outside Spain. What really concerns us is not the individual poet himself but the whole current of Spanish poetry of which he forms part.

It may be as well to prepare the reader by some general account of that current. Immediately after the Civil War, the favorite models for young writers were the Spanish poets of the 16th and 17th centuries rather than their 20th-century predecessors. Many of the latter had been on the other side in the conflict and had gone into exile. Never since the Renaissance had so many sonnets been written in one country in one epoch. This revival of the poetical example of Spain's "Golden Age" (1500-1650, approximately) was known in Spain as "Neoclassicism." The term was used so frequently and so insistently that it is impossible to avoid it here, even at the risk of confusion with the quite different Neoclassical movement in European poetry of the late 17th and the 18th centuries.

Naturally a reaction came to this "Neoclassicism." As time went on—and up to the present day—Spanish poetry has tended to fall into one of two groups. The first was a poetry of the inner life, inspired by Catholic values, though often not devotional. The second was what Spaniards call "social" poetry, which means that the writer implies criticism of the society he lives in. He writes, in fact, from a left-wing or even Marxist point of view. The example of the South American poets César Vallejo (1895-1938) and Pablo Neruda, both of them of the extreme Left, encouraged Spaniards to imitate them. The stability of the government in Spain and the unlikeliness of a revolt probably helped to make revolutionary verses popular.

Taken as a whole, the modern poetry of Spain has great vitality

xiii

and range, not to speak of volume of output. Justice has hardly been done to it in other countries. Some translations, mostly of the "social" poets, have appeared in France. Mr. J. M. Cohen has written several articles about it, in the *Times Literary Supplement* and other periodicals. The poet he seems to prefer is Blas de Otero, and many Spaniards would agree with him, but there is no real reason for specially admiring that poet rather than others.

When Gerardo Diego published an anthology of contemporary Spanish poets in 1932, the poets included were all asked to give their opinions about poetry. We thought it would make the present book more direct and personal if we asked the poets chosen for special comment in the first eight chapters to reply to a questionnaire. Their answers are to be found in Chapter 11. An occasional reference to the opinions expressed there will be found in earlier chapters. The poets who had already given their views in Diego's anthology were not included in our questionnaire. Of the remaining poets approached, only one preferred not to reply.

This introduction is closed with a shortened version of a lecture given at the Instituto de España, London, in November, 1959. It may serve to explain why we set out to write this book, and how it is a result of direct contact with Spanish literary life.

"I read Spanish at Cambridge. . . . In the summer of 1934 at Santander I went to see some interesting productions of old Spanish plays by what I understood was a student company. It was called La Barraca. . . . One of the works performed was *Los hijos de Alvargonzález,* a narrative poem by Antonio Machado. It was performed in mime, with a voice reading the words behind the scenes. I regret to say that I described that voice in my diary as monotonous and droning. Later I learned that it was García Lorca who had read the lines. . . .

"In 1938, I was the first person to translate a play of Lorca's into English, *Mariana Pineda,* which was performed at the Barn Theatre, Sheer. The 17-year-old Peter Ustinov had the fundamental part of the villain Pedrosa, prowling about the stage like a tiger and making full use of the sinister shadows thrown by the spotlights. . . .

"After I had lived in Portugal for six years, the British Council transferred me from Lisbon to Madrid in 1943. The scholarly poet Don Dámaso Alonso was one of the people I was privileged to meet constantly. He was very much occupied at that time with preparing his two books of poems, *Oscura noticia* and *Hijos de la ira,* for publication. He would recite them frequently, over a glass of wine in a tavern. . . . When he recited, all were silent, deeply impressed. Later those very poems were the ones that were to have the most widespread effect in Spain of any written in those years. . . .

"I busily enquired about new names and I learned that I certainly ought to visit the Gran Café de Gijón. There a group called the Juventud Creadora used to meet, especially on Saturday nights. . . . The center of the group was José García Nieto, the editor of *Garcilaso,* the review in which all the young poets wrote at that time. . . . There could have been no friendlier atmosphere than the one García Nieto created in that café. Before long I found myself trying my hand at writing verses in Spanish, some of which were printed in *Garcilaso* and other poetry reviews. . . .

"I had, in fact, reached Madrid right in the middle of the so-called 'Neoclassical' movement. Perhaps this movement would not have been so important, if it had not been for the compelling force of García Nieto, who drew the whole group round himself. He was to say, much later, in a broadcast: 'La Juventud Creadora era yo realmente.' (The Juventud Creadora was really I.)

"Other poets, living in the provinces, had their own poetry reviews. Some of them, such as Eugenio de Nora and Victoriano Crémer in León, Rafael Molina in Córdoba, and Gabriel Celaya in San Sebastián, would attack the Juventud Creadora. But when they visited Madrid, they always spent some time in the Gijón. . . . Yet it was at the Poetry Congresses of 1952, 1953, and 1954 that the Spanish poets met most coherently as a whole. What mattered was not what was said there, but the fact of being together. 'How fine it is to wander down medieval streets,' said Aleixandre in Segovia on the eve of the first Congress. Then Roy Campbell turned up. The Spanish poets had never seen anyone quite like him before. He talked all the time and always had a glass of wine at his elbow. . . .

"As to the actual poetry being written at the present time in Spain, it started with the advantage of having all the experiments behind it. The language and symbols had been sifted. There were no schools left. The poet had to stand or fall according to the excellence or weakness of his own poetry."

NOTES TO INTRODUCTION

1. *Selected Poems: Edith Sitwell* (London, 1952), p. xv.

2. The dates of a poet's birth and death are mentioned when he has not been given a special section in the following chapters. If he has, his dates will be given at the head of his section. In the case of a living poet, naturally only the date of birth is given.

1

Poets in Spain up to 1939

To compare the poetry written in Spain from 1939 onwards with that written before the Civil War is like observing the similarities of Restoration drama to the work of playwrights before the closing of the London theaters. The style of the one clearly derives from that of the other. There are of course important differences. In 1660 all the older dramatists except Shirley had died, whereas many of the older generation of Spanish poets are still alive and writing even today. The gulf of time was much greater in Restoration England and foreign influences were far more at work than in contemporary Spain. But, in both cases, we are conscious of a literary continuity after a major social and political upheaval. So that just as we could not adequately discuss Dryden, Wycherley, or Otway without referring to Shakespeare, Jonson, Massinger, and others, so we need to know something of Juan Ramón Jiménez, Machado, Lorca, Alberti, and Jorge Guillén before we can properly understand the poets writing in Spain at present. The aim, therefore, of this present chapter is to say something of certain twentieth-century Spanish poets now dead or in exile before discussing the work of their successors after 1939.

Spanish critics and literary historians speak of the appearance of a new poetic style at the beginning of the twentieth century which they call *modernismo*. The French Symbolists were a powerful influence on it. The *modernistas* found the poetry of such poets as Campoamor, Núñez de Arce, and Gabriel y Galán too didactic and grandiloquent; and they were fortunate enough to possess a greater poet than their predecessors and rivals—the Nicaraguan, Rubén Darío.

Rubén Darío (1867-1916)

Emmy Neddermann writes:

> Da die *Prosas Profanas* in erster Linie ihr Entstehen literarischen Erlebnissen Daríos zu danken hatten, so fanden die spanischen

1

Dichter eine Unzahl von Anregungen darin, die sie hauptsächlich
auf die moderne französiche Dichtung hinwies.[1]

Though the *Prosas Profanas* owed their existence to the literary
experiences of Darío, nevertheless the Spanish poets found an
immense number of suggestions in them which drew their attention above all to French literature.

Darío's greatest debt was to Verlaine, the "padre y nuestro mágico"
(father and our magician). Verlaine's "Art poétique" insists on "la
musique avant toute chose" (music before everything). Darío cultivated a greater variety of meters than any of the nineteenth-century
Spanish poets,[2] or than even Verlaine himself. The English poet who
is nearest Darío in this respect is Swinburne, though he has not
Darío's variety of subject-matter.

Darío said that in Spain, "la juventud vibrante me siguió"[3] (the
young who were most alive became my followers). Before his time
we find the languors of late Romanticism or the novel-like narrative
verse of Campoamor's "El tren expreso." After him there came the
Machados and Juan Ramón Jiménez—younger *modernistas*—who
were even more different from Spanish poets before 1900 than Darío
was.

The literature of France and other countries sometimes supplied
Darío with themes:

> Shakespeare va por la floresta,
> Heine hace un *lied* de la tarde . . .
> Hugo acompasa la fiesta
> Chez Thérèse. Verlaine arde[4]

> Shakespeare wanders through the forest;
> Heine writes *lieder* to evening . . .
> Hugo beats time to the fiesta
> Chez Thérèse. Verlaine is ardent

But he assimilated these authors well, especially Verlaine. He
could write that complicated but beautiful line "Que púberes cané-
foras te ofrenden el acanto" (May canephorous pubescents offer you
the acanthus), or one of a great and almost tragic simplicity, such
as "Francisca Sánchez, acompáñame" (Come with me, Francisca
Sánchez). After two hundred years during which Spain had produced less fine poetry than any other of the larger European countries, he supplied by himself alone much of what had been lacking

from Romanticism onwards. Thus, though he himself was typical of the nineteenth century, he prepared the ground for the poets of the twentieth century, all of whom admire him as a master.

Antonio Machado (1875-1939)

"It is a question," writes Thomas Hardy in *The Return of the Native,* "if the exclusive reign of . . . orthodox beauty" in natural scenery "is not approaching its last quarter. The new Vale of Tempe may be a gaunt waste in Thule: human souls may find themselves in closer and closer harmony with external things wearing a sombreness distasteful to our race when it was young." Was it not some such new austere taste in landscape which made Unamuno, Azorín, and Machado find great and unsuspected beauties in the countryside of Castile? For the Castilian plain appeared to them, as Egdon Heath had to Hardy, "a thing majestic without severity, impressive without showiness, emphatic in its admonitions, grand in its simplicity." Hardy, writing in 1878, had foreseen quite clearly a coming change in the sense of what was beautiful. The pessimism bred in Spain by the defeat of 1898 was by no means the only cause which made Spanish writers view the external world and their own emotions with a solemn sobriety unknown to their predecessors.

Darío had renewed the technical possibilities of expression in Spanish poetry. It was left to Unamuno and Machado and others to apply the poetical instrument thus perfected to the expression of later values that came in with the new age. One of the great prose classics of the present century is called *À la recherche du temps perdu.* Proust "finds" time by fixing his recollections of the past in the more lasting mold of literature. By the same means Unamuno sought to perpetuate his love of Salamanca or his emotion on visiting Madrigal de las Altas Torres. The poetry of Antonio Machado, according to Julián Marías, also shows an "esencial temporalidad . . . que la impregnó desde el principio" (essential feeling of the temporal . . . which imbued it from the first).

> Ni mármol duro y eterno,
> ni música ni pintura,
> sino palabra en el tiempo.[5]

> Not the hard eternal marble,
> Nor music, nor painting either,
> But a word existing in time.

Machado's sense of time is something more than Wordsworth's "emotion recollected in tranquillity" when he writes:

> Mi corazón está donde ha nacido,
> no a la vida, al amor, cerca del Duero . . .
> ¡ El muro blanco y el ciprés erguido! . . .[6]

> My heart is in the place where it was born,
> Not to life but to love, beside the Duero . . .
> The white wall with the cypresses above it.

Time and place guard within themselves the poignancy of his loss. The past lives again in the poem. In another sonnet, Machado's father, who had died young, looks compassionately at the grey hairs of his son now grown old. Time is recaptured by the poem.

Another feature of Machado's poetry, pointed out by Bousoño, is his manner of implying his own state of mind by the words he chooses in order to depict an outward scene. When he is apparently speaking of a village square, we read "negro," "cipresal," "humean," and "muertas," and are given an impression of a melancholy which is not actually referred to. Similarly, in writing of Soria he makes it live geographically:

> . . .¡ Campos de Soria
> donde parece que las rocas sueñan,
> conmigo vais! ¡ Colinas plateadas,
> grises alcores, cárdenas roquedas!

> He vuelto a ver los álamos dorados,
> álamos del camino en la ribera
> del Duero, entre San Polo y San Saturio,
> tras las murallas viejas
> de Soria—barbacana
> hacia Aragón, en castellana tierra—.
> Estos chopos del río que acompañan
> con el sonido de sus hojas secas
> el son del agua cuando el viento sopla,[7]

> You fields of Soria
> In which the very stones seem to be dreaming,
> You go where I go, hills marked out in silver,
> Grey rocky summits and discolored boulders.

> Now I have once more seen abeles all golden,
> Abeles along the path beside the River
> Duero, between San Polo and San Saturio,
> Beyond the ancient ramparts

Of Soria, that barbican
On the earth of Castile out against Aragon.
Those poplars by the river which accompany
The murmur of the water when the wind blows,
Because their dry leaves rustle when it passes,

In this passage things are regarded as people and the historical past lives in the present. Rocks appear to be dreaming; the poplar leaves play an accompaniment to the sound of the river. Though a military incursion from Aragon would have been possible only in a very remote past, Machado thinks of Soria as still preserving all the spiritual and poetical values of Castile against the different world of Aragon to the east.

In such ways as this, Machado is a *modernista*. The line backwards is clear, through Darío and the Symbolists to Baudelaire's "Correspondances":

La Nature est un temple où de vivants piliers
Laissent parfois sortir de confuses paroles;
L'homme y passe à travers des forêts de symboles
Qui l'observent avec des regards familiers.[8]

Nature is like a church where living pillars
Sometimes let muffled sounds come out of them;
Man passes down it through a wood of symbols
Which watch him with a glance that sees inside him.

Juan Ramón Jiménez (1881-1958)
(Nobel Prize, 1956)

Juan Ramón Jiménez, who was awarded the Nobel Prize in 1956, began as a *modernista*. Rubén Darío and Valle-Inclán personally suggested the titles to him for his first two books of poetry, and Villaespesa was one of his greatest friends. He, too, wished to give permanence to what he saw and felt to be beautiful. He wrote of the Parque del Oeste in Madrid:

Me paro una y otra vez, ¿cómo irme, cómo dejar sola esta radiante belleza, que si yo no veo no ve nadie, que no se ve?[9]

I keep stopping. How can I go and leave this bright loveliness to itself? For if I do not see it, no one sees it, it is not seen.

The transmission of this "beauty" seemed to Jiménez a form of religion:

lo poético lo considero como profundamente relijioso, esa relijión inmanente sin credo absoluto que yo siempre he profesado.[10]

I consider what is poetic to be deeply religious with that imma-
nent religion which has no absolute creed and which I have always
professed.

And he was one of those poets who believe that their past poetry
always can be improved. In his old age he was still polishing the
poems he wrote as a young man, altering words which now sounded
pedantic to him.[11]

Gerardo Diego says of him:

> Para él la poesía es la esencia misma del espíritu y de la inteli-
> gencia . . . Si otros poetas quieren practicar una poesía humana,
> Juan Ramón Jiménez parece obstinarse en invocar una humani-
> dad, un universo todo poético, que si realmente existen es sólo
> para que él los sueñe en sus poesías. Y él sueña para que los
> otros despierten y los contemplen.[12]

> For him poetry is the very essence of the spirit and the intelli-
> gence. . . . While other poets wish to create a human poetry,
> Juan Ramón Jiménez seems to persist in evoking a purely
> poetical humanity and world which, if they really exist, only
> do so in order that he may dream about them in his poetry. And
> he dreams so that others may awake and view them.

That is the reason why he dedicated his selected poems "A la inmensa
minoría (To the vast minority) and why his finest love-poem is
written to the spirit of poetry whom he hates in splendid garments
but loves in unadorned nakedness.

Thus he seeks for aesthetic perfection which expresses what is
best for him in human experience: "¡No le toques ya más, / que así
es la rosa!"[13] (You must touch it no more, / This is how the rose
is!) Society and religion, as usually understood, are not his concern
in his poetry. In this respect, he became the grandfather of the post-
Civil War "Neoclassical" Movement, which we shall study in a later
chapter.

One of his main differences from Rubén Darío is that he uses only
a limited number of fairly simple poetical forms. The sonnet undoubtedly suits him very well and the *Sonetos espirituales* is one of
his best and most characteristic books.

His aesthetic ideas were at one with his age. A Spanish edition
of Croce's book on aesthetics was published with a preface by Unamuno.[14] Ortega y Gasset wrote his *Deshumanización del arte*,[15] a
book which maintains that the "human interest" in a work of art

or literature is impure and that artists of contemporary schools, such as the Cubists, show their excellence by concentrating on the technical representation of the forms of things in preference to speaking to the emotions. Meanwhile the Abbé Bremond in France said that the purest poetry did not depend on its associations but on creating a receptive state of appreciation in some ways comparable to that attained to by the true practice of prayer in religious life.[16] Though Jiménez could not be likened to a Cubist painter and was not a "pure" poet either, he had resemblances to both. He regarded poetry as an end, not as a means. He believed in poetic expression for itself, not for its relation to the emotion it sought to express.

Jorge Guillén (1893-   )

After the Machados and Juan Ramón Jiménez, there came a group of younger poets of what is known as the *generación de la Dictadura.* The title indicates that these writers began publishing during the Dictatorship of General Primo de Rivera. However, it was actually at the beginning of the Republican period, in 1932, that Gerardo Diego's *Poesía española antología*[17] gave what might almost be called artistic coherence to the group. The aestheticism of Juan Ramón Jiménez, his cult of the *inmensa minoría* seems to have had a more immediate influence on these poets than the example of Antonio Machado. The effect of Machado was slower and, in the end, probably deeper. It becomes quite apparent only in poetry written some time after 1939 by an even later generation.

We can find something of Jiménez in Guillén's belief in a "poesía bastante pura, ma non troppo"[18] (poetry quite pure, but not too pure) and even in the use of certain "popular" themes by Lorca and Alberti, precedents for which can be found in some of the poetry of Jiménez.[19] At the same time, the poetry of Cernuda, Altolaguirre, Alberti in *Sobre los ángeles,* Lorca in *Poeta en Nueva York,* and Gerardo Diego and Larrea in their *creacionista* work has some relation to Surrealism. Certainly some of them are attempting to draw on their unconscious for part of their imagery, though it might be very difficult to say which part. Jorge Guillén, on the other hand, is a particularly conscious poet.

Jorge Guillén has published four editions of his *Cántico,* in 1928, 1936, 1945, and 1950, to each of which he has added more poems. The special qualities of Guillén's poetical style give these books unity. He uses the present tense with great frequency and is even fond of exclamations without verbs. This is all part of his desire to express that plenitude which he says, in his dedication to Salinas, the latter poet also eagerly seeks. In expressing plenitude he seldom even refers to emotions or incidents connected with any kind of sadness or tragedy. Even on the very rare occasions when he does write of death, he views it with great poetical serenity, as Professor E. M. Wilson has shown in comparing "Muerte a lo lejos" with Quevedo's much sadder sonnet, "Avisos de la muerte."[20] He heads it with a serene quotation from his friend and (in certain things) master, the pure poet Valéry: "Je soutenais l'éclat de la mort toute pure." (I had to endure the flash of death at its utmost.) And when he writes a four-line poem on the death of García Lorca, he does not lament but speaks of the peace of death amidst the confusions of war.

But why does Guillén so often use the present tense? Certainly Valéry uses it even more consistently, and his example may have been important to Guillén, but that is only a subsidiary reason. Surely the true reason is that he wishes to perpetuate the singleness of various moments of time in the artistic form of poetry, to do, in fact, something similar to what Proust does in prose. Thus Guillén's plenitude might be called a "fullness of time." His joy is that of the artist who has found his true means of expression, and what he communicates to the reader is really his own feeling of creativeness. Hence the absence of those emotions objectively expressed which are the subject of most of the lyric poetry of the past.

The technical devices Guillén uses all aim at the same effect of expressing plenitude. Dámaso Alonso points out how his frequent *enjambements* in short-lined poems contribute to this end.[21] Guillén also wishes to avoid any easily-recognizable literary references to passages in other poets. That is one of the reasons why he often avoids words which belong to poetry rather than to prose or formal speech. Yet he is not colloquial either, but has built up his own literary vocabulary. Words like *raudo* (precipitant) and *alud* (avalanche) are not common in ordinary Spanish usage; but Guillén repeats them because they fit well into his personal word patterns.

Guillén uses metaphors sparingly and *para ojos mentales* (for mental eyes). He is much further along the road coming from Baudelaire's "Correspondances" through the Symbolists than are either Antonio Machado or Juan Ramón Jiménez.

"Todo, en el aire, es pájaro"[22] (All in the air is bird), writes Guillén, meaning not that the air is completely full of birds, but that the whole air of the countryside, where he can hear birds singing, fills him with joy. A swan is described as a "tenor de la blancura" (tenor of whiteness), meaning that its whiteness is like a beautiful aria sung by a fine tenor and thus referring obliquely to the legend that the swan when dying is possessed of a marvellous gift of song. "Les parfums, les couleurs et les sons se répondent" (Scents, colors and sounds reply to each other), as Baudelaire said. And all this helps to convey the central idea of fullness.

Guillén's most recently published work forms part of a second book, which will be called *Clamor,* still in process of composition. He still uses the present tense. As if *Cántico* had been too lyrically removed from the present day world, he now brings in satire, humor, political protests. Included is a long attack on dictatorship, called "Potencia de Pérez," and also a poem on the Nazi concentration camps—and long prose poems in an ironical and prosaic style which recall several contemporary French poets. Clearly he now wishes to write a definitely impure poetry ("ma non troppo?") as a contrast to the style of his earlier book. The "clamor" referred to is usually the noise of the modern world, though in one of the poems it is the sum of the noises when rushing along in a motor-car. There is a long monologue by Lucifer. This style of poetry is so different from that of the Guillén of *Cántico* that we feel we should wait for the eventual publication of the whole book before commenting finally on it.[23]

The Góngora Revival

The Góngora Revival of 1927 showed the interest of the young Spanish poets at that time in the author of the *Soledades.* And in France, also, Paul Valéry put the line "En roscas de cristal serpiente breve" (Brief serpent in spirals of crystal) at the head of one of his books.[24] In that line there is clearly not the same voluntary mixture of impressions received by two different senses and the idea they suggest, as there is in Guillén's "tenor de la blancura." Yet Góngora has the same intellectual delight in finding aptness in what at first sight seems disparate. The Spanish poets of the Dictatorship sought in Góngora what their English contemporaries sought in Donne: "heterogeneous images . . . yoked by violence together." There is, of course, an interesting difference between England and Spain here. Donne's imagery often bears witness to his interest in science; Góngora's is drawn from ancient pastoral mythology or from aristocratic splendor; Donne speaks of "stiff twin compasses" and Góngora of "roscas de cristal"; Donne's imagery is complex; Góngora's language is involved. But a detailed comparison might show that the same desire for a new kind of expression impelled them both.

Federico García Lorca (1898-1936)

When a group of poets wishes to write in a manner different from its immediate literary forerunners, it turns to some poet or poets in the past whom it considers to have been unduly neglected. In 1927 and after, not only Góngora but the poets of the late Middle Ages were read with a new interest by the Spanish poets. Dámaso Alonso collected a very fine anthology of these poets.[25] And Lorca, with his musical talent and his interest in stage productions of the classical dramatists, was extremely conversant with all that was best in what are called "popular" music and poetry. He helped Falla in his researches into the "folk" music of Andalusia. And just as Falla used the popular music in his compositions, so Lorca imitated the literary style of the folk-songs in his poetry. Both in his lifetime and afterwards, the *Romancero gitano*[26] has been by far the most popular of his books. The images in that book are by no means those generally used by poets before the 20th century. For instance: "Las piquetas de los gallos/ cavan buscando la aurora . . ."[27] (The pickaxes of the cockerels/ Dig down as they look for daybreak . . .) That is not an exact description of what happens in the early morning but a reminder of the association between cocks and dawn, avoiding the usual reference to their crowing. It is easier to understand than many of the images of Guillén.

It may seem surprising that a book strewn with passages of this sort should win public favor, until we remember that even Shakespeare, who has held the most varied theatrical audiences for centuries, is hardly an easy poet. Readers could overlook what they found obscure in a book that presented the Andalusian Gypsy lore with greater skill and power than ever before. Yet, even so, we must acknowledge that it is the simplest of the poems in the book that so many Spaniards, even the least cultured, know by heart—"La casada infiel."

Not only did Lorca draw on the folklore of the Andalusian gypsies and peasants; he also wrote nursery-rhyme poetry in somewhat the same style as the early Edith Sitwell in England: "El lagarto y la lagarta/ con delantaritos blancos."[28] (The he-lizard and she-lizard/ with their spotless little aprons.) But there is a note of sadness about such a poem that a child would hardly care for: "¡Ay cómo lloran y lloran,/ ¡ay!, ¡ay!, cómo están llorando!" (How they go on weeping and weeping./ Oh, oh, how they go on weeping!) He is a very impersonal poet, for he hardly ever refers to his own joys and sorrows or gives us his own direct impressions.

By the 1930's a new influence began to affect Spanish poetry—Surrealism. Though this French literary and artistic movement—deriving actually from Freud—was never completely acclimatized in Spain, a number of Spanish works would not have been written but for its example. Even in the twenties, Gerardo Diego and Larrea had composed *creacionista* poems (see Chapter 2) which had affinities with Surrealism. Lorca's residence in North America from 1929 to 1930 resulted in his writing his *Poeta en Nueva York*.[29] Though these poems were probably not written in the Surrealist manner—"automatic writing"—they were very largely in the Surrealist style. (And there is some flavoring of Surrealism in the allusive imagery of Guillén and Lorca of which we have been speaking.) Indeed it was only in these partially Surrealist works of Diego, Larrea, Lorca, Alberti, Cernuda, Neruda, and others that free verse began to be used to any appreciable extent in Spanish poetry. Later, other poets, not particularly akin to the Surrealists, were to write free verse; but it has not up to the present been so generally accepted as, for example, it has been in modern English poetry.

Rafael Alberti (1902-   )

Alberti's poetic development ran parallel to Lorca's for a time, though his (partially) "Surrealist" phase in *Sobre los ángeles* was followed by a period of political propaganda, unlike Lorca. Later still, at an age which Lorca never reached, Alberti returned to a poetry which was a maturer, more thoughtful form of his earlier style.

His early books, such as *Marinero en tierra*[30] can be set side by side with the early work of Lorca. There is even a similarity of imagery:

> Si no robé la aurora de los mares,
> si no la robé,
> ya la robaré.[31]

> If I have never stolen the sea's daybreak,
> If I have never stolen it,
> Still, I will steal it.

Yet, direct statement is very common as in the famous lines:

> Si Garcilaso volviera,
> yo sería su escudero;
> que buen caballero era.[32]

> If Garcilaso returned here,
> I'd carry his shield beside him.
> For he was a gallant gentleman.

Alberti is trying to find new modes of writing poetry just as consciously as Lorca. He is even more fully experimenting in adapting the past poetical styles of Spain to modern poetry, especially those of the *siglo de oro*. He was very successful with the sonnet, and when the Góngora Centenary came in 1927, he produced *Cal y canto*,[33] in which a style adapted from Góngora is used for such subjects as trams or the bullfight. As Salinas says:

> Los temas son, muchos de ellos, temas de la vida real moderna: estaciones, baños, ascensor, telegramas, aviación, "foot-ball," asoman por estas páginas. Pero todo ello sublimado al nivel de arriscada altivez poética, en donde el ideal gongorino quería colocar las realidades.[34]

> Many of his subjects are taken from everyday life: stations, baths, a lift, telegrams, aviation, and football make their appearance in these pages. But this is all heightened to that level of perilous poetical arrogance on which it was Góngora's ideal to place reality.

Alberti's next free-verse Surrealist phase was previous to Lorca's. We may even suspect that the example of *Sobre los ángeles*[35] may have contributed to the composition of *Poeta en Nueva York*. Alberti's book, however, is the less Surrealist of the two. It is built on a definite plan of interpreting each of several different states of mind by its tutelary angel, whereas Lorca's book is born of the confusion caused in his mind by a vast modern industrial city. *Sobre los ángeles* is Alberti's last deliberate experiment in style, though Sir Maurice Bowra sees in it the poet's spiritual despair at the loss of all his former values.[36] Alberti, shortly after publishing it, joined the Communist party and set out to use his art for political purposes. Poetically speaking, he returned to his early fondness for direct statement:

> Estáis,
> estáis de acuerdo,
> aunque a veces algunos de vosotros pretendáis ignorarlo.[37]

> You are,
> You are in agreement,
> Though sometimes some of you try not to know it.

But much of the imagery, though easy to understand, is in the style which we have found in Guillén, Lorca, and Alberti's own early poems:

> A "Niebla," mi perro

> "Niebla," tú no comprendes: lo cantan tus orejas,
> el tabaco inocente, tonto de tu mirada,
> los largos resplandores que por el monte dejas
> al saltar, rayo tierno de brizna despeinada.[38]

> To my Dog, "Niebla"

> "Niebla," it's all beyond you. But it sets your ears singing
> And the innocent, silly tobacco of your pupils,
> And the long, gleaming flashes when, in the open country,
> You spring like a tender ray of a wisp dishevelled.

The dog's ears sing. His eyes are of tobacco. He leaves gleams of light behind him. He is a flashing wisp. All these metaphors are clearly of the "Correspondances" variety.

Some of Alberti's poetry written in exile is still finer than what he wrote in Spain. But as it develops from his former styles there is no need to discuss it here. Few would deny that he is the best and most definite of the Spanish revolutionary poets. He has not the doubts as to his own genuineness and usefulness which assault later Spanish poets. And he does not make us feel he is perhaps writing to order, as Miguel Hernández (see Chapter 2) does in his Civil War poems, even though Hernández was perhaps as sincere in his Communism as Alberti.

Luis Cernuda (1904-   )

The earlier poems of Cernuda are sufficiently obscure for some of them to have been printed in the *Antología del surrealismo es-*

pañol.[39] But the passage of time has rendered him clearer than any of his contemporaries. The comparison of two excerpts will show this. The first is from *Los placeres prohibidos* (1931) :[40]

> Pero si la ira el ultraje el oprobio y la muerte
> ávidos dientes sin carne todavía
> amenazan abriendo sus torrentes
> de otro lado vosotros placeres prohibidos
> bronce de orgullo que nada precipita
> tendéis en una mano el misterio
> sabor que ninguna amargura corrompe
> cielos relampagueantes que aniquilan.[41]

> But if anger and outrage opprobrium death even
> Like greedy teeth which have no meat as yet
> Threaten by the unleashing of their torrents
> On the other side you forbidden pleasures
> Bronze of a pride which nothing can precipitate
> In one hand grasp at mystery
> The savor which no bitterness corrupts
> The heavens with their lightning which annihilates.

The lack of punctuation gives at first an impression of disorder, but the syntax of this long poetical sentence is really very strictly observed. The images certainly do not harmonize very satisfactorily. It is hardly clear why the teeth need flesh, why bronze should be thrown, or why pleasures should be skies. But the allusive quality is almost lacking, and the only shade of a *correspondance* is when a bitterness corrupts a taste. The "bronze" is merely a quality expressed by the metal in which statues are molded; Shakespeare uses "marble" in much the same way: "Not marble, nor the gilded monuments . . . ," Sonnet LV. So that hidden behind the façade of the lack of punctuation we find a poet more traditional, less in the Baudelaire-Symbolist line than any of his predecessors or contemporaries. And yet he is not entirely outside it either, since he can write, for instance: "Un día comprendió cómo sus brazos eran/ Solamente de nubes . . ."[42] (One day he realized that his arms were/ Only of clouds . . .)

Now here is an example of Cernuda's later style to contrast with his earlier one:

> Recuerdo bien el sur donde el olivo crece
> Junto al mar claro y el cortijo blanco,
> Mas hoy va mi recuerdo más arriba, a la sierra
> Gris bajo el cielo azul, cubierta de pinares,

Y allí encuentra regazo, alma con alma.
Mucho enseña el destierro de nuestra propia tierra.
¿Qué saben de ella quienes la gobiernan?
¿Quienes obtienen de ella
Fácil vivir con un social renombre?
De ella también somos los hijos
Oscuros. Como el mar, no mira
Que aguas son las que van perdidas a sus aguas,
Y el cuerpo, que es de tierra, clama por su tierra.[43]

I remember the South with the olive trees growing
By the clear ocean and the white farmhouses,
But today my remembrance goes higher, to the mountains,
Grey under the blue sky, covered with pine trees,
And finds itself a lap, spirit to spirit.
There is much to be learned in exile from our country.
For what do those who govern her know about her,
Receiving from her
An easy livelihood and social credit?
But we too have come from her, we, her obscurer
Children. Like the sea, she is careless
As to what waters mingle with her waters,
And the body, which is of earth, clamors for its earth.

There is an increased clarity of expression. The idea of the verse is complex, but the poet's mastery does not allow us at first to notice this. The memory seeks a refuge, soul to soul, amid the countryside of the Guadarrama. To know one's land one should be banished from it and not be in successful authority over it. The land is like the sea and receives all her sons, even obscure exiles. And the human earth of the exile's body feels the need of the parent earth of his land.

Thus we see that the complexity of the passage depends, not on the way it uses imagery or the eccentricity of its forms of expression, but on its half-mystical conceptions. Memory and the countryside are souls, and it is in this sense that the land receives its exiles, though they are absent.

Religious themes have become increasingly commoner in the poetry of Cernuda. His "Noche del hombre y su demonio,"[44] for example, is a dialogue between the poet and a being which he calls his demon but which may be another part of himself or God. Another of his themes is his solitude in contrast to the human need for love. So that, whereas Lorca is the most impersonal of the poets of his generation, Cernuda is the most personal, though he tells us his deepest feelings and not mere anecdotes of his existence.

Pablo Neruda (1904-   )

The Chilean poet, Pablo Neruda, had a considerable effect on the Spanish poets at the time of the Republic. Lorca and he appeared in public together in South America. From 1934 to 1938 Neruda was Chilean consul in Madrid, thus emulating Rubén Darío who on more than one occasion represented Nicaragua there. Germán Bleiberg says: "Después de Rubén Darío es quizá el único poeta americano que ha influído en la lírica peninsular."[45] (After Rubén Darío he is perhaps the only American poet who has influenced the poetry of Spain.) His effect on Spanish poetry in the thirties, however, was much less marked than Darío's at the beginning of the century, for he found awaiting him a number of good poets whose style was already formed. He helped to lead Spanish poetry further along the road to Surrealism—which neither it nor Neruda ever altogether reached. He published a poetry review in Madrid called *Caballo verde para la poesía*.

At this period, Neruda was writing in imagery woven in the somnambulistic manner of the Surrealist, though a Byronic Dark Hero, who is the poet himself, may be observed among the shadows. He was a friend of Vicente Aleixandre, whose poetry at this time was in a similar style, though there is no reason to suppose that either of them imitated the other. Indeed the real impact of Neruda was to be several years later when the example of his political poetry began to be admired by Spanish revolutionary poets in the fifties (Chapter 7).

Effect of These Poets

What remains is to inquire how the writings of all these poets affected the art from 1939 onwards. The general renewal of poetic technique by Rubén Darío was an advantage to all the poets after him. The example of Machado—especially of his nature poetry— has helped later poets in the production of some of their best work. Jorge Guillén, Salinas, and even Altolaguirre have their imitators, Lorca and Alberti far fewer, though their poetry looks easy to copy. The inferior words of Flamenco musical reviews may model themselves on the *Romancero gitano,* but serious poetry has avoided such mimicry.

Rubén Darío, Machado, and Jiménez are accepted as masters by all modern Spanish poets. Later poets are open to more criticism,

and each one of the *generación de la Dictadura* group has his de-
tractors among the new poets after 1939. Yet, though Jiménez is
no longer questioned as a poet, his theories as to what poetry should
be are certainly not universally accepted. The phrase "A la inmensa
minoría" does not please those who tend towards the left. Opinions
of Jiménez such as "lo espontáneo de un espíritu cultivado no puede
ser más que lo perfecto"[46] (spontaneity in a cultivated mind can
only mean perfection) find more of an echo in the practice of García
Nieto and the "Neoclassical" school (Chapter 3) than in those who
followed Aleixandre (Chapter 4) and the revolutionary poets (Chapter 7). But, as we have said, Jiménez was accepted as a great poet
by all these groups.

Jiménez never visited Spain again after the Civil War. He did
however publish both prose and verse in Spanish reviews[47] and was
interested in the poetry being produced in Spain. This can be seen
by the poem he wrote to Juana García Noreña[48] and by private letters to various Spanish poets.

Several of the exiled poets have by now published in Spain again.
Luis Cernuda brought out a second edition of *Ocnos*,[49] with addi-
tional prose poems included, but the final passage affirming that God
does not exist was omitted, with the author's permission, to avoid
possible trouble with the censorship. Cernuda also published his
translation of *Troilus and Cressida* in Spain. Guillén has published
Lugar de Lázaro (1957). He now comes to his native land from time
to time. Various books by Salinas have appeared posthumously.[50]
Altolaguirre used to make short visits to Spain, on one of which
he died as the result of a motor accident in 1959. The poet who has
had no contact with Spain since 1939 is Alberti. Some of his books
are even forbidden to enter, but he is always included in anthologies.
Some lesser poets have even returned to live in Spain.

The gulf between Spanish poets in and outside Spain is thus much
narrower than it was before. Immediately after the Civil War works
of the latter were very hard to obtain. Their influence therefore diminished, though their earlier works were of course known to everyone interested in modern poetry. Even so, it was their simpler poems
which were most admired in the early years after the Civil War.
We can see this, for example, from Alfonso Moreno's anthology of
Poesía española actual.[51] Fifteen of the twenty-one poems by Alberti
there were written before *Sobre los ángeles*. Early poems like "Qui-

siera estar solo en el Sur"[52] are chosen to represent Cernuda, though some of his poetry of exile in *Las nubes*[53] is also selected. It is perhaps significant that it was *Ocnos,* his simplest book in the period after 1939, that appeared in Spain.

It may have been a need for simplification that made poets after 1939 turn to Garcilaso rather than to Góngora, as we shall see in the next chapter.

NOTES TO CHAPTER 1

1. *Die symbolistichen Stilelement im Werke von Juan Ramón Jiménez* (Hamburg, 1935), p. 2.
2. "Los elementos de que extrae este nuevo caudal estético pueden agruparse así: a) un estudio profundo de la tradición poética española (clásicos y primitivos); b) el conocimiento de las escuelas francesas postrománticas: parnasianismo y simbolismo. De la primera, acaudillada por Leconte de Lisle, extrae Darío el gusto por el verso bien tallado, recortado a cincel, bruñido y sonoro; de la segunda, presidida por Verlaine, el matiz inefable, el tono menor y las 'correspondances' entre las diversas sensaciones que había cantado Baudelaire, y c), finalmente, el contacto con un grupo de poetas hispanoamericanos— Gutiérrez Nájera, Díaz Mirón, José Martí—que a su manera inician también una reacción contra la tradición literaria del siglo XIX." (Guillermo Díaz-Plaja, *La poesía lírica española* [Barcelona, 1937], p. 354).
3. Pedro Salinas, *La poesía de Rubén Darío* (Buenos Aires, 1948), p. 40.
4. *Obras completas* (Madrid, 1953), p. 1004 ["Dream"].
5. *Diccionario de literatura española* (Madrid, 1949), p. 371.
6. *Poesía española antología, 1915-1931* (Madrid, 1932), p. 95.
7. *Ibid.,* p. 82.
8. *Les Fleurs du Mal* (Garnier edition, Paris, 1957), p. 14.
9. Clemencia Miró, *John Keats: Poesías* (Madrid, 1946), p. 20.
10. *Animal de fondo* (Buenos Aires, 1949), p. 114.
11. In "Carta a Carmen Laforet," *Insula* (Madrid), No. 15 (January, 1948).
12. *Poesía española antología (contemporáneos)* (Madrid, 1934), p. 180.
13. *Segunda antolojía poética* (Madrid, 1933), p. 296.
14. (Madrid, 1912).
15. (Madrid, 1925).
16. *La Poésie pure* (Paris, 1926).
17. See note 6.
18. *Poesía española antología, 1915-1931,* p. 195.
19. Especially in "arte menor."
20. In *Atlante,* I (London, 1950).
21. *Poetas españoles contemporáneos* (Madrid, 1952), p. 214.
22. *Poesía española antología, 1915-1931,* p. 200 ["Cima de la delicia"].
23. The most comprehensive collection of Guillén's new poems is to be found in *Maremágnum* (Buenos Aires, 1957).
24. *L'Idée fixe* (Paris, 1932).
25. *Poesía española. Antología. Poesía de la Edad Media y poesía de tipo tradicional* (Madrid, 1935).
26. (Madrid, 1928).
27. *Obras completas* (Madrid, 1954), p. 362 ["Romance de la pena negra"].
28. *Ibid.,* p. 299 ["El lagarto está llorando"].

29. (Mexico, 1940).
30. (Madrid, 1925).
31. *Poesía, 1924-1944* (2nd edition, Buenos Aires, 1946), p. 15.
32. *Poesía española antología, 1915-1931,* p. 322.
33. (Madrid, 1929).
34. *Literatura española siglo XX* (Mexico, 1949), p. 196.
35. (Madrid, 1929).
36. *The Creative Element* (London, 1949).
37. *Poesía española antología (contemporáneos),* p. 472.
38. *Poesía, 1924-1944,* p. 237.
39. *Verbo* (Alicante), Nos. 23-25 (1952).
40. *La realidad y el deseo* (Mexico, 1940), pp. 87-111.
41. *Poesía española antología (contemporáneos),* p. 525.
42. *La realidad y el deseo,* p. 67 ["Desdicha"].
43. *Ibid.,* p. 258 ["El ruiseñor sobre la piedra"].
44. *Como quien espera el alba* (Buenos Aires, 1947), pp. 87-92.
45. *Diccionario de literatura española,* p. 430.
46. Prologue to *Segunda antolojía poética* (Madrid, 1922).
47. For example, "Recuerdo a José Ortega y Gasset," *Clavileño* (Madrid), 24 (November-December, 1953).
48. *Poesía española* (Madrid), 12 (December, 1952).
49. (Madrid, 1949).
50. Including a book of poems, *Confianza* (Madrid, 1955).
51. (Madrid, 1946).
52. *La realidad y el deseo,* p. 52.
53. *Ibid.,* pp. 179-263.

Here, as in the Notes to subsequent chapters, the name of an author is not mentioned when it is clear from the text of the chapter. The place and date of a book's publication is given the first time it is mentioned in any chapter.

2

Poets who remained in Spain

The gulf existing between the exiled poets and those in Spain in the years following the end of the Civil War has been recalled. Though in many ways this chapter is a continuation of the last one, it is primarily concerned with poets, known to the Spanish poetry public before 1939, who continued to live and to write in Spain. We are also more directly concerned with these poets than with those in the last chapter, since their post-Civil War work falls within the scope of this study. Yet the poets we are about to discuss are also interesting for the effect they had on younger men, which was of course all the greater because of their physical presence in Spain.

The Civil War cleft Spanish intellectual life, leaving the smaller of the two sections in Spain. Blas de Otero describes it as "un golpe . . . que destierra los ángeles mejores"[1] (a blow . . . which exiles the best angels). Besides this, the post-war atmosphere was not propitious to literary experiment, which was for a time all too readily equated with left-wing politics. A change came about eventually, some of which was due to the work of writers we shall examine in this chapter. An appreciation of that evolution is of course one of the principal aims of our general survey.

Manuel Machado (1874-1947)

Of the poets who had become known at about the turn of the century, there was only one of particular note left in Spain in 1939—Manuel Machado. His poetry is *modernista* and his technical perfection shows him to have been a good disciple of Rubén Darío. Some of his poems have a conventional Andalusian setting. He can also write well in *soleares* and other forms of popular verse which people associate with his native Seville. Among the best-known of Manuel Machado's poems are his historical sonnets which weave an exotic pattern out of the past and often end dramatically. By 1939 he had

20

become a highly respected and respectable citizen, but was not to write anything more of any value. When he did write, there was little in it to inspire the young poets. They paid him honor, thinking more of his brother—and of his whole generation—than of him himself.

Gerardo Diego (1896-   )

Though Manuel Machado was little more than a symbol, young poets in Spain looked to Gerardo Diego, Vicente Aleixandre, and Dámaso Alonso to supply the place of the *mejores ángeles*. They were expected to continue writing important poetry worthy of the Dictatorship Generation, and in fact did so. This was their opportunity; they were to help to restore a broken poetical tradition. The first of the three to make his influence felt was Gerardo Diego. Diego writes poetry in so many styles that he is almost a generation in himself. Significantly enough, the most important of his poetical publications is the *Primera antología de sus versos*.[2] This contains a selection from all the various "books" that Diego has been composing simultaneously throughout his life. Some of these are unpublished, others have had two editions with a space of years in between, the second containing new poems.

Some of Diego's poems show the influence of Jiménez. Like Antonio Machado, he has written poems on Soria. He was one of the modern masters of the sonnet whom the post-war "Neoclassicals" studied. But he also writes *creacionista* poems. *Creacionismo* is a poetical movement akin to the French *ultraisme*. Its first Hispanic exponent was the Chilean, Vicente Huidobro (1893-1948), who wrote poetry both in French and Spanish. He was soon followed by Diego and Larrea. *Creacionismo* was one of the precursors of Surrealism and therefore was invented before "automatic writing" came to be practiced. It was not the unconscious which was to be drawn on. On the contrary, as Huidobro says: "El poema creacionista nacerá solamente de un estado de supraconsciencia o de delirio poético"[3] (The Creationist poem will be born only of a state of super-consciousness or poetic delirium.) Clearly, however, there is something similar between such a delirium and the passive state needed for automatic writing. It is, of course, an attempt to track poetry down to its essentials. Jorge Guillén explains:

... cabe ... la fabricación—la creación—de un poema compuesto únicamente de elementos poéticos en todo el rigor del análisis; poesía poética, poesía pura. ... Es lo que se propone, por ejemplo, nuestro amigo Gerardo Diego en sus obras creacionistas.[4]

It is possible to imagine ... the confection, the creation of a poem composed exclusively of poetical elements in the strictest sense —poetic poetry, pure poetry. ... This is the aim, for example, of our friend Gerardo Diego in his Creationist works.

Here is a *creacionista* poem by Diego from *Biografía incompleta*. It is given both in the anthology of *Poesía española* and in the *Primera antología de sus versos,* so that the author presumably considers it one of his most successful poems in the genre.

Esperanza

¿Quién dijo que se agotan la curva el oro el deseo
el legítimo sonido de la luna sobre el mármol
y el perfecto plisado de los élitros
del cine cuando ejerce su tierno protectorado?

Registrad mi bolsillo
Encontraréis en él plumas en virtud de pájaro
migas en busca de pan dioses apolillados
palabras de amor eterno sin
carta de aterrizaje
y la escondida senda de las olas[5]

Hope

Who said there is exhaustion for curves gold desire
the lawful sound of moonlight upon marble
and the perfect fold of the elytrons
of the cinema exercising its tender protectiveness?

Search my pocket
You'll find feathers in it in virtue of the birds
crumbs in search of bread moth-eaten gods
words of eternal love without
air landing cards
and the hidden pathway of the waves

Clearly such a poem is similar to those paintings which are labelled "An Old Mill," for instance, and consist of a number of lines and circles which resemble nothing. Many people would probably prefer the picture to be called "Geometrical Pattern." But the artist was genuinely thinking of an old mill when he was painting, only he is using a personal imagery which is virtually impossible for others to follow. Diego's poem is slightly more comprehensible than that. He does, in fact, speak of "palabras de amor eterno sin/ carta de aterrizaje" which may be considered a symbol of hope, as may the other things in the poet's pocket. And then there is the inexhaustible curve of the first line. This is one of the most coherent of Diego's *creacionista* poems, but, even so, the imagery is extraordinarily personal and we may all the time be supposing something quite different from what the poet meant. Yet all we know of Diego and the *creacionistas* leads us to suppose that he has a personal understanding of what he wants to say.

The Surrealist, on the other hand, has been taught by Freud that everything in the unconscious falls into a pattern which can never be fully understood by the conscious mind of the individual. He therefore does not even need to understand what he creates himself. This is an important difference. It implies, for one thing, that the *creacionista,* on the contrary, needs to arrange and polish his material to his own satisfaction. That is why we do not find in Diego's poems of this kind those repulsive images in which Surrealist poems are apt to abound. Apart from that, for the unprejudiced reader the line of demarcation between the two schools is very faint indeed.

Diego says that poetry is "aritmética, aritmética pura" (arithmetic, pure arithmetic), though he adds that "Crear lo que nunca veremos, esto es la Poesía"[6] (Creating what we shall never see—that is Poetry). This explains why he is just as at home with traditional forms such as the sonnet as with *creacionismo*. Julián Marías says:

> Gerardo Diego, en todas sus formas, en todas sus tendencias, en todos sus metros—desde las formas clásicas a las que no quieren ser ni siquiera formas, desde la inspiración en Lope, Machado o Juan Ramón hasta el ultraísmo y el creacionismo—, ha conservado la conciencia de que la poesía es divertimiento y producción de una irreal belleza, que se apoya más o menos en las cosas del mundo, pero siempre se agrega a ellas y las excede.[7]

> Gerardo Diego in all his forms, in all his phases and in all his meters—from classical verse forms to those which do not pretend to be forms at all, from what he has written under the inspiration of Lope de Vega, Machado or Juan Ramón to his Ultraism and Creationism—has always been conscious that poetry is an amusement and the production of an unreal beauty, resting more or less on the things of this world, but always adding to them and exceeding them.

That is to say that his art is really *deshumanizada* in Ortega's sense. Many poets are continually trying to express their personal feelings and thought, but Diego is much more concerned with producing a poem which shall be as perfect an example as possible of its particular genre. The emotion, if it is there, grows out of the form or the subject. When he writes the poem "Rosalía," he wishes to recreate the poetic impression which Rosalía de Castro's lyrics give him:

> Pajarillos, fuentes, flores
> —ahí va la loca—decían,
> —ahí va la loca soñando—.
> La loca yo, Rosalía.[8]

> Small birds and the springs and flowers,
> They said, "There goes the mad woman,
> There goes the mad woman dreaming."
> The mad woman, I, Rosalía.

The "Romance del Duero,"[9] written in Soria, mingles the effect Machado's poetry has on him with a traditional ballad-meter.

> Río Duero, río Duero,
> nadie a acompañarte baja;
> nadie se detiene a oír
> tu eterna estrofa de agua.[10]

> River Duero, River Duero,
> No one walks down there beside you;
> And no one lingers to listen
> To your lasting verse of water.

Neither in this "Romance del Duero" nor in "Rosalía" is he speaking directly as Gerardo Diego. In spite of this, we are conscious of Diego the artist, if not of Diego the individual. He never wishes to confess himself in public as a Romantic poet might or even a Surrealist who, after all, publishes the unadorned overflowings of his unconscious. That is why the physical presence and the example of Diego were important in Spain in the years immediately following 1939 when perfection of form became for a time the prime concern of a poet. For the poetry of Diego, like that of Jiménez before him, led naturally on to the "Neoclassical" movement. Before tracing the rise and decline of that trend the work of other younger poets will be surveyed for their importance to it.

Miguel Hernández (1910-1942)

Though Miguel Hernández was known to the small poetry-reading public before the Civil War, he achieved much greater fame with his propaganda poems during the conflict. Even in England, John Lehmann in a survey of modern poetry mentioned Hernández but presented him as a rough soldier of the Republic, inspired by the struggle to write.[11] No doubt Mr. Lehmann was misled by the preface to his war-book, *Viento del pueblo*.[12] Therein Tomás Navarro Tomás presented him as a man of the people who learned to write poetry by reading the books in his local workers' center; a friend who was a student lent him some. He was certainly born of a peasant family and began life as a herdsman. But he was exceptionally deeply read in the Spanish poetry of the *siglo de oro* by the age of twenty-two, when his first poems appeared in a review in Orihuela, his native town. At twenty-three he published *Perito en lunas,* a poem in the style of Góngora, doubtless inspired by Diego's *Fábula de Equis y Zeda* (of the Góngora Centenary year).[13] He was even more successful than Diego in capturing Góngora's style in a slightly modernized form.

In 1934, Hernández went to live in Madrid, where he worked for the publishing firm of Espasa Calpe. The poems he had written in Orihuela won him a welcome from the poets of Madrid. In the autumn of the same year, he published his *auto sacramental, Quien te ha visto y quien te ve* in *Cruz y raya*.[14] As in *Perito en lunas* he had reproduced the style of Góngora, so he wrote this play in that of Calderón, with some suggestion of the modern world, as when Man's Five Senses, personified, organize a revolutionary strike. We also find here a "wind" theme in a passage of this play. This was to become almost a *leit-motiv* in Hernández's poetry (see the analysis of one of his poems in Chapter 9).

Hombre-niño: Padre, ¿y qué hay luego, detrás del viento?
    Esposo: Más viento en pos.
    Hombre-niño: ¿Y detrás del viento?
    Esposo: Dios.
    Hombre-niño: ¿Nada más Dios?
    Esposo: ¡Nada más![15]

    Man-Child: Father, what's behind the wind?

Husband:		Still more wind.
Man-Child:	And behind the wind?	
Husband:		God.
Man-Child:		Nothing
	But God?	
Husband:		Nothing but God.

In Madrid he became a close friend of "Bergamín, el chileno Neruda, Aleixandre y José María de Cossío"[16] and of Antonio Oliver and his wife, Carmen Conde.[17] The sympathies of this group, as of most of the intellectual world at that time, were politically of the Left, and Hernández soon became a Communist.

In 1936 he published *El rayo que no cesa.*[18] In this book political opinions do not seem to have affected the poetry, any more than they did that of Cernuda or Germán Bleiberg. The poetic form of the poems in Hernández's book is almost entirely taken from the Spanish poets of the first half of the seventeenth century. The sonnets, for instance, are, according to Guerrero Zamora,[19] in the style of Quevedo. The imagery, on the other hand, is very indirect and allusive. Let us see an example of this strange mixture of the Renaissance, the Baroque, and the twentieth century. This passage is taken from his "Elegía" on the death of Ramón Sijé, his great friend in Orihuela who had published a review there with him:

> Tanto dolor se agrupa en mi costado,
> que por doler me duele hasta el aliento.
>
> Un manotazo duro, un golpe helado,
> un hachazo invisible y homicida,
> un empujón brutal te ha derribado.
>
> No hay extensión más grande que mi herida,
> lloro mi desventura y sus conjuntos
> y siento más tu muerte que mi vida.
>
> Ando sobre rastrojos de difuntos,
> y sin calor de nadie y sin consuelo
> voy de mi corazón a mis asuntos.[20]

> So much of sorrow crowds into my side
> That, for my pain, even my breath is pain.
>
> A sightless axe performed the homicide,
> A cuff from a hard fist, a frozen blow,
> A brutal shove has cast your life aside.

There's nothing wider than my wound. I know
My bitter loss and weep for what's ahead.
Your death, more than my life, saddens me so.

I walk upon the stubble of the dead
And, with no warmth from anyone, or comfort,
Leaving my heart, towards my affairs I tread.

(For over a decade "Neoclassical" poets were to try to find the secret of writing as magnificently as that—but without success.) *Aliento* is the breath of life, life itself—the "wind" theme. The moral blow given by hearing of the death of a friend is "frozen" because it gives a feeling of spiritual numbness akin to the physical sensation produced by great cold. There is nothing wider than this moral wound because he feels that the death of his friend affects everything for him. Memory makes him tread upon the remains of the dead because he remembers his friend wherever he goes. For the same reason he is, as it were, travelling from the sadness of his heart to his everyday business. The images are all related to the poet's feeling but they are disconnected from each other. The poetry of the Renaissance, which Hernández in many ways followed so closely, sustains an image for much longer. Here is the first part of a sonnet by Quevedo:

A fugitivas sombras doy abrazos;
en los sueños se cansa el alma mía;
paso luchando a solas noche y día
con un trasgo que traigo entre mis brazos.
Cuando le quiero más ceñir con lazos,
y viendo mi sudor, se me desvía:
vuelvo con nueva fuerza a mi porfía,
y temas con amor me hacen pedazos.[21]

Fugitive shadows are what I embrace;
My soul tires of the dreams along its way;
Alone I struggle both by night and day
Against a goblin that my arms enlace.
When closely round him all my snares I trace
He notices my toil and will not stay,
So I gather fresh force for the assay
And love, persistent, tears me in the chase.

Like Hernández, Quevedo tells us that a feeling, this time of love, haunts him everywhere. But his metaphorical pursuit of a dream is almost a narrative. We can, if we wish, even forget that he is speaking of love and attend only to what he says of his vision. How-

ever, when we reach the last line of Quevedo's sonnet, we have a
foretaste of twentieth-century imagery: "hago correr tras ella el
llanto en ríos" (I make rivers of weeping run towards the vision). To
make a river of tears follow a phantom is hardly an exact classical
image. This shows that the new imagery of modern Spanish poetry
is not entirely without precedents in the past.

As can most great Spanish poets—Saint John of the Cross, for
example—Hernández can at times write with an extraordinary
simplicity and economy of words:

> Aunque bajo la tierra
> mi amante cuerpo esté,
> escríbeme, paloma,
> que yo te escribiré.[22]

> Even though my loving body
> Beneath the earth is lain,
> Write to me still, my darling,
> I'll answer you again.

The first half of this straightforward little verse is phrased in a
manner proper only to poetry; but the second—even including the
word *paloma*—is in the language of speech. Some critics, such as
Guerrero Zamora, think that the quality of such love-poetry and
the references to the life of the countryside show the sensibility of
the unspoiled peasant. There is no reason altogether to set aside this
biographical explanation, but Hernández's simplicity is, nevertheless,
as fully in the Spanish poetic tradition as his complexity.

The propaganda poetry of Hernández, written during the Civil
War, was addressed to a much wider public than his previous writings.
He was obliged to be much less Baroque than before. Yet the style
is the same, only simplified. Here is a passage from "Canción del
esposo soldado":

> Morena de altas torres, alta luz y ojos altos,
> esposa de mi piel, gran trago de mi vida,
> tus pechos locos crecen hacia mí dando saltos
> de cierva concebida.[23]

> Your towers are tall, your light is tall, your eyes are tall, my
>   swarthy
> Wife with a skin as mine is, deep draught my life has swallowed,
> Your mad breasts grow towards me, leaping up with the leaping
> Of a doe that is pregnant.

Clearly the insistence on height and the references to *mi piel* and *trago* are neither an exact description of appearance or sensations, nor are they really metaphors; they are *correspondances.* Yet they are so skilfully introduced that most readers would pass over them without noticing.

His second book of propaganda poems, *El hombre acecha,* was never published, though proof sheets were printed of it, some sets of which have been preserved.[24] In some of these poems we can see the poet's disillusion when he began to realize that his cause was failing. The feeling of bitterness naturally continued in his final poems, written in prison between 1939 and 1942. They are his best. Writing for the general reader had made him less Baroque and his style was now less like that of the poets to whom he was originally indebted. His writing had become more personal, whether to tell of his own feeling of defeat (as in the poem examined in Chapter 9) or to speak of his wife or of his little son, as in the following poem where the *seguidilla* form suggests the simplicity of childhood and the images the father's disillusionment and bitterness:

Al octavo mes ríes
con cinco azahares.
Con cinco diminutas
ferocidades.
Con cinco dientes
como cinco jazmines
adolescentes.

Frontera de los besos
serán mañana,
cuando en la dentadura
sientas un arma.
Sientas un fuego
correr dientes abajo
buscando el centro.

Vuela niño en la doble
luna del pecho:
él, triste de cebolla,
tú, satisfecho.
No te derrumbes.
No sepas lo que pasa
ni lo que ocurre.[25]

The eighth month you're laughing
With five orange blossoms,
With five very little
Ferociousnesses.
Five teeth appearing,
As it were, five jasmins
All in their young days.

They'll be the frontier of
Kisses tomorrow
When you feel that your jaws have
A weapon in them,
A fire within them
Flowing down and seeking
Its center deeper.

Fly, dear child, in the double
Moon of the bosom.
It is saddened by onions
But you are satisfied.
Don't you be cast down.
You don't know what's going on
Or what is happening.

The teeth are like orange-blossom and jasmins but they also foretell future fierceness. They are also a weapon for love or hate (for "arma" and "fuego" are almost certainly an intentional ambiguity, a device much rarer in Spanish than in English poetry). The mother's breasts show that she is not fully nourished, but the child is happy and does not yet know the tragedy he is born into.

In these last poems of Hernández's the image has at last become secondary and the poet stretches out to feelings that are beyond the poem, that are only suggested as a consequence of what he says. That is why our account of the images in this poem is different in kind from those of other poems above.

Hernández's prison poems have now been published,[26] but, for a long time, only a few typewritten copies of them were available. Partly for this reason and partly because they express a maturity of feeling that can be acquired but not imitated, it was really only the work of this poet before the Civil War which influenced "Neoclassical" poetry after 1939. These last poems of Hernández's are possibly the finest poems which have been written since 1939.

Germán Bleiberg (1915-   )

Juan Ramón Jiménez, Gerardo Diego, and Miguel Hernández are three poets on whom the "Neoclassicals" modelled their work. But there was another poet who had written a book of *Sonetos amorosos* in 1936,[27] whom they felt even closer to them than these three. This was Germán Bleiberg.

For a time, Bleiberg's life ran parallel with that of Hernández. He published sonnets in the *siglo de oro* style in 1936. In the same year, the Lope de Vega prize for drama was shared between them. They had the same political views. Immediately after the Civil War, they were in the same prison, and Bleiberg's earlier prison poems even resemble those of Hernández. But there the likeness ceased, for Hernández died and Bleiberg returned to his home and to the life of letters.

Germán Bleiberg was in the Petrarchan tradition of ideal love when he wrote the *Sonetos amorosos*. But his immediate model was Garcilaso de la Vega. He placed two quotations from that poet's Eclogues at the beginning of his book.

> . . . y aquel sonido
> hará parar las aguas del olvido.
> > Garcilaso. *Egloga* III

> . . . at that sound will
> The waters of forgetfulness stand still.
> > Garcilaso. *Eclogue* III

> por ti la verde hierba, el fresco viento,
> el blanco lirio y colorada rosa
> y dulce primavera deseaba.
> > Garcilaso. *Egloga* I

> For you the green grass and the cooling breezes
> And the white lily and the crimson roses
> And the sweet Spring were all things that I wanted.
> > Garcilaso. *Eclogue* I

These quotations tell us more of what Bleiberg took from Garcilaso than reading longer passages of that Renaissance poet would. Bleiberg does not revive the pastoral convention. He only sometimes uses a word as Garcilaso might have done, as when he makes *azucena* (lily) express the whiteness of skin. But Bleiberg's images are taken from natural objects, flowers, birds, water, the wind and, above all, light. The result is something like Garcilaso without Arcadia, or like the above quotations separated (as they are) from the long poems that contain them. These quotations are not disimilar to Bleiberg's:

> Un viento dócil tu rubor acrece,
> con la blancura en flor de acacia nueva.[28]

> A docile wind adds to your blushing redness
> The flowering whiteness of the young acacia.

or

> El alma te construye entre azucenas
> sobre el paisaje que la brisa hiere,
> donde los aires tiemblan en tu ensueño.[29]

> The spirit gives you form among the lilies
> Within the countryside the wind has wounded
> Where all the air is trembling at your daydream.

The imagery of this second passage is as insubstantial as most of Bleiberg's. The lilies and the wounds and trembling of the breeze are not real, but only part of the half-pleasurable, half-painful emotion the poet experiences in thinking of his absent beloved. Bleiberg seems almost indifferent to the visual effect of his words. Words that look familiar have another meaning. Some are even repeated very insistently. *Luz* appears in sixteen of the seventeen sonnets and in some of them twice. *Voz* is another key-word, as we might call it. *Aire* is frequently used. Let us quote a quatrain in which the three are found together:

> Me duele el aire de tu voz señera
> contraria al aire de mi voz perdida,
> en ti me encuentro y en tu luz olvida
> mi corazón la luz que le prefiera.[30]

> The air of your unfurled voice gives me pain;
> It stands against the air of my lost voice.
> I find myself in you and, by your light,
> My heart forgets the light which would prefer it.

To understand this we are almost bound to take just the few less usual words, because the key-words lead us into the same sort of labyrinths as those sentences in Don Quixote's favorite books which helped to drive him mad. *Señera:* it is not quite clear whether this means marked with a banner or isolated, in any case it refers to the signal excellence of the beloved; *perdido:* he is lost, we do not know exactly why, but "en ti me encuentro." The two last lines presumably mean that the thought of his beloved drives all other former thoughts from his mind. There is also the word *contraria* in the second line, which suggests that love is a conflict, as well as a meeting ("en ti me encuentro," as above). The more we examine this quatrain the more it seems to crumble apart; but immediately we read it through quickly, it acquires meaning.

But let us return to the key-words *voz* and *luz* once again. *Voz* is used in the first and second lines, *luz* in the third and fourth. We could however change the two pairs round without making any appreciable difference to the quatrain. We may now begin to wonder whether the key-words have a real meaning at all and whether these sonnets which invoke the name of Garcilaso have not been far more deeply affected by Surrealism than the casual reader would ever suspect.

The use of key-words is not peculiar to Bleiberg in modern Spanish poetry. Hernández and Rosales, two poets very closely knit to him in the history of Spanish poetry, use them also. Hernández, for instance, at times used the word *costado:* "Tanto dolor se agrupa en mi costado."[31] *Costado* here is equivalent to "heart." As to Rosales, his style in the sonnet is almost identical with Bleiberg's. *Luz* is one of his key-words, too, and nearly always appears.

But the sonnet is by no means the only form in which Bleiberg has written. Both before and after the *Sonetos amorosos,* he has composed many poems in different meters, especially in free verse. Some of these poems were written in prison between 1939 and 1943. The language of the *Sonetos* recurs constantly:

> ¿Qué voz la vuestra, pálidos labios del otoño,
> voz apenas escuchada,
> cuando en un vasto día estival
> todo fué sol en mi anhelo más íntimo?[32]

> What a voice is yours, pale lips of Autumn,
> A voice hardly heard
> When, on a vast Summer's day,
> All things were sunshine to my inmost yearning?

Voice, autumn, summer, and sun are all really symbols for the poet's state of mind. But Bleiberg alternates this kind of writing with more direct phrases, as when he says of his unhappiness in prison:

pero, sobre todo, que no llore nadie conmigo,
porque mi soledad es lo único cierto que poseo,
mi soledad y mi llanto
y mis pálidas hojas mustias del Otoño.[33]

But, above all, let no one weep with me.
My solitude's the one sure thing I have,
My solitude, my weeping
And my pale leaves all withered in the Autumn.

The autumn leaves are still symbolic, but the passage is in the tone of direct statement, easily understood.

Another example of this kind of writing is in *La mutua primavera,* Bleiberg's latest book. He speaks of his home as a ship:

¡Oh nave fingidamente anclada
en una céntrica calle de ciudad,
nave que visitan los amigos
con mensajes de laurel y de victorias![34]

Oh ship anchored, as it were,
In a central street in a city,
Ship visited by friends
With messages of laurels and of victories.

To his wife and daughter he says: "Pero no temáis, mis dos pasajeras." (But do not fear, my two passengers.) The image of a home in a town as a ship on the sea of life is a striking one; *laurel* is in the *Sonetos amorosos* style.

Luis Rosales (1910-   )

According to Vicente Gaos, *Abril*[35] by Luis Rosales is the source of the whole "Neoclassical" movement and he takes this to include Hernández and Bleiberg.[36] But, though García Nieto and other members of the *Garcilaso* group have read what Gaos says, they insist that their immediate inspiration came from reading Bleiberg. And Bleiberg's views on poetry personally affected Ridruejo. Besides Rosales, even in *Abril,* cultivates a diversity of styles, including free verse. He now says that he no longer believes in the aesthetic ideal of beauty as he did when he was a forerunner of the "Neoclassicals." Also, as a Catholic, he finds this ideal too near to a mere game, too removed from the true seriousness of life.[37] He thinks that *La casa encendida*[38] is his best book; this is a long poem in free verse, half narrative, half a dream. A passage from it was included in the *Anto-*

logía del Surrealismo español. Though he is grateful to this anthology for what he takes to be a compliment, he himself considers the poem positive and explicit, an expression of the whole flow of his life and therefore not Surrealist at all.

Luis Felipe Vivanco (1907-   )

Vivanco's first book of poems appeared in 1936.[39] After the Civil War, he formed a group with Rosales and Leopoldo Panero and, to a lesser extent, with Dionisio Ridruejo. These poets were the nucleus of those writing in the review *Escorial.* All had begun writing during the time of the Republic. They were very much concerned with reviving the poetical atmosphere of that period, so far as was possible, in the years following the Civil War. Ridruejo had republished the poetry of Antonio Machado (see Chapter 3). *Escorial* also published some of the post-Civil War poetry of Manuel Machado. Thus it prepared the literary public for the books of Aleixandre and Dámaso Alonso which appeared in 1944. (See the end of this present chapter.)

Vivanco specifically presents himself as a Catholic poet,[40] and this claim is supported by his brother-in-law Valverde.[41] His importance as a poet is that he was one of the first to write in a style resembling Antonio Machado.

He writes quite vividly of his love for his family and of the countryside. Here is a description of Finisterre:

> Las islas que se alejan . . . Los escollos postreros.
> (Vivir en una isla que es un suelo cubierto
> de tojos y conejos. Vivir en una aldea
> que, si talan los pinos, sepultará la arena
> movediza en las dunas.) De madrugada, en sueños,
> suenan, se acercan, llegan, y se alejan los zuecos.[42]

> The islands in the distance. Further, the shoals in ridges.
> (I'm living in an island, which is a soil all covered
> With furze-bushes and rabbits. I'm living in a village
> Which, if they cut the pines down, will soon be buried under
> The shifting dunes.) At daybreak, still half asleep, half dreaming,
> The sound of clogs grows nearer, reaches us, then grows fainter.

This is in the Machado manner. The poet reproduces the effect of the scenery on him by words bearing some suggestion of desolation, *tojos, suelo, talan, sepultará, arena movediza.* The repetition of *vivir en* gives an impression of remoteness. *Madrugada* leads on to three significant diphthongs, *sueño, suenan,* and *zuecos;* in the last line we can perhaps fancy we hear the sound of the clogs.

Leopoldo Panero (1909-   )

As a young man, Panero published in Neruda's review *Caballo verde para la poesía.* He did not publish in book form till 1949, when *Escrito en cada instante* appeared. The poetry of Panero, like Vivanco's, often resembles Antonio Machado's:

> ¡Lejos, hondo, fragante, vasto aliento
> dorado del pinar! El viejo estío
> —la luna en el canchal, el son del río—
> al alma torna mientras gime el viento.[43]

> Far-off, profound, and fragrant, the vast golden
> Breath of the pinewood. The old days of Summer—
> The moon on stony ground, the river's murmur—
> Come to the mind again. The wind is groaning.

Hondo, viejo and *gime* are relieved by *dorado.* Leopoldo Panero's brother Juan (1908-1937) had, as a sonneteer, been another precursor of the "Neoclassicals": "durmió mi voz el corazón herido/ por soberana luz de luz segura."[44] (My voice was set to sleep by the heart wounded/ By sovereign light coming from light unquestioned.) And he himself often writes in the "Neoclassical" idiom: "¡Oh, fluye, fluye en mí, total marea/ que moja cuanto soy de amor supremo.[45] (Oh, flow, flow, into me, you total flood-tide,/ Moistening all that I have of highest loving.) These two lines, however, are very different from those we have seen of Bleiberg's, almost certainly because *total* and *supremo* suggest spiritual greatness; adjectives of this kind can be used to adorn high tragedy; there is a finality about them; they receive the strongest stress in the line and are quite outside the Petrarch-Garcilaso-Bleiberg tradition. Yet the imagery is still cloudy.

We might, in fact, call Vivanco and Panero poets of the Machado revival (which came after Ridruejo published his edition of Antonio Machado). This was, however, overshadowed by the Aleixandre revival in 1944.

Vicente Aleixandre (1898-   )

Aleixandre had been the greatest poetical rebel of the Republican period. He seems to have been the only poet definitely to set out to write under the "influencia . . . de un psicólogo de vasta repercusión literaria"[46] (influence . . . of a psychologist who caused vast literary repercussions), that is to say, of course, of Freud. Aleixandre was thought of in early life as a revolutionary in every way. Hernández dedicated *Viento del pueblo* to him with the words: "Nosotros venimos brotando del manantial de las guitarras acogidas por el pueblo" (We have sprung from the source of the guitars the people received for their own), a phrase, by the way, even less applicable to Aleixandre than to Hernández himself, though Aleixandre at that time wrote a ballad in a more or less popular form about a hero in the defence of Madrid.[47]

Aleixandre began with a book called *Ambito*[48] which both by the form of the verse and the use of images reminds us of Guillén:

> La noche en mí. Yo la noche.
> Mis ojos ardiendo. Tenue,
> sobre mi lengua naciendo
> un sabor a alba creciente.[49]

> Night is in me. The night is I.
> My eyes are shining. And, tenuously,
> A savor of growing daybreak
> Is finding birth on my tongue.

The first two sentences are exclamations with no main verb. The third is a typically Guillénesque *correspondance*. But soon Aleixandre was to read Freud and try to apply psycho-analysis as a poetic method. (He was not alone in this, naturally. Many others, all over the world, were making the same experiment at the same time.) In the prose-poems of *Pasión de la tierra*[50] he wrote in dream-symbols. His other poetry, in a highly rhythmical free-verse, used the same sort of symbols but subordinated them to some theme, usually of love, interspersed with clear statements about his emotions and thoughts. Aleixandre does not induce in himself the trance Surrealists require; instead, he voluntarily creates a pleasing though rather stark pattern with unusual images:

Se querían de noche, cuando los perros hondos
laten bajo la tierra y los valles se estiran
como lomos arcaicos que se sienten repasados:
caricia, seda, mano, luna que llega y toca.

Se querían de amor entre la madrugada,
entre las duras piedras cerradas de la noche,
duras como los cuerpos helados por las horas,
duras como los besos de diente a diente sólo.[51]

They loved during the night-time, when the dogs of the deepness
Bark underground. The valleys seem as if they were stretching
Like the backs of archaic beasts which can feel a stroking.
Caresses, silk, a hand and a moon which comes and touches.

They loved with true affection just as the dawn was breaking,
Among the hard, serrated stones which surround the night-time.
They were hard as those bodies which many hours have frozen,
They were hard as those kisses given tooth to tooth only.

The poet affirms that the dogs are underground and the valley
stretches out, simply because that is the impression they give; in this
kind of poetry an impression is the same as a reality. In the same way,
night contains hard shut stones and the hours freeze bodies. Aleixandre
sets us on the border-line between sensation and thought. There is
also something wild and almost animal about his poems, full of extravagant images; and we must not try to understand these logically,
lest they become absurd.

As a further illustration of his technique let us take a description
from "El vals" (quoted by Dámaso Alonso in *Poetas españoles contemporáneos*):

Pechos exuberantes en bandeja en los brazos,
dulces tartas caídas sobre los hombros llorosos,
una languidez que revierte,
un beso sorprendido en el instante que se hacía "cabello de ángel,"
un dulce "sí" de cristal pintado de verde.

Un polvillo de azúcar sobre las frentes[52]

Exuberant breasts on a tray in the arms,
Sweet cakes which have fallen over the weeping shoulders,
Languidness overflowing,
A kiss compressed to the instant of changing to cotton candy,
A sweet crystal Yes painted green,

Powdered sugar on brows.

Many poets in the past have of course chosen the sensuality of the dance as their subject. Byron wrote of the waltz, attacking the then new custom of dancing entwined:

> Hot from the hands promiscuously applied,
> Round the slight waist, or down the glowing side,
> Where were the rapture then to clasp the form
> From this lewd grasp and lawless contact warm?
> At once Love's most endearing thought resign,
> To press the hand so press'd by none but thine;
> To gaze upon that eye which never met
> Another's ardent look without regret;
> Approach the lip which all, without restraint,
> Come near enough—if not to touch—to taint;[53]

Alfred de Musset, on the other hand, dwells on the waltz with sensuous pleasure. He is waltzing with an Italian dancer:

> Au moindre mouvement de mon bras, je la sentais plier comme une liane des Indes, pleine d'une mollesse si douce et si sympathique, qu'elle m'entourait comme d'un voile de soie embaumé[54]
>
> *(Confession d'un enfant du siècle)*
>
> At the least touch of my arm, I felt her bend like liana of the Indies, full of a softness so sweet and so pleasant that it wrapped me round like a veil of embalmed silk.

Byron contrasts the behavior of waltzers with that of chaste lovers. Musset uses images of comparison taken from things traditionally considered beautiful—liana and silk. It was left to Aleixandre to compare, in his Freudian manner, the sensuality of the dancer to the kind of extremely sweet food usually served at dances; there is even a displeasing suggestion of indigestion. Also one image does not follow on from another, but merely suggests it as in a dream; the "pechos" are "dulces tartas . . . sobre los hombros"; a kiss becomes a sweetmeat; and a "yes" is painted green. The idea appears to be that incontinence in eating sweet things at a dance leads to the thought of another sort of incontinence.

When the Civil War ended, Aleixandre remained in his house in Madrid, an invalid. Cernuda said that Aleixandre was "Enfermo y solo, vivo allá en el suelo/ Que fuera el mío"[55] (Ill and alone, alive there in the land/ Which once was mine). He was not, however, alone for long. Soon the young poets began to visit the sick man in his villa; they discussed poetry and read their own compositions to this surviving figure of the Spanish poetical *avant-garde*.[56]

Gerardo Diego in 1941 spoke of the fondness of the young poets of the day for sonnets, "aunque yo creo que un cambio de aire en las veletas haría ya bien a la salud"[57] (though I believe that a change of air in the vanes would be good for the health). This change of air came with the publication of Aleixandre's *Sombra del paraíso*[58] in 1944. The effect of the book had been prepared for by the previous publication of some of the poems in literary reviews. There was some political significance in the reception given to this book by the literary world. It followed up the effect of Ridruejo's edition of Antonio Machado in 1941. Hitherto the stage had been largely held by poets who had supported the Nationalists during the struggle, such as Manuel Machado and Adriano del Valle (1895-1957).[59] Dámaso Alonso, though he spent the time of the Civil War in Valencia and wrote an essay there on *La injusticia social en la literatura española*,[60] had never been a revolutionary poet and was soon back at Madrid University after the end of the hostilities. He was, however, one of a number of writers with more liberal ideas who in 1944 contributed to a special number of the poetry review *Corcel* totally devoted to Aleixandre. It is worth while remarking that the only one who was at any time really a member of the "Neoclassical" group was Vicente Gaos, though Morales was not far from "Neoclassicism" at the beginning.

Many things that were happening in 1944 were partly symbolized by the appearance of Aleixandre's book. That the Nazis were being defeated had become obvious to everyone in Spain except the most fanatical pro-Germans. Most of the minor Republican intellectuals who had been imprisoned when the Civil War ended had by that time been released. They formed another group different from the "liberal" one writing in the Aleixandre number of *Corcel*. The former soon merged with the rest of the literary life of Spain and, as might be expected, they approved of Aleixandre. The point of view of these ex-prisoners began to influence literary opinion; the most important of them was, of course, Germán Bleiberg.

If *Sombra del paraíso* had been as full of personal and Freudian images as Aleixandre's former books, it would hardly have satisfied all the expectations it aroused. It would probably never have appeared, for the authorities might have felt suspicious of the poet's cryptic utterances. As it was, the book was recognizably in the Aleixandre style and probably an improvement on his former writings, but the general meaning was plain and the whole had a unifying tone.

The *Ciudad del paraíso* is Málaga, where the poet spent his childhood:

> . . . ciudad de mis días alegres,
> ciudad madre y blanquísima donde viví, y recuerdo,
> angélica ciudad, que, más alta que el mar, presides sus espumas.[61]

> . . . city of my happy days,
> Very white mother-city, where I lived, and I remember,
> Angelic city, that higher than the sea, you preside over its foam.

But this "Paradise" of his childhood is also that of his early experiences of sensual love, as we can read in "Luna del paraíso" and "Muerte en el paraíso." Love, even in its more brutal aspects, is regarded as inevitably good, just as the wild animals of literature which haunt these pages are thought of as inherently admirable because of their force. It is clear that Aleixandre had read and been impressed by Blake's "Tyger," perhaps in Juan Ramón Jiménez' translation.[62] Indeed according to these poems, everything that is violent is good, even suicide.[63]

The poems of *Sombra del paraíso* had been written in the 1930's. The poetry Aleixandre was actually writing in the 1940's was to appear later, particularly in *Historia del corazón* (1954).[64] This suggests that Aleixandre is one of those poets who thinks, with Pope and Eliot, that poetry should be kept to mature like wine and not hastily delivered to the public. Thus his published work represents a slow development, not to be hurried by external events in Spain or the world, however far-reaching in their effects. If some historian, in a very distant future age, is left with Aleixandre's books as the only record of the present age he will probably assume that nothing of note took place in the times through which this poet lived. There is only a gradual change in Aleixandre's style, of a kind we might have expected in all the poets of his generation had there been no Civil War. Yet the young were looking for something new in poetry and this was where they found it.

Within a remarkably short time of the publication of *Sombra del paraíso,* one of the young poets who formed his circle presented a study of this book, and of some of the poems later included in *Historia del corazón,* as a thesis for a doctorate at Madrid University.

This poet was Carlos Bousoño and the thesis appeared in book form in 1950 under the title of *La poesía de Vicente Aleixandre*.[65] Perhaps we may obtain from this work some notion of what the young in 1944 were looking for and found in Aleixandre's poetry.

What appears to impress Bousoño more than anything else about Aleixandre's poetry are the images. These he divides into three classes, *el símbolo, la imagen visionaria continuada* (the continued visionary image) and *la visión*.

The "symbol," for Bousoño, is more or less what we have called an "allusive image." It is *espiritual* and *intangible*[66] and "no traduce miembro a miembro una esfera real, sino de modo conjunto"[67] (it does not transpose a real sphere bit by bit, but as a whole). The *imágenes visionarias continuadas* are different from "symbols" because several aspects of the image in question are used as points of comparison throughout the poem or some considerable portion of the poem. *La visión,* on the other hand, is an "atribución de cualidades o de funciones irreales a un objeto" (attribution of unreal qualities or functions to an object), as Bousoño explains. His example is the following passage from Aleixandre:

> . . . tus pies remotísimos sienten el beso postrero del poniente
> y tus manos alzadas tocan dulce la luna,
> y tu cabellera colgante deja estela en los astros.[68]

> Your very far-off feet feel the last kiss of the setting sun,
> Your raised hands touch the moon sweetly,
> And your streaming hair leaves its wake among the stars.

And Bousoño explains:

> Es una visión porque el poeta atribuye a un objeto real (cuerpo humano) cualidades que no puede poseer (tamaño cósmico).[69]

> This is "vision" because the poet attributes to a real object (the human body) qualities it cannot possess (cosmic size).

But surely that is not what gives the passage its peculiar character. Let us take an example from an earlier (English) poet of a human body being given cosmic size. It is from Thompson's *The Hound of Heaven* (Aleixandre probably knew this poem in Muñoz Rojas's translation but there does not appear to be any direct influence on the passage Bousoño quotes. We are simply comparing.):

> Even the linked fantasies, in whose blossomy twist
> I swung the earth a trinket at my wrist,

Are yielding; cords of all too weak account
For earth with heavy griefs so overplussed.[70]

The passage from *The Hound of Heaven* is just as much an example
of *visión* as that from Aleixandre. We might, also, describe it as a
cosmic conceit (in the Elizabethan sense) or, alternatively, as an
imagen visionaria continuada, though perhaps it is not sufficiently
long sustained for that. Certainly Thompson adds one surprising
image to another throughout his poem with a profusion and a success which is denied to Aleixandre. The difference lies in the thread
knitting the kaleidoscopic images together. In Thompson it is pro-
vided by the course of the poet's spiritual life which he is expressing
in this highly imaginative way. Whereas, in Aleixandre, there is
only a dream-connection between one image and another. The poet's
feet can touch the sunset, his hands can reach out to the moon and
his hair is among the stars because a dreamer can do anything—and
always without the least sense of strangeness, for a dreamer is never
amazed.

Perhaps a nearer comparison to Aleixandre's dream-vision may
be found in the end of one of Yeats's sonnets: "love fled,/ And
paced upon the mountains overhead,/ And hid his face amid a crown
of stars."[71] There is still a difference, since Yeats is speaking of an
allegorical figure—Love—and Aleixandre of a living poet. But Yeats
is imagining the dreams of an old woman looking into the fire, so
that he comes nearer to Aleixandre's dream-method than Thompson
does.

A verse from one of Aleixandre's love-poems will perhaps make
this continual presence of dream-imagery in his work plainer:

Muslos de tierra, barcas donde bogar un día
por el músico mar del amor enturbiado,
donde escapar libérrimos rumbo a los cielos altos
en que la espuma nace de dos cuerpos volantes.[72]

Thighs of earth, like two boats, one day to row about in
On the musical sea of love which is turbid,
Where one escapes so freely under way to the high heavens
In which the foam is born of two bodies flying.

The earthy thighs become boats. These boats are rowed over the sea
of tarnished love. The sea is musical, since in a dream-state we might
connect a sea of love with music. The boats escape towards the high
heavens and in them the bodies of the lovers are creating the foam

of the ocean upon which they are floating. That is to say that through sensuality the body becomes the soul and love becomes spiritual. One image suggests and fades into another as in dreams.

We have found some analogy between Aleixandre's *visión* and a couple of passages from English poetry. Bousoño has something to say about *visión* and the English poets:

> la poesía de orden visionario madruga en Inglaterra extraordinariamente, comenzando con los mismos albores del romanticismo. Tanto Shelley como Keats, y antes Blake, son, en este sentido, típicamente modernos:[73]

> Poetry of a visionary kind appears extraordinarily early in England. It begins there in the very dawn of Romanticism. Both Shelley and Keats, and Blake before them, are, in this sense, typically modern.

This might explain Aleixandre's use of Blake's "Tyger" mentioned above. The same poem may have been at the back of his mind when he said "romantically" in his speech on entering the Spanish Academy of Language:

> Y en el fasto de las plumas del ave del paraíso, como en la fuerza preciosa del tigre despoblador estamos viendo algo de lo que gemirá después dulcemente en la pupila intacta de la enamorada.[74]

> And in the pomp of the feathers of the bird of paradise, as in the splendid strength of the depopulating tiger, we see something of what will later groan sweetly in the intact pupil of the beloved.

Aleixandre's great skill in *Sombra del paraíso* was to write in his own "visionary" style and yet give a general impression of coherence, even compose poems each with a definite theme in a book which has a certain unity of mood. Naturally the young poets felt encouraged by his remarkable example. Perhaps they also found in his "visionary" quality that something which Bousoño is conscious of in Blake, Keats, and Shelley but which had hitherto been very little known in Spanish poetry.

In the years following the publication of *Sombra del paraíso,* Aleixandre ceased to appear such a unique figure in Spanish poetry. Much poetry of a more varied nature was written in Spain and the work of Spanish poets abroad became much more easily available. Aleixandre was no longer a survival from a revolutionary age but an academician and a master.

His *Historia del corazón* (1954)[75] is, however, just as important a part of Aleixandre's achievement as *Sombra del paraíso,* even though it may not have been as enthusiastically received. Dámaso Alonso says:

> . . . el retorno a lo que (inexactamente, pero para entendernos) podemos llamar "emoción directamente humana" . . . se intensifica aún en el libro *Historia del corazón,* escrito entre 1945 y 1948.[76]

> . . . the return to what (inexactly, but so as to understand each other) we may call "direct human emotion" . . . becomes even more intense in his book *The Heart's Story,* written between 1945 and 1948.

The language and imagery are plainer, more pedestrian, the dream-quality less persistent. For instance, he speaks almost prosaically of

> . . . ése que vive ahí, ignoro en qué piso,
> y le he visto bajar por unas escaleras
> y adentrarse valientemente entre la multitud y perderse.[77]

> . . . the man who lives up there I don't know in which flat,
> Whom I've seen coming downstairs
> And boldly enter the crowd and get lost among it.

The master even becomes rather pedantic at times. A child's hoop is an "aro gayo de rodantes colores" (gay ring of rolling colors); he would hardly have used that adjective *gayo* in his earlier books; nor do we feel he would have spoken of the "viviente aromar"[78] (living scentedness) of flowers. This implies that when Aleixandre leaves the dream for the day-to-day world he is in danger of falling into a traditional literary rhetoric.

As to the subject-matter of these poems, they are generally about a love in which the soul and body are thought of as one. Passion founded on sensuality appears to be all that comforts the poet in his stony pessimism. Life is aimless, meaningless, cruel and brief. Rubén Darío had written that we do not know "adónde vamos ni de dónde venimos" (where we are going or where we come from) but Aleixandre replies: "Sabemos adónde vamos y de dónde venimos. Entre dos oscuridades, un relámpago."[79] (We know where we come from and where we are going. A lightning flash between two darknesses.)

Dámaso Alonso (1898-   )

Dámaso Alonso's *Hijos de la ira*[80] appeared a few weeks after *Sombra del paraíso.* This second book by a poet of the *generación de la Dictadura* did not perhaps seem so important at the time, but it has been one of the few modern Spanish books of poetry to appear abroad in translation. A German rendition was published in about 1954,[81] at a time when relatively little poetry was being printed in Germany, even by native poets. The preface speaks of Alonso with an enthusiasm usually accorded abroad only to Lorca.

Alonso's poetical production before 1944 had been slight. Diego's Anthology of Contemporary Poetry only includes ten of his poems. This is less than Salinas, Guillén, Larrea, Diego himself, Lorca, Aleixandre, Cernuda or Altolaguirre. In fact Alonso's reputation had hitherto depended more on such things as his prose paraphrase of Góngora's *Soledades* or his anthology of medieval Spanish poetry[82] than on his own poetry. And it had been the medieval lyric which had guided him in the composition of his own work before.

His latest poems in this style may be found in *Oscura noticia,*[83] also published in 1944. He chooses his words with fastidious care.[84] Some of the images are remarkable, but they are more often metaphorical, in the traditional manner, than allusive. Here is a description of unborn children which may illustrate this:

> . . . !Ay de esos cieguecitos
> de leche no cuajada,
> de tierna pulpa vegetal, dormida,
> pellitas de manteca,
> aun con rocío y música,
> entre las verdes hojas de los úteros![85]

> . . . Oh, poor little blind things
> Of milk not yet congealed,
> Of tender, sleeping, vegetable pulp,
> Little pats of butter,
> Music and dew still round them,
> Among the green leaves of their mothers' wombs.

The only "dream" word here is *música,* which we have come across above in the passage from Aleixandre's love-poem. The rest of the verse simply describes an embryo by other objects resembling it. The adjective *tierna* gives the tone and *leche, manteca, rocío* and *verdes hojas* maintain this note of tenderness.

Hijos de la ira was in a completely new manner, at least for Alonso. It was written in free verse and had a Biblical wealth of repetitions and of visualized abstractions:

porque fantasmas eran, son, sólo fantasmas,
mis interiores enemigos,
esa jauría, de carlancas híspidas,
que yo mismo, en trailla, azuzaba frenético
hacia mi destrucción,
y fantasmas también mis enemigos exteriores,
ese friso de bocas, ávidas ya de befa,
que el odio encarnizaba contra mí,
esos dedos, largos como mástiles de navío,
que erizaban la lívida bocana de mi escape,
esas pezuñas, que tamborileaban a mi espalda, crecientes, sobre
el llano.[86]

Because they were ghosts, yes, they are only ghosts,
My inner enemies,
The whole pack of them, with the spikes on their collars,
That I myself hallooed frantically, holding their leash,
To my destruction,
And ghosts, too, were my outer enemies,
That palisade of mouths, avid for mockery,
Which hate had fleshed against me,
Also those fingers, long like the masts of ships,
With which the livid gulf of my escape was bristling,
Those hoofs which drummed at my back, increasingly, over
the plain.

(The last line is made to sound like a horse galloping.) This is
"visionary" writing. But the purpose of it is different from the examples we have seen in Aleixandre. Alonso is piling up images of
horror in order to communicate to us the state of spiritual torment
he has been through. His method is rhetorical. (An earlier writer
would probably have used one long simile, in the Homer-Virgil style,
somewhat in the following way: "Even as a man beset with hounds,
etc., etc., . . . so I . . . .")We are reminded of Rimbaud:

Sur toute joie pour l'étrangler j'ai fait le bond sourd de la bête
féroce. J'ai appelé les bourreaux pour, en périssant, mordre la
crosse de leurs fusils. J'ai appelé les fléaux, pour m'étouffer avec
le sable, le sang.[87]

I have leapt unheedingly, like a savage beast, on every joy to
choke it. I have called to the executioners, so as to bite the butts
of their rifles as I perish. I have called to catastrophe to stifle
me with sand, with blood.

Dámaso Alonso, in 1943, at the age of forty-five—as he repeats many
times—finds himself in Madrid:

Madrid es una ciudad de más de un millón de cadáveres (según
las últimas estadísticas).
   A veces en la noche yo me revuelvo y me incorporo en este
nicho en el que hace 45 años que me pudro,[88]

Madrid is a city of over a million corpses (according to the latest
statistics).
   Sometimes at night I toss about and sit up in this niche where
I have been rotting for forty-five years.

The book is full of monsters. Even the insects which buzz around his
table at night assume gigantic and horrible proportions in his ex-
asperated imagination. And the most powerful poem in the book
depicts the terrifying loneliness of an old servant-woman, whose re-
lations and friends have all died; she is described as travelling in a
horrible empty train running along with nobody else in it and nobody
driving it. Nora has taken this as a symbol for the despairing feeling
contemporary Spanish poets have about their work.[89] But Alonso
has contrasted this poem with others in which God saves him from
the despair of the world of monsters:

Yo no he tenido un hijo,
no he plantado de viña la ladera de casa,
no he conducido a los hombres
a la gloria inmortal o a la muerte sin gloria, . . .[90]

I have never had a son,
I have never planted a vine on the slope by my house,
I have never led men
To immortal glory or to death without glory, . . .

Though he is unworthy, the prayers of his mother and his wife will
finally save him, in the form of two wings bearing him up to Heaven.
   "Dios me ha tocado de su dedo" (God touched me with His
Finger), Dámaso Alonso explained at a public reading of these poems.
There is in them a great spiritual conflict. This was a very different
thing indeed from the almost purely formal "Neoclassical" poetry
which had been written before 1944.
   Hijos de la ira has led on to the greater maturity of *Hombre y
Dios*.[91] Here Dámaso Alonso sometimes writes in free verse, some-
times in sonnets, thus merging two currents in modern Spanish poetry.
In these poems the writer contrasts outer and inner reality. The object we perceived becomes, on another plane, a spiritual reality. For
example, Alonso's *dulce miopía* (sweet short-sightedness) is not only

his actual physical state; his soul does not see as it might, either. He is an elderly monkey, that is to say a miserable sinner. And, while the other passengers in the airplane to America read *Life,* Alonso imagines that he sees the world below covered with blood. *Hijos de la ira* had been the story of a conquest over monstrous and meaningless uncertainties; *Hombre y Dios* is an affirmation of faith. Alonso has shown how fine religious poetry can be written in modern Spain; few have followed his example.

After *Hombre y Dios* comes *Gozos de la vista.*[92] The "sweet short-sightedness" of *Hombre y Dios* has suggested the central theme of this book. Everything in these poems is centred in the idea of sight. The blind fight against the evil buffetings of unseen forces. Light is the good thing which gives man most joy. Brightness and darkness have, of course, become good and evil, but here the symbol and what it symbolizes are so much at one that the images never become metaphors. This was already so in *Hombre y Dios,* but it is even more evident here. The sense of sight conquers the monsters of the old days.

We have now seen what the poets who had begun writing before 1936 had to offer to those writing after 1939, from the renewed cultivation of the poetic forms of the Renaissance, through the Machado revival, to Aleixandre's half-Surrealist technique and Alonso's revival of religious poetry. The time has now come to see their influence in action on other less fully formed poets.

NOTES TO CHAPTER 2

1. *Angel fieramente humano* (Madrid, 1950), p. 54 ["Puertas cerradas"].
2. (Madrid, 1941).
3. *Agora* (Madrid), 15-16 (January-February, 1958), p. 34. ["Arte poética"].
4. *Poesía española antología, 1915-1931* (Madrid, 1932), p. 195.
5. *Biografía incompleta* (Madrid, 1953), p. 40.
6. *Poesía española antología, 1915-1931,* pp. 264-265.
7. *Diccionario de literatura española* (Madrid, 1949), p. 184.
8. *Primera antología de sus versos* (1st popular edition, Buenos Aires, 1941), p. 146 ["Rosalía"].
9. *Poesía española antología, 1915-1931,* pp. 267-268.
10. *Ibid.,* p. 267.
11. *New Writing in Europe* (London, 1940).
12. (Valencia, 1937).
13. (Mexico, 1932).
14. (Madrid, July-September, 1934).
15. *Obra escogida* (Madrid, 1952), p. 256. See also Juan Guerrero Zamora, *Noticia de Miguel Hernández* (Madrid, 1951), p. 58.

16. *Diccionario de literatura española,* p. 302.
17. See *Noticia de Miguel Hernández,* pp. 24-25 (letter to Carmen Conde and Antonio Oliver).
18. (Madrid).
19. *Noticia de Miguel Hernández,* p. 38.
20. *Obra escogida,* p. 133 ["Elegía"].
21. *Obras completas. Verso* (Madrid, 1943), p. 51 ["En vano busca la tranquilidad"].
22. *Obra escogida,* p. 79 ["A mi Josefina"].
23. *Viento del pueblo,* p. 127.
24. Selected poems from *El hombre acecha* are included in *Obra escogida.*
25. *Obra escogida,* p. 245 ["Nanas de la cebolla"].
26. In *Obra escogida* and previously in certain poetry reviews such as *Halcón* (Valladolid), 9 (May, 1946).
27. (Madrid, 1936).
28. *Más allá de las ruinas* (Madrid, 1947), p. 27.
29. *Ibid.,* p. 28.
30. *Ibid.,* p. 20.
31. See note 20.
32. *Más allá de las ruinas,* p. 95 ["Años de presagios"].
33. *Ibid.,* p. 88 ["Elegía de las hojas otoñales"].
34. (San Sebastián, 1948), pp. 25-26.
35. (Madrid, 1935).
36. "De Luis Rosales a José García Nieto," *La estafeta literaria* (Madrid), 25 (1946).
37. Opinion expressed in private conversation.
38. (Madrid, 1949).
39. *Cantos de primavera* (Madrid).
40. "Alabadle, mis años
de madurez católica, a sabiendas
de todo lo que cuesta
ser católico en vez de vitalista." (*Continuación de la vida,* [Madrid, 1949], p. 110).
"Praise him my years
Of Catholic maturity, fully knowing
All that it costs one
To be a Catholic instead of a vitalist."
41. See José María Valverde, *Estudios sobre la palabra poética* (Madrid, 1952), p. 196.
42. *Continuación de la vida,* p. 57.
43. *Escrito en cada instante* (Madrid, 1949), p. 21 ["El viejo estío"].
44. *Poesía española actual* (Madrid, 1946), p. 461 ["Soneto amoroso"].
45. *Escrito a cada instante,* p. 14 ["Invocación"].
46. Vicente Aleixandre, *Pasión de la tierra* (Madrid, 1946), p. 11.
47. Published in *Romancero de la Guerra Civil* (Madrid, 1936) ; the title is "El fusilado."
48. (Málaga, 1928).
49. *Antología de poetas españoles contemporáneos* (Barcelona, 1946), p. 458 ["Posesión"].
50. (Mexico, 1935).
51. *Antología de poetas españoles contemporáneos,* p. 456 ["Se querían"].
52. *Poesía española actual,* p. 300.
53. Current Oxford University Press edition of *The poetical Works of Lord Byron,* p. 145 ["The Waltz"].
54. (Flamarion edition; Paris, n.d.), p. 117.
55. *Como quien espera el alba* (Buenos Aires, 1947), p. 44 ["A un poeta futuro"].
56. See special Aleixandre number of *Corcel* (Valencia), 5-6 (1944), and an article by José García Nieto in *Juventud* (Madrid), (July 4, 1944).

57. *Alondra de verdad* (Madrid, 1941), p. 71.

58. (Madrid).

59. Adriano del Valle's most important book of poems was *Arpa fiel* (Madrid, 1942) which was awarded the National Prize for Literature.

60. In *Hora de España* (Valencia), 2 (February, 1937).

61. *Poesía española actual,* pp. 315-316.

62. "un tigre / soberbio la sostiene" ("a magnificent tiger bears her"). (*Sombra del paraíso* [2nd edition, Buenos Aires, 1947], p. 50 ["Diosa"].) Jiménez' translation of Blake's "Tyger" appeared in *Obra en marcha* (Madrid, 1928).

63. "besé su muerto azul, su esquivo amor" ("I kissed her dead blue, her elusive love"). (*Sombra del paraíso,* p. 111 ["Muerte en el paraíso"].

64. (Madrid).

65. (Madrid).

66. *Ibid.,* p. 19.

67. *Ibid.,* p. 16.

68. *Ibid.,* p. 26. The quotation from Aleixandre is taken from *Sombra del paraíso,* p. 11 ["El poeta"].

69. *Ibid.*

70. [Sir] A [lgernon Methuen Marshall] Methuen, *An Anthology of Modern Verse* (14th School Edition, London, 1927), p. 223.

71. *Ibid.,* p. 237.

72. *Poesía española actual,* p. 314.

73. *La poesía de Vicente Aleixandre,* p. 174.

74. Aleixandre was received into the Spanish Royal Academy of Language on January 22nd, 1950. Dámaso Alonso spoke the speech of welcome which, together with Aleixandre's own address, was printed in pamphlet form, at the latter author's expense, and distributed to those attending the ceremony of his reception, as is usual on those occasions. The quotation is on p. 12.

75. See note 64.

76. From Alonso's speech mentioned in Note 74; p. 48 of the publication quoted.

77. *Historia del corazón,* p. 56.

78. *Ibid.,* pp. 90 and 91.

79. *Ibid.,* p. 183.

80. (Madrid, 1944).

81. *Söhne des Zorns* (Munich, n.d. [1954 ?]).

82. (Madrid, 1927) and (Madrid, 1935).

83. (Madrid).

84. Note the title *Dafodelo original* on p. 67, the result of much self-questioning and enquiry as to the correct Spanish name for a daffodil. Also, in translating Eliot's *Journey of the Magi,* Alonso consulted twenty people and kept the printers waiting a fortnight in order to find the right Spanish equivalent for the phrase, "Set down this." (See T. S. Eliot, *Poemas* [Madrid, 1946], p. 52.)

85. *Poesía española actual,* p. 269.

86. *Ibid.,* p. 277.

87. *Une saison en enfer* (Paris: Mercure de France, 1932), p. 8.

88. *Hijos de la ira,* p. 13 ["Insomnio"].

89. See Note 46 to Chapter 7.

90. *Hijos de la ira,* pp. 152-153 ["Las alas"].

91. (Málaga, 1955).

92. Poems from *Gozos de la vista* have appeared in various reviews, *Insula, Papeles de Son Armadans, Cuadernos Hispanoamericanos,* and *Clavileño;* also in Dámaso Alonso, *Antología: Creación* (Madrid, 1956).

3

"Neoclassicism"

Between 1939 and 1944, most of the poetry published in Spain was in one of the traditional verse-forms and in a language resembling that of Spain's Renaissance poets. We have seen that a few poets writing in the days just before the Civil War adopted the style of Góngora, Quevedo, or Garcilaso. But now such neo-Renaissance writing (known in Spain as "Neoclassical") became a general custom. Young poets deliberately schooled themselves in the classical Spanish forms in order to make suitable contributions to García Nieto's review, *Garcilaso*.

During the Civil War, many sonnets had been published on the Nationalist side, especially on political themes such as José Antonio or the Alcázar at Toledo; Ridruejo's are the prototype of these. Rosales was probably regarded at that time as the leading Nationalist poet. Ridruejo's *Primer libro de amor* was published almost immediately after the end of the Civil War.

There were two main reasons for the excessively traditional nature of the poetry written in Spain in the years immediately after 1939. First, a war (and particularly a civil war) blunts people's sensibilities and makes them suspicious of anything which appears unconventional. Secondly, many young men of the new generation, whose first contact with the adult world had been the Civil War, were very well satisfied with the new Government's religious and social policy. If they were poets, they did not feel called upon to guide their readers at all on, say, theological, philosophical or social questions. These had already been solved by others more competent than they and therefore no longer concerned them. They read Giménez Caballero's *Arte y estado*[1] *(Art and the State),* which spoke of the writer and artist filling a natural place in a better-organized society, and they were convinced that this applied to themselves. Their problems as poets were concerned with using traditional forms as perfectly as possible, and their chief models as to how this should be done were Hernández' *El rayo que no cesa* and Bleiberg's *Sonetos amorosos.*[2]

We have already noticed the extraordinary vagueness of the language and imagery of those *Sonetos amorosos.* This was one of the things the young imitated to the extent that in certain of their works, particularly their sonnets, the absence of exact meaning and the disconnection of the images became very confusing. The reader seeking to understand literally what was said might well feel himself in a world of dream-symbolism similar to that of the Surrealists. A good example of this sort of "Neoclassical" vagueness can be found in the sonnet by García Nieto analyzed in Chapter 9.

Some justification is needed for the constant use of the term "Neoclassical" in the present work. Our reason is that we do not think there is any other to replace it. Certainly this modern Spanish "Neoclassicism" has nothing to do with that of writers of the age of Boileau and Pope or with a strict adherence to the rules of Aristotle and Horace. The Neoclassicism of eighteenth-century Europe was a serious and, some think, a very fruitful attempt to revive ancient Roman standards in life and art. Contemporary Spanish "Neoclassicism" merely wished to recapture the styles of Spain's "classical" Golden Age. "Neoclassical" is not perhaps an ideal term for this, but Neo-Golden Age sounds very halting and "neo-Renaissance" will not really do, as it suggests too much.

There are, however, one or two similarities between the old Neoclassicals of the age of Boileau and Pope and the modern Spanish ones. The first is an avoidance of anything personal or emotional. The second is stylistic. The contemporary Spanish "Neoclassicals" choose their words so carefully that the limitation of their vocabulary recalls that of the eighteenth-century writers. Certain words are repeated again and again. We have found *voz* in Bleiberg, Rosales, and Juan Panero; it recurs constantly in such "Neoclassicals" as Ridruejo and García Nieto. *Costado,* a favorite word with Hernández, appears so frequently in García Nieto that a satirical poem (published anonymously and really by García Nieto himself) said: "Este es Nieto, el del *costado.*" (This is Nieto, the poet who writes "costado.")

The subject-matter of the poem is usually very conventionally treated; indeed, it is reduced to a minimum and sometimes hardly exists at all. This is particularly the case with the love-poetry. To the reader, the beloved is an abstraction, as shadowy as Petrarch's Laura or the ladies who inspired the Renaissance sonneteers. Also, the reader does not obtain any very clear visual picture of what he is reading about. This is because the "Neoclassicals" are more concerned with the sound of their verses and their rhetorical effect than with visual exactness. The deliberate use of key-words mentioned above also contributed towards this result.

Dionisio Ridruejo (1912-   )

Dionisio Ridruejo published a small book of poems called *Plural*[3] in 1935. It was printed in the provinces and attracted no notice. Ridruejo claims that the influence of Antonio Machado is *patentísima* (very obvious) in these poems, but it is not so obvious as he thinks. His enthusiasm for Machado in these early days is worth noticing, for it was Ridruejo who republished Machado's complete poetical works. This required considerable moral courage at that time, since Machado unconditionally supported the Republic during the Civil War; several poems and prose passages attest this. Ridruejo was, however, determined that Machado should be read and admired in Spain again, for the good of Spanish poetry and civilization, and he effected this. He wrote the introduction:

> Yo no escribo este prólogo como poeta joven para el libro de un maestro muy amado. Yo escribo este prólogo como escritor falangista con jerarquía de gobierno para el libro de un poeta que sirvió frente a mí.[4]

> I am not writing this preface as a young poet for the book of a much-loved master. I am writing this preface as a Phalangist writer with a government post for the book of a poet who served on the side opposite to me.

He makes Machado's political bias quite plain:

> No hemos querido mitigar este hecho, ni aun la existencia de las raíces que de él haya en toda su vida. Nos parecería una hipocresía estúpida, una puerilidad de avestruz. Ahí están los pocos versos que puede ser un antecedente, ¡tan inocentes, sin embargo![5]

> We did not want to minimize this fact, nor even the existence of the roots of it throughout his life. That would seem to us to be a stupid piece of hypocrisy, the folly of an ostrich. For the few verses which can serve as an antecedent are there. And yet, how innocent they are really!

But, if Machado was the master of the young Ridruejo, another contemporary also influenced him—perhaps even more than he realized.

> La amistad buena, aunque casual, con un poeta—Germán Blei-berg—me influye entonces considerablemente, inclinando mi in-augurada dirección hacia un mayor formalismo, casi preciosista.[6]

> A good, though fortuitous, friendship with a poet—Germán Blei-berg—had a considerable influence over me at that time. It in-clined my early steps towards a greater, an almost precious cultivation of form.

Much later, in the early 1940's, Ridruejo was connected in *Escorial* with Panero and Vivanco, the poets of what we have called the Machado revival. Yet Ridruejo's own imagery long remained "Neo-classically" vague. Not till his poems on Russia do we find objects in Nature observed for their human meaning—as in Machado.

In order to write for the Republicans, Hernández had been obliged to simplify his style. But the young poet of the Nationalists, Ridruejo, made no concessions of that sort at all. Obviously, even when the subject-matter was political, he was primarily interested in the formal beauties of the verse.

> El taller descolgaba sus martillos
> para abatir los mármoles ilustres
> y las manos ternísimas del lirio
> muerto sobre la larga encrucijada.[7]

> So they unslung the hammers in the workshops
> That they might strike down the illustrious marbles
> And the hands—oh, so tender—of the lily
> Where it lay dead at the enormous crossroads.

Doubtless the *taller* was revolutionary Spain, the *mármoles ilustres* the traditional values of Spain and the *lirio* the religion of Christ. But all this can only be understood after some experience of the new "Neoclassical" style. Such writing can have had no popular effect, even if it was intended to.

In 1939 Ridruejo published his *Primer libro de amor,* a long book of poetry in the Petrarch-Bleiberg style, except that Ridruejo's imagery is rather more sophisticated.

> Quien pula aristas al diamante bruto,
> quien vuelva al ave su perdida guía,

quien haga soledad y compañía,
voz y silencio, al cántico absoluto.

Quien me devuelva todos mis mensajes
y sea, en mis quietudes recogida,
costa anhelada y vela de mis viajes.[8]

She who can polish facets of rough diamonds,
Who gives the bird its leading-strings again,
And who can turn the absolute in singing
To solitude and company, voice and silence.

She who can answer all my messages,
And be to me, retired within my quietness,
The longed-for coast and sail of all my voyages.

But, as in Bleiberg, the expressions are generally not visualized;
thus the sail of his ship and the shore towards which he is sailing
are merged together. A detailed analysis of one of Ridruejo's sonnets
from another book, *Sonetos a la piedra,*[9] is given in Chapter 9.

After a short term as Director of the Spanish Press, Ridruejo
joined the Blue Division and took part in the invasion of Russia
in 1941. He describes this in *Poesía en armas (Cuadernos de la cam-
paña de Rusia).*[10] For the first time he really describes something—
the countryside through which he is advancing. He finds it strange
and says "la inmensa mole de planeta / sin acabar, eleva su desierto"[11]
(The immense bulk of an unended planet / Has raised its desert
here), choosing words such as *mole, planeta,* and *desierto* which
Machado too might have used to describe the scene.

He is crossing the Russian forests which are silent and full of
mud and chaos. The snow begins to fall. He feels the fear of the
unknown and the grip of the cold. God Himself is in the force of
Nature. The elements and the long muteness of the Russian countryside are more terrible than man. The inhabitants live in "tristes
aldeas de madera" (sad villages of wood). They have "Ojos mansos /
de larga esclavitud y pobre tierra"[12] (Eyes which are mild / Because of their long slavery and poor soil).

A friend is killed and has to be buried in the snow-covered earth;
this adds to the poet's feeling of sadness amidst the snowy solitude,
though that too has its beauty. The enemy's fire breaks up the silence.
A battle begins and a feeling of pleasure in the combat wakes in him.

He is living within a little circle of snow, girt round by a wood,
and he feels at one with his companions. The countryside is very

beautiful with the white of the sky and that of the snow fading into a single harmony. He and his companions in the trenches pray together, and he feels that his bastion of honor can resist all things. The corpse of an enemy makes him think of the difference between himself, living, and his friends who have been killed. And yet he knows they have gone to eternal life.

> No es aprendido;
> revelado a mi ser, inseparable
> de mí mismo lo sé.[13]

> It's not been learned,
> It's revealed to my being, and inseparable
> From myself, as I know.

In January, 1942, the poet was in a hospital in Berlin. There he wrote his first free-verse poem. He contrasts little Spain, with its sharply defined rivers and mountains, with the vastness of Russia. But he finds fault with what he considers the lukewarm neutrality of his ruined country.[14]

The poet returns to the front. The Russian winter shows signs of coming to an end. He is travelling in a horse-sleigh, and his feeling for Nature is heightened by the touch of the first breezes of Spring. He describes the countryside, with a primitive village, a ruin, a mill, an ancient monastery by the wood-side, and a frozen lake on the borders of which the snow shows blacker. A distant town rises with its towers and cupolas which once were Christian. Spaniards killed in this land belong here also. The dead make him feel the greatness of his cause. He begins his journey home to Spain in April when the gradual thaw is bringing to the surface the remains of those lost in battle.

The final poem of his Russian book was suppressed by him in the 1950 collected edition of his poems; but he says in the Preface that he does not retract the opinions expressed there. This poem is a comment on the international implications of the war with Russia. England is vituperated for her alliance with the Soviet Union. But, in the midst of his attack, the poet pays her a real compliment by calling her people "Extranjeros en Europa, aunque hayan añadido/ algunas de las cuerdas más bellas de su estrofa"[15] (In Europe they are foreigners, though they've added/Some of the loveliest strings to her song's stanza).

After his return, he continued from time to time to write descriptions of natural scenery in what we might call his Machado manner. There are poems of his on the countryside near Malaga, on the Gredos mountains, and on the scenery around Ronda. He is, for instance, near to Machado in these lines on Gredos:

> Por fuera
> de los pinares sube la montaña
> verde, amarilla, gris, blanca en la cumbre,
> eternamente enaltecida y mansa.[16]

> Outside,
> Beyond the pinewoods the mountain goes upwards,
> Green, yellow, grey, and then white at its summit,
> Eternally so mild and yet exalted.

After the adjectives of color, come others which are normally only applicable to persons; we have seen an example of this in Machado himself.

There is even something of a fusion of the two styles, the "Neoclassical" and the Machadoesque. In some passages, however, Nature is seen as a Baroque pattern:

> aquí rosa y clavel, pasto de olores;
> allí dalia, en el tacto, vagamente.

> La azucena a brazada y en la frente
> la estrella del jazmín, blancos honores.[17]

> Here the rose and the pink, a food for perfumes,
> The dahlia there, through the sense of touch, vaguely.

> The lily, in an embrace, and, on the forehead,
> The star of jasmin, that white badge of honor.

Each individual flower is given a certain value for its own particular beauties. These are not the abstract *azucenas* of Bleiberg's *Sonetos amorosos,* where they are really a key-word. And in the following passage "A un almendro" we find direct observation of the coming of Spring, though the tone is "Neoclassical":

> Por ti, por ti, de marzo en los alcores
> se puebla la inocente maravilla
> y decide la tierra a alzar, pausada,
> la rica desazón de sus olores
> y el descanso feraz de su verdura.[18]

For you, for you upon the hills of March
The innocent marvel spreads itself on all sides,
And the slow-moving earth decides to save
The rich insipidness of all its flavors,
The fruitful restfulness of all its verdure.

Ridruejo's latest book of poems, *Elegías*,[19] shows a great change in the poet in every way. Exile to Ronda, for reasons which have never been made public and, later, marriage seem to have matured Ridruejo. He also felt the turn of international politics to be a defeat of the ideas he supported. Such an attitude was quite common among certain Spaniards between 1945 and 1948; not only men of so outstanding a position as Ridruejo, but even those whose only possible crime was occupying some minor and badly-paid government post supposed that as a result of the allied victory a revolution was imminent in which they would lose their lives.

All this is symbolized by the change in Ridruejo's poetical style. The *elegías* are in free verse; the language is no longer "Neoclassical," though he uses powerful terms proper to rhetoric—"castles," "banners," "diamonds," and so on. From the beginning Ridruejo liked to use images with some aristocratic flavor in them, and these words evoke a distant idea of medieval chivalry. Even his metaphors from Nature have grandeur:

Miradla [man's pride] cuando rompe contra su propia furia
y salpica la arena de diminutas gotas,
de diminutos hombres solitarios que no se reconocen.[20]

Look where man's pride breaks against its own fury
And splashes the sand with tiny drops,
With tiny, solitary men who do not recognize each other.

This is the kind of visionary imagery which Bousoño has commented on in the poetry of Vicente Aleixandre. In these elegies Ridruejo tends to lose his thread in long unrhythmical lines. The best of the poems and the one which maintains the most consistent tone is "Umbral de la madurez." Here Ridruejo says that all he has believed in has become diminished by the passing of youth—youth which had brought illusion with it from the womb. But, though the heroic mood no longer holds him, he does not wish to disillusion the youth of others who come after him.

Ridruejo's complete poems up to 1948 have been published in a single volume under the title *En once años*.[21] The impression the volume gives as a whole is disappointing. After he has launched post-Civil War "Neoclassicism," we follow him through his experiences in Russia to his poems of disillusionment on reaching the age of maturity. Here we have a valuable human record of a man whose integrity and intellectual courage are remarkable. But he always seems to miss that final mastery of his medium which makes Hernández, Machado, and Alonso true masters in the three successive styles he has cultivated. These are a revival of the manner of the Renaissance poets, the poetry of man in the face of Nature, and that of the stress of spiritual conflict.

At present, this man who was once the leading poet of the Nationalists seems to have become opposed to the régime, and this has twice led to his imprisonment. Ridruejo's recent political opinions and the consequences of his expressing them have been widely commented on abroad. He is not known, however, to have presented them in poetic form, so that they fall outside the scope of this book.

José García Nieto (1914-   )

Of all the poets of modern Spain, García Nieto is the one who has adhered most consistently to traditional verse-forms. In one of his recent free-verse poems, written no doubt to show that no style was beyond him, he expressly says that the form does not suit him.[22]

His technical ability is beyond question. He has turned his facility to account in winning far more *juegos florales* (floral games or poetical competitions) than any other Spanish poet past or present. He can charm the most stupid audience by reading them just the right poem. His serious poetry, however, has never been really liked in literary circles in Spain. They complain that he is "cold," but that is really what he sets out to be. As a "Neoclassical," the passions are almost entirely excluded from his poetry which seeks another aesthetic, Petrarchan, Garcilasian excellence of its own, from which the feeling in Petrarch and Garcilaso is absent.

García Nieto wrote his first book of poems *Víspera hacia ti*[23] in a Republican prison, where he was constantly reading Bleiberg's *Sonetos amorosos*. Other poets he was reading very carefully at this time were Hernández *(El rayo que no cesa)* and Altolaguirre. Above all, Bleiberg was his especial influence, together with the poets of the Renaissance, with Garcilaso at their head. But there was a real difficulty in emulating the latter. The sixteenth century was steeped in classical Latin culture. To recapture its spirit completely today a profound knowledge of Latin and the Latin poets would be of inestimable service, even though a poet so great as Hernández has been able to dispense with it. But none of the poets after 1939 we are discussing was a Latin scholar. García Nieto, for one, did not study at a university.

García Nieto was one of a group of young Madrilenian poets who first began to meet at the time of the Civil War. Their sympathies were Nationalist and most of them were in prison at some time between 1936 and 1939 for this reason. The others were José Luis and Carlos Prado, Jesús Juan Garcés, Rafael Romero Moliner, and the journalist Jesús Revuelta. Of these only Garcés and Romero Moliner attended a university. But they imposed a training on themselves as poets, reading Spanish poetry of the past and present very thoroughly and imitating it. In 1943, this group was responsible for launching the poetry review *Garcilaso;* they became the nucleus of the *Juventud Creadora.*

These poets at first showed a particular preference for the sonnet. García Nieto used the form very skilfully; he makes us admire his technical handling of the *enjambement,* for example. As a sonneteer, García Nieto, following Bleiberg and Ridruejo, consciously seeks not to be too precise and not to recount anything.

At a public recitation in 1942 García Nieto attacked the *poetas deshumanizadores*[24] who had divorced poetry from the general public. Yet García Nieto's sonnets are as dehumanized in their way as any of the poems of the least communicative of the poets of the *generación de la Dictadura.* We have already suggested that there is something strangely akin to Surrealism in some modern "Neoclassical" Spanish poets. Is there not an element of this in, say, García Nieto's sonnet analyzed in Chapter 9? Certainly García Nieto sometimes says in conversation that he has read all the works of Freud and that he accepts the conclusions of psychoanalysis in so far as they do not conflict with Catholic orthodoxy. The absence of a logical sequence of ideas in some of his poems perhaps bears witness to this.

In any case, it is not the thought or the emotion which is important in García Nieto's sonnets, but the play of words and images:

A un espejo que va perdiendo el azogue

Qué fracaso del aire, qué cadenas
rotas aquí un momento, qué caída
de la ilusión ya casi conseguida,
derribada de pronto en las almenas.[25]

To a Looking-Glass which is losing its Quicksilver.

What a failure in the air, oh, what a chain
Is, for a moment, broken, what a fall
Of those high hopes that almost achieved all,
Swiftly cast from the battlements again.

Cadenas and *almenas* are what we called key-words when discussing Bleiberg's *Sonetos amorosos*. They are not real or even metaphorical chains and battlements, since what is being described is the loss of quicksilver from a looking-glass. "Broken chains" simply means something that disintegrates and "battlements" something that stands upright. Yet, at the same time, the poet wants us to feel the rhetorical force of the original meaning of these words.

Let us now turn to poems by García Nieto not in sonnet form. With him, as with many poets vitally interested in technical skill, the influence of former writers is hardly disguised at all. His "Cantar de tierra," one of the finest poems in *Poesía*,[26] clearly recalls Alberti's "A un capitán de navío."[27] Alberti writes "fuiste condecorado por un golpe de mar" (By a wave of the sea you were invested) and García Nieto, "vendrás armado en lunas caballero/ y con la Cruz del Sur condecorado" (The moons will dub you knight when you return here/ And with the Southern Cross you'll be invested). In another poem, the line "Aldebarán amigo" reminds us that Unamuno wrote a long poem to that star[28] and that Alberti began a sonnet with the name.[29]

García Nieto has written in most of the traditional forms. His *auto* in verse, the *Retrato del ángel, el hombre y la pastora,* was acted in 1944 and published in 1945.[30] Hernández' *Quien te ha visto y quien te ve* seems to have been in his mind when writing it, since the allegorical theme is almost identical, though the treatment and the style are different. In "Toledo"[31] García Nieto writes *soleares* and neat little poems in the popular vein; but he has not really the lightness or humor to be successful at these. He is more at home when, in a style with something of Machado in it, he describes the innocent ardors of early love in a cane-brake:

Dentro de aquellas salas,
verdes columnas, angustiosas puertas,
de aquel brillante, fiel, nutrido bosque,
dejaba huir mis ojos
hasta el mundo feliz de un primer día,
bebiendo el más oscuro
rincón de tus cabellos.[32]

Within those rooms,
With their green pillars and their anxious doors,
In that bright, faithful, and abundant wood,
I let my eyes flee outwards
Towards the world, happy on its first day,
Whilst I drank in the darkest
Corner of your hair.

The second line is especially reminiscent of Machado, with its two adjectives and substantives in opposition. Many examples can be found in Machado, in a similar meter:

¡Y día adolescente
cuando pensaste a Amor, junto a la fuente,
—ojos claros y músculos morenos—,[33]

That day of adolescence
When you thought about love beside the fountain.
How clear the eyes were and how brown the muscles.

Again: "¡Colinas plateadas,/ grises alcores, cárdenas roquedas"[34] (The hills marked out in silver,/ Grey on the heights, the rocks of livid colors). The rest of the passage rather resembles Machado, but not so closely. This is partly because it is a country scene.

In two poems of *Del Campo y soledad*[35] he ceases to be a "Neoclassical" cultivating impersonality and a lack of emotion. In the first of these two poems he is looking at a photograph of himself as a child. He reflects on how time is passing and how sad life will be at the age of ninety. But he also feels joy in remembering his childhood's first sense of wonder at the world:

Era también un niño
porque apenas palabras
salían de sus labios,
apenas nombres, formas de las cosas,
señales luminosas de un encuentro.
Aquí, *tarde;* aquí, *amor;* un poco antes,
Madre—sí, con mayúscula—;
muerte siempre detrás, porque era un Hombre.[36]

He was also a child
Because it was merely words
Which came forth from his lips then,
Merely the names, the shapes of things around him,
The luminous impressions of a meeting.
Here the *evening,* there *love;* a little before that,
Mother—yes, with a capital;
Death always behind him—he was a man-child.

There is an echo here of Unamuno's "Era un muchacho pálido"[37] (He was a pale boy). And, like Unamuno, he approaches the prosaic without ceasing to be poetic.

García Nieto is even more personal in the second of the two poems, "Poema ante un otoño," which is in alexandrines and makes full use of the rhetorical surge of the rhythm of that verse-form. The occasion for writing the poem was that José Luis Prado had written a fine poem (in the same form) which will be discussed in its proper place; in it he had spoken of the punishments God had sent him for his sinful pride. One of these was an estrangement between him and García Nieto (who had been his companion in prison). García Nieto replies to this poem: "¿No ves que soy un río profundamente triste/ cruzando por orillas no elegidas por mí?" (Can you not see I am a river of deep sorrow/ Flowing between banks which are not those that I should have chosen?) Yet, for all his sadness, he never loses his religious faith:

Sustento de la tierra, pasto oscuro del lodo
serán mis ojos, fijos al último paisaje;
antes que tú lo sepas, yo lo habré visto todo,
dirás a Dios mi nombre, y aliviará mi viaje.[38]

Sustenance shall my eyes be for the earth and a pasture
For the mud, when they're fixed on the last of my landscapes.
Before you know about it, I shall have looked at all things,
You'll say my name to God, then, and that will ease my journey.

The "Neoclassical" is still present in these quotations. When the poet describes himself as a "river," he is using a key-word frequently found in "Neoclassicals" for "existence" or "person"; but in the next line he does something rather "unneoclassical," which is to develop the key-word into a metaphor.

Both the poems we have just examined speak of death. It is death which gives the sadness to the poems, a sadness which would be despair if it were not for the poet's faith. There has been an inward struggle of which the poet would normally prefer not to speak, but which cannot help revealing itself in these two poems.

None of García Nieto's love-poetry was as personal as this, except on one occasion when he wrote a book under an assumed name and in an assumed character. This book is called *Dama de soledad*[39] and is ostensibly by a poetess called Juana García Noreña. (No writer of that name exists, though someone was found to impersonate her.) But the first letters of one of the poems[40] spell out the real author's name.[41]

The poems are written on one of the oldest themes of poetry in the world—the sorrow of a girl who has been abandoned by her lover. We find it, for instance, in such widely differing poems as Ovid's *Heroides,* the Portuguese *cantares de amigo,* Góngora's *romance* about "La más bella niña," and Julia's letter in Canto I of Byron's *Don Juan.* These masculine representations of how a woman might feel are eminently successful; in literature emotion transposed to another person is often more affecting than a direct expression of the author's feelings. This is clearly what has happened in *Dama de soledad.*

One of the reasons for García Nieto's publishing the book in such a way was that he wished to show that he could write poetry that was not "cold." So long as people thought this work was by a real poetess, they praised its emotion. Juan Ramón Jiménez wrote a poem to Juana García Noreña.[42] But as soon as people knew who *Dama de soledad* was really by, they ceased to be moved by it.

Most of the book is in the Neoclassical style:

> Galanes que me desposan,
> ruiseñores que me cantan,
>
> ciudades que se me ofrecen,
> alas que me llevan, alas . . .[43]

> Gallants who wish to marry me,
> Nightingales which sing about me,
>
> Cities which are offered to me,
> Wings to bear me, wings to bear me.

These are four images of or allusions to happiness. They mingle into one imprecise impression of emotion. In other passages the feeling is much more forcefully expressed:

Cuando de tu dulcísimo arbolado
regreso a mis praderas de congoja,
una gota de sangre en cada hoja
pienso que el amor mío te ha dejado,[44]

When, from the sovereign sweetness of your wood,
I come back to the meadows of my pain,
On all your leaves, I think, there has been lain,
In my love's memory, a drop of blood,

This is the myth of the nightingale and the rose, though the expressions are chosen for their effect as poetical rhetoric rather than because they form an exact picture, which they do not. Here is another passage:

No son los clavos, no, los que me hieren,
sino la soledad, donde se mueren
las horas del amor de cualquier modo.

También yo estoy sin luces en mi ermita,
y con mi rosa de papel escrita,
y con mi puerta sin cerrar del todo.[45]

No, no. It's not the nails with which I'm torn,
But the long loneliness which must be borne
While all my hours of love die desolate.

No light can in my hermitage be found,
Although my paper rose is writ around,
And slightly open stands my little gate.

The last three lines compare three aspects of the life of a hermit to the feelings of a girl left by her lover. The sadness belongs to the girl, not the hermit.

Tregua[46] is written in brief poems of short lines. He has tried to surpass his other work. He tells us in his answer to the questionnaire that all his poetry is like an apprentice's workshop and that therefore he prefers *Tregua* to his earlier poems—as more technically perfect, presumably. Certainly we should have difficulty in assigning influences to these poems and, in that sense, García Nieto is a more original poet in this book. On the other hand, the hopes we might have conceived from *Del campo y soledad* and *Dama de soledad* that he would become a more personal lyric poet are not fulfilled.

Aparezco lleno de oro
si en su caudal hundo mis brazos,
pero la carne sola sabe
qué hombre sostiene aquí clamando.

No sois, érais; no estáis, estábais;
conmigo fuísteis al milagro,
y hoy vuelvo solo—¿os veo hermosas
porque érais mías?—y aun os amo.[47]

I appear with gold covering me
If I plunge my two arms into its treasure,
But only the flesh has knowledge
What sort of man it bears up here exclaiming.

You are not, you were; you do not, you did.
You went with me to work the miracle.
Now I've come back alone. I see you're beautiful,
Because you were mine? And still I love you.

The poem is a study of the poet's relation to his own poems. If he has recourse to what he has written he can appear remarkable (like someone plunging his arms into a pile of gold). But his real being is unaffected by this. The poems are a miracle of time now past and are no longer part of him, though he loves them. The style is "Neoclassical," with a very slight mixture of the prosaic.

Religious faith is above the artist's aesthetic ideal:

Gracias, Señor, porque estás
todavía en mi palabra;
porque debajo de todos
mis puentes pasan tus aguas.[48]

My thanks, oh Lord, because You are
Still in the words which I utter,
Because Your waters are under
My bridges, flowing beneath them.

Puentes and *aguas* are prevented from being typical key-words because they are woven into a single image.

Thus the impersonality of "Neoclassicism" has in the long run proved unsatisfactory, though we cannot say García Nieto had as yet found anything very much in place of it. He acknowledged this in a lecture given in the Ateneo in Madrid in 1950, "Doble confesión de un poeta católico" (Double Confession by a Catholic Poet) (unpublished). The poets before him, he told his hearers, had fallen to worshipping their own creations or had tried to build up a world of poetry out of all the *suciedades y entrañas* (dirt and entrails) revealed by Freud. Then the *Juventud Creadora* ("Neoclassicals") had come forward in *Garcilaso* cheerfully accepting *limitación* and *modestia*. A new poetical discipline had made renovation possible. The formal beauties and the tenderness of Garcilaso de la Vega had rendered him a suitable paragon for the *Juventud Creadora*. But now "no es Garcilaso la tabla de salvación" (Garcilaso is not the plank which will save us). The poet must turn to God. For this he will need new forms of expression:

> tendrá que operar con delicadísimos materiales, y estará más lejos que nunca de lo meramente formal, de lo literario y de lo retórico. Porque la huella de lo divino será siempre esencia y síntesis, y los materiales humanos que lo reflejan estarán lejos siempre de lo sobrado, de lo floral y de lo meramente descriptivo.

> he will have to work in very delicate materials, and he will be further than ever from what is merely formal, literary, and rhetorical. For the trace of divinity will always be an essence and a synthesis, and the human materials which reflect it will always be something very different from the superabundant, the florid, or the merely descriptive.

He says nothing more definite as to his idea of what this future Catholic poetry will be like. One suspects that it might be a poetry of the type of Machado, or Jiménez, or Unamuno, but in the Catholic tradition of Saint John of the Cross or Fray Luis de León. The interesting thing is that García Nieto has become dissatisfied with the search for an impersonal poetical perfection. The more personal poems of *Del campo y soledad,* the vicarious emotion of *Dama de soledad,* and the self-questionings about his poetry in *Tregua* (more prosaically explained in his lecture) all lead us to conclude this. The truth is that García Nieto felt he could not write what really mattered. By a different path he had reached the same despondency as Ridruejo.

García Nieto, in 1957, received the Fastenrath Prize of the Spanish Royal Academy of Language for the book of poems called *La red.* Half of this little book consists of sonnets, written with the author's usual skill and very definitely "Neoclassical." One of them is to his "creature" J.G.N. (Juana García Noreña), whom he has devoured as Saturn did his children. "Dije lo que alguien no me dijo / jamás"[49] (I said what somebody never said to me), he explains, thus suggesting that the origin of Juana may have been some sentimental incident in his life.

The second part of *La red* consists of four free-verse poems, and of one rhyming poem. García Nieto's free verse is remarkable because, at its best, it is as formal as that of Dámaso Alonso, whose example one would not have expected him to follow. He uses long similes, much like those of *Hijos de la ira*. Here is the beginning of one of four very long consecutive similes in a poem called "Elegía de amor":

He sido como ese borriquillo de la noria,
girador incesante y vendado
alrededor de un agua apenas oída que nunca corrobora su
 presencia,
de la que no le será dado jamás el arrebatador trago radiante[50]

I have been like that little donkey at the well-wheel,
A ceaseless, blindfolded turner,
Round water hardly heard which never corroborates its presence,
The ravishing, radiant draught of which shall never be given it.

So far as this goes, García Nieto is treating free verse as a form of poetry possibly even more complex to write than sonnets. But in another free-verse passage, he insists on the external fact that he is writing on the typewriter.

One of his latest works, *El parque pequeño*,[51] is a long octosyllabic poem with an assonance on every second line. It is a mature man speaking. The scene is his home and through his window he can see the grassy courtyard where his children play. God is present as a force watching over the courtyard, watching over everything. To walk with his little son reminds him of walking with his own Father in childhood.

The images are still rather formal and addressed rather to the ear than to the visual imagination—which is hardly a fault in poetry, though no doubt the ideal thing is that they should address both senses at once. "Cielo mínimo del cautivo" (the prisoner's minimum of sky) is an example. It has force and originality and recalls the poet's youthful prison experiences, of which we have spoken earlier in this chapter. In "Neoclassical" times, we should hardly have found so vivid an expression in any poet. And this is only one isolated example in *El parque pequeño*.

Thus García Nieto too, though far more slowly than Ridruejo, has finally moved right away from "Neoclassicism." Still, traces of it can be found in Spanish poetry at the present time, even among quite young poets.

Vicente Gaos (1919-   )

Gaos has said in a private letter: "Dámaso Alonso ha señalado la influencia de Antero de Quental y de Unamuno sobre mi poesía.

Estoy de acuerdo, aunque en ese momento no había leído a Quental."
(Dámaso Alonso has pointed out the influence of Antero de Quental
and Unamuno on my poetry. I agree, though at that time I had not
read Quental.) Gaos is like the Portuguese poet Quental in two ways.
They both wrote in sonnet form when composing their best work
and both expressed what might be called a religious feeling of disbelief. Unamuno also expressed this.

The sonnets of Gaos's first book, *Arcángel de mi noche*,[52] belong
to the "Neoclassical" period and he has a polished command of his
form. But he does not restrict his vocabulary or use key-words, which
makes his writing nearer to that of the Renaissance poets. But no
poet in the sixteenth or seventeenth centuries would have written
the line in Gaos's second book *Sobre la tierra:* "Existe al menos tú,
si Dios no existe."[53] (Exist yourself at least, though God does not.)

The whole tone in which he speaks of religious faith is modern:
"Oh, sálvame, Señor, dame la muerte,/ no me amenaces más con
otra vida."[54] (Oh, give me my salvation, Lord, my death,/ And do
not threaten with another life.) Notwithstanding, the last poem of
Arcángel de mi noche suggests the triumph of belief:

> Cosa imposible fué, rebelión mía,
> intento de negar a Dios y al mundo,
> relámpago infeliz, ángel caído.

> Yo no sabía, no, yo no sabía
> que sólo Tú, con tu callar profundo
> dabas al universo su sentido.[55]

> The thing could not be. It was my revolt,
> My attempt to deny God and the whole world,
> Unhappy flash of lightning, fallen angel.

> I did not know, oh no, I did not know,
> That only You, from the depths of Your silence,
> Had power to give the universe a meaning.

Even in Gaos there is a certain imprecision of imagery which
would not have seemed fitting to a poet of the Golden Age. A "rebellion" is compared disparately both to a flash of lightning and to
a fallen angel; the fallen angel is presumably thrust down by a thun-
derbolt, but this synthetic way of saying so is modern. Also *callar
profundo* giving *sentido* mingles the idea of not speaking with depth
and, at the same time, with giving meaning. This is trying to express
an almost certainly heterodox religious idea by a *correspondance*.

After the Aleixandre reaction, Gaos has written more and more in free verse, but this work is less interesting. In spite of that, some people prefer his poetry to that of García Nieto, for he received more votes for the *Antología consultada* (see Chapter 7). He has been a university lecturer in the United States and has translated Shelley and Eliot.

Other "Neoclassical" poets were Jesús Juan Garcés,[56] Luis López Anglada,[57] and José María Alonso Gamo,[58] to mention only three of the most outstanding. "Neoclassicism" could of its nature only be a temporary fashion. One of its main uses was to train a rather less cultivated generation of poets in technical skill. Young men are encouraged to publish poetry in modern Spain, as can be seen by the large number of government-subsidized reviews in which poetry has been printed. "Neoclassicism" trained them in their art.

NOTES TO CHAPTER 3

1. (Madrid, 1935).
2. Both published in Madrid in 1936.
3. (Segovia).
4. Preface to Machado's poetical works (Madrid, 1941), p. xiii.
5. *Ibid.*
6. *Entregas de poesía* (Barcelona), 9 (1944) ["Confidencia literaria"].
7. *En once años* (Madrid, 1950), p. 171 ["Al 18 de julio"].
8. *Poesía española actual* (Madrid, 1946), p. 569.
9. (Madrid, 1943).
10. (Madrid, 1944).
11. *En once años,* p. 235 [Poem I of "Soledad"].
12. *Ibid.,* p. 238 [poem II of "El Volchow," "De Nowgarod a Possad"].
13. *Ibid.,* p. 254 [poem XIV of "El Volchow"].
14. *Ibid.,* pp. 257-263 ["A España ante la guerra del mundo"].
15. *Poesía en armas,* p. 160.
16. *Poesía española actual,* p. 582.
17. *En once años,* pp. 330-331 ["La mentida nostalgia"].
18. *Ibid.,* p. 318 ["A un almendro"].
19. (Madrid, 1948).
20. *En once años,* p. 440 ["Todavía"].
21. See Note 7.
22. *La red* (Madrid, 1955), p. 54 ["Carta a Juan Alcaide Sánchez"].
23. (Madrid, 1940).
24. In the printed but unpublished Anthology of *Filmófono,* Madrid, 1942. The reference is, of course, to Ortega's *Deshumanización del arte* and to the poets in Diego's Anthology who shared or were influenced by Ortega's attitude.
25. *Juego de espejos en doce sonetos* (Santander, 1951), p. 16.
26. (Madrid, 1944), pp. 79-83.
27. *Poesía española actual,* p. 345.
28. *Ibid.,* pp. 14-18.
29. See *1616* (London), 2 (1934).
30. (Madrid).

31. In *Fantasía* (Madrid), 3 (1945).
32. *Segundo libro de poemas* (Madrid, 1951), p. 140 ["Cañaveral"].
33. Angel del Río, *Antología general de la literatura española* (Madrid, 1954), 2, 630.
34. *Ibid.*, p. 622.
35. (Madrid).
36. *Ibid.*, p. 26 ["Momento para un retrato"].
37. *Antología general de la literatura española*, 2, p. 499.
38. *Del campo y soledad*, p. 45.
39. (Madrid, 1950).
40. *Ibid.*, p. 47 ["La otra muerte"].
41. JO/SE/GA/R/CI/A/NI/E/T/O.
42. In *Poesía española*, 12 (December, 1952) ["Eco de dama de soledad"].
43. *Dama de soledad*, p. 47 (see Notes 40 and 41).
44. *Ibid.*, p. 54 ["El daño"].
45. *Ibid.*, p. 60 ["La ermita"].
46. (Madrid, 1951).
47. *Ibid.*, p. 39.
48. *Ibid.*, p. 15.
49. *La red*, p. 20 ["Saturno"].
50. *Ibid.*, p. 47.
51. *El parque pequeño y Elegía de Covaleda* (Madrid, 1959).
52. (Madrid, 1944).
53. (Madrid, 1945), p. 28 ["Adolescencia"].
54. *Arcángel de mi noche*, p. 61 ["La noche"].
55. *Ibid.*, p. 80 ["Mi creación"].
56. (1917—). Till now, he has only published one book of poems, *He venido a esta orilla* (Madrid, 1949).
57. (1919—). His name figured as editor of *Halcón*, which published his book, *Al par de tu sendero* (Valladolid, 1946). He published a single time in *Garcilaso* (Madrid), 34 (February, 1946). The Adonais series includes his *La vida conquistada* (1952) and *Aventura* (1956).
58. (1913—). He published a book of poems written during and about the Spanish Civil War, *Paisajes del alma en guerra* (Buenos Aires, 1943). He won the National Prize for poetry with *Tus rosas frente al espejo* (Valencia, 1952), a book of "Neoclassical" sonnets.

4

The group round Aleixandre

What we have called the Aleixandre revival began with a few
poets going daily to Vicente Aleixandre's house to discuss poetry
with him. They did not imitate Aleixandre in their writing and many
of them did not at once abandon the stylistic mannerisms of "Neoclassicism." But they helped to supersede it. Aleixandre's most frequent visitors were José Suárez Carreño, José Luis Cano, Rafael
Morales, and above all Carlos Bousoño. Poets from the provinces
such as José Luis Hidalgo and Eugenio de Nora also went to see
him when visiting Madrid.

"Neoclassicism" had excluded all political and religious doubts;
even if these existed, they had no place in poetry. But now a poetry
of discontent was beginning to be written again. Gaos had been one
of the first to write it, with his prayer to God for annihilation after
death. Aleixandre's visitors, besides, felt more or less dissatisfied
politically, except Bousoño, who was indifferent to such questions.
In their poetry the influence of Machado was more marked than that
of Juan Ramón Jiménez. As Bousoño wrote in 1948:

> Maestros y jóvenes han coincidido sobre todo en tres puntos
> concretos: clarificación de la expresión poética, humanización
> del fondo vital de la poesía, y nueva complacencia en la línea
> Quevedo-Machado frente a la línea Góngora-Juan Ramón
> Jiménez, antes preferida.[1]

> Both the established masters and the young are in agreement
> as to three specific points: the clarification of poetic expression,
> the humanization of the vital background, and a new penchant
> for the Quevedo-Machado line of poetry rather than the Góngora-
> Jiménez line which had been preferred before.

Sombra del paraíso was accepted as the message of a whole older
generation, of a former world. Now that it had appeared, there was
no need to obey strict rules of versification any more or to cultivate
the sonnet. José Luis Cano (1912), for instance, whose *Sonetos a la*

bahía[2] had won praise in "Neoclassical" days, now wrote his psalm-like *Voz de la muerte*,[3] the first book in free-verse to appear in the Adonais series—of which Cano himself was the editor. And, almost immediately after *Sombra del paraíso,* José Luis Hidalgo published *Raíz,* a book of poems in a style like Aleixandre's, illustrated with drawings which could be described as Surrealist.

José Suárez Carreño (1915-   )

We should, on the other hand, have difficulty in showing the trace of Aleixandre's poetry on Suárez Carreño's. Yet he definitely tells us, in his answers to the questionnaire, that he began to write poetry under the influence of Aleixandre's *Espadas como labios.*

Suárez Carreño's first book consisted of poems written in the Nationalist army during the Civil War. It was published in 1943 under the title of *La tierra amenazada.*[4] Suárez Carreño's poems do not show which side he had fought for. There are no political references.

> Van los mulos de la sombra
> por las tierras desoladas.

> Son las cinco de la tarde.
> Alguien dice: noche larga.[5]

> The mules of the shadow are going
> Across the desolate countryside.

> It's five o'clock in the evening.
> Someone says: "This will be a long night."

The writer is just a soldier alone in the night of war; he might belong to either side. In 1944, Julio Maruri (1920-   ), a younger poet, then doing his military service in Santander, lent the book round the barracks and found that it had a strong appeal for people who normally never read poetry.

His second book, *Edad de hombre* (1944),[6] won the *Adonais* Prize in 1943, and is therefore also prior to the Aleixandre revival. It is entirely composed of sonnets. He writes of fierce, egotistical love and of death as the end of all. The meaning and the emotion are very clear but the imagery is very tenuous and "Neoclassical." Yet he was one of the most fervent of Aleixandre's supporters.

José Luis Hidalgo (1919-1947)

Neither *Raíz* nor Hidalgo's second book—a very short one—*Los animales*[7] is worth commenting on here. But he showed himself a fine poet in *Los muertos*,[8] published a few days after his death from tuberculosis. The book was being rushed through the press in order that he might see it before he died, but he only knew it in the form of proof-sheets; a copy of it was buried with him. There is the same conflict between faith and bitterness in *Los muertos* as in Gaos' poems. The poems are in regular traditional forms and in what Bousoño would call the Quevedo-Machado style. Here is the last verse of a poem called "Flores bajo los muertos":

> ¿Y qué? Todo es lo mismo; crecer o derrumbarse,
> tener sobre la carne una nube o la muerte,
> doblarse ciegamente, doblarse como un río,
> con estas blancas flores, leves y detenidas.[9]

> So what? It's all the same, then, to grow or be demolished,
> Whether one has a cloud or has death on one's body,
> Or double oneself blindly, as if one were a river,
> With these white flowers around one, which are so slight and
> lingering.

There is some vagueness of imagery here; words like *nube* and *río* might be what we have called key-words. But the verse is emotional rather than contemplative, in the school of Machado rather than that of Jiménez. The poet expresses a longing for belief in God, while professing the same nostalgic scepticism as Gaos and Blas de Otero. He is, actually, more bitter than they are. In a poem addressed to Christ he says:

> Has bajado a la tierra cuando nadie te oía
> y has mirado a los vivos y contado tus muertos.
> Señor: duerme sereno, ya cumpliste tu día,
> puedes cerrar los ojos que tenías abiertos.[10]

> You have come down to earth here, when no one listened for you,
> And you looked at the living and counted your dead men.
> Lord, you may now sleep quietly, your day has been
> accomplished,
> And you may shut those eyes now, which before were wide open.

Rafael Morales (1919-   )

Rafael Morales published in *Garcilaso*. The sonnets in his first book *Poemas del toro*,[11] written while he was a student in Madrid, show the influence of Hernández' *El rayo que no cesa.* But Morales says that he has never considered himself a "Neoclassical." He claims to be the interpreter of outward Nature:

> Me impresionaba aquel revuelo de pajaritos que ofrecieron sus tiernas alas pardas a mis primeros versos; con ellas, volaba en rimas mi imaginación de niño. No era posible que entonces, al hacer el poemilla, buscase otra cosa que expresar un sentimiento. Exactamente como me ocurre ahora.[12]

> I was impressed by the flight of the little birds that offered their tender grey wings to my first verses; with them my childish imagination flew in rhyme. It was not possible at that time, when I wrote a little poem, for me to try to do anything but express a feeling. Just as it is with me now.

This approach is certainly different from that of a true "Neoclassical" poet, who would be mainly concerned with the perfection of his form. Yet if "Neoclassicism" emulates the poetry of the Golden Age, so does Morales:

> Toda la noche suena y se estremece,
> y fundida con toros y paisaje
> rueda redonda, caudalosa crece.[13]

> So all the night is full of sounds, and trembles
> And, fused together with the bulls and landscape,
> It circles round and copiously increases.

The mixture of different sense-impressions is modern, but the rhetorical close is in the style of Quevedo. And the sonnets of the *Poemas del toro* (one is analyzed in chapter 9) are sufficiently like those of the "Neoclassicals" to make it hard to dissociate Morales' from the others.

In his answers to our questionnaire, Morales says that he is very glad "que el sentimiento cristiano de mi poesía pueda hacer un bien" (that the Christian feeling in my poetry may do good). This might refer especially to the feeling for the unfortunate which he particularly expresses in his poems *Los desterrados.*[14] Morales believes that poetry is to be sought everywhere, including the unhappy things of life and in people who are bowed under affliction: "Buscadla también en los ojos de los ahorcados o en las manos sucias de los trabajadores."[15] (Look for it also in the eyes of the hanged or in the dirty hands of the workers.)

In *Los desterrados,* his desire to be humanitarian leads to some absurdities. This is how he addresses the leper:

Ay, mírala, qué bella es la muchacha,
qué delicada y pura junto al aire.
Pero no la desees: olvida, olvida.
No sirves ya, leproso, para amante.[16]

Oh, look at her. That girl is very lovely,
How delicate and pure with the air round her.
You must not desire her. Forget, forget her.
Now you are useless, leper, as a lover.

The exhortation to contemplate followed immediately by another to forget is not really very skillful. *Aire* looks like a "Neoclassical" key-word. But in general this book shows that Morales had abandoned "Neoclassicism" without acquiring a satisfactory new manner. That was to come in *Canción sobre el asfalto.* There he writes about common objects, especially those which have connections with poverty —a dustbin, a wheel going along a dusty road, an old coat, or a pair of shoes: "tienden dos alas de cuero / para sostener mi vida."[17] (Putting out two wings of leather / So as to sustain my life.)

Morales is one of the most read poets of his generation. His poems have been reprinted more frequently than those of any other poet after 1939.

Carlos Bousoño (1923-   )

The poets we have just been commenting upon certainly associated themselves with Aleixandre in their successful attempt to enlarge the poetical field of post-Civil War Spain. But they were not followers of his as Carlos Bousoño was. While he was still a student, his poems won praise from Aleixandre and Dámaso Alonso. Aleixandre was to write of Bousoño's poetical language that it "obedece hasta un grado de apuramiento en la belleza que no creo haya sido superado en nuestra lengua"[18] (attains to a degree of purified beauty which I do not believe has been surpassed in our language). Indeed Bousoño was, he said, "la voz más pura que haya sonado nunca, acaso, en la poesía española"[19] (the purest voice which has ever sounded, perhaps, in Spanish poetry). These quotations are from the first piece of prose writing that Aleixandre published after 1939—the preface to Bousoño's second book, *Primavera de la muerte* (1946). That

Aleixandre had consented to write the preface at all was considered a great honor for the young Bousoño. Though the tone of prefaces and even book reviews is largely eulogistic in contemporary Spain, Aleixandre went beyond the bounds convention would have sanctioned.

We might therefore expect Bousoño's poems to be in fairly strict conformity with Aleixandre's ideas of what poetry should be. But here again Bousoño's manner of writing is fairly unlike Aleixandre's. Bousoño generally writes in regular meter and, though his imagery is "allusive," he is not nearly so hard to understand as Aleixandre. Indeed, his meaning is as immediately clear as, say, that of Bécquer. There is even a Becquerian tone about at least one of the poems in Bousoño's first book, *Subida al amor*.[20] Bousoño writes:

> Tal vez la aurora sea pura,
> el aire delicado, claro el día.
> Mas muchos hombres hay como la lluvia
> oscura e infinita.[21]

> Perhaps the daybreak may be pure and
> The air be delicate and daylight limpid,
> Yet there are many men like the rain falling
> Infinitely and darkly.

This is sufficiently like:

> pero aquellas [madreselvas] cuajadas de rocío,
> cuyas gotas mirábamos temblar
> y caer, como lágrimas del día . . .
> esas . . .¡no volverán! (Rima LIII)[22]

> And yet those honeysuckles set with dew,
> The drops of which we could see when they trembled
> And fell, like tears because the day was coming,
> These—shall return no more.

Being dark and infinite and like the rain has a hint of Romantic self-pity about it. The poet might be supposed to be thinking of himself as a minor Byronic hero if a non-Romantic modesty did not make him use the plural. But in both passages—Bécquer and Bousoño—water represents sadness or tears; in Bousoño, the rain is the image, in Bécquer, the dew. The form of the verse, too, is very similar.

His answers to the questionnaire show that Bousoño admires both Bécquer and Espronceda, though the latter is an unpopular poet nowadays and seldom mentioned in the other replies to our question-

naire. In Bousoño's poems to God we find something of the grandiloquence of Espronceda:

> Como el león llama a su hembra, y cálido
> al aire da su ardiente dentellada,
> yo te llamo, Señor. Ven a mis dientes
> como una dura fruta amarga.[23]

> Just like a lion calling his mate and hotly
> Gnashing out at the air with ardent biting,
> I call to You, oh Lord. Come to my teeth now
> Like a fruit hard and bitter.

Though Father Lama calls Bousoño an *auténticamente místico* poet,[24]
this passage has the same rhetorical insincerity as the final verse of
Espronceda's "Himno a la inmortalidad":

> Hombre débil, levanta la frente,
> pon tu labio en su eterno raudal;
> [that is to say, the torrent of immortality]
> tu serás como el sol en Oriente;
> tu serás, como el mundo, inmortal.[25]

> Weak man, raise up your forehead
> And place your lip at the eternal torrent.
> You will be like the sun on the horizon,
> You will be like the world and be immortal.

Bousoño's poem is really far more extreme than Espronceda's. Espronceda's poem speaks of being as famous as the sun and the world;
but Bousoño is a lion with God Himself for a lioness. The image
is a monstrous one from every point of view and probably few paral-
lels to such presumption could be found in literature. Eliot's "Christ
the tiger" is a symbol of the power of God, even if rather an unusual one. Bousoño's lion does not remind us of Eliot, but of the
wild animals of Aleixandre's poems. Bousoño's "Oda a España"[26]
also uses violent imagery. In order to say that the hand of God lies
heavy on Spain (in Spanish, that she is *tocada de la mano de Dios*)
Bousoño writes:

> Y yo te veo tierra,
> tierra sólo y herida por el hacha
> de Dios, y vas sangrando, y cae
> toda tu sangre por mi cara.[27]

> I can see you as earth,
> Earth only and earth wounded by the axe

Of God, and you are bleeding and your blood
All sheds down on my face.

A similar language of violence is used at times by Dámaso Alonso in *Hijos de la ira* and by Aleixandre. An image of this sort might well appear in Surrealist poetry. We are beginning to see the effects of the Aleixandre revival more clearly in Bousoño than in Suárez Carreño, Hidalgo, or Morales. Bousoño may not write free verse like Aleixandre's but they both admire energy or violence for its own sake. We can find examples of Mr. Empson's "ambiguities" in Bousoño's poetry. He speaks in the following manner of a woman he remembers from his childhood:

> Yo te vi siempre, siempre, paseando
> tu enorme cola por la triste estancia,
> mientras yo golpeaba mi luz dulce,
> mi niña luz, mis suaves luces ávidas.[28]

> I always, always saw you walk with
> Your vast train [or tail] around the sad apartment,
> And I beat at my sweet light as you did so,
> My childish light, lights which were soft and avid.

Whether the *cola* is the train of a dress or the tail of a peacock (and it is both) it represents vanity, not a real object in the past, for we can hardly believe that any woman at the time of Bousoño's childhood can have habitually worn a train. The lights are meaningless if taken literally; they are an indirect image of childish happiness, very nearly a key-word.

In "Cristo adolescente" there are two lines describing the childhood of Christ: "Pasabas por los bosques como un claror liviano,/ por los bosques oscuros donde tu Cruz crecía."[29] (You crossed the woods like an uncertain radiance,/ The somber woods, in which Your Cross was growing.) Bousoño says of these lines that he, the poet

> está viendo simultáneamente dos tiempos distintos: un tiempo presente, en que el árbol es aún árbol, y un tiempo futuro en el que este árbol se convertirá en cruz, en la Cruz de Cristo.[30]

> sees two different times simultaneously, a present time at which the tree is still just a tree and a future time at which this tree will become a cross, the Cross of Christ.

Bousoño apparently thinks that this passage is one which shows a contemporary poetical sensibility, but surely this is very like the "dramatic irony" so freely used in Shakespeare's tragedies and histories, when characters unwittingly refer to their future tragic ends. Bousoño is trying to prove that his poetry is more "contemporary" than it in fact is. Actually he sometimes follows Aleixandre and sometimes older conventions. In the following verse, the young poet regards himself as the prematurely-aged debauchee of the Byronic tradition:

> Escúchame, muchacho. Yo te hablo
> con lenguaje de monte antiguo y bronco
> por donde mucha lluvia fue dejando
> su sabio estigma silencioso.[31]

> Now listen to me, boy, for I am speaking
> With the tongue of an old and rugged mountain
> On which much rain is gradually leaving
> Its wise and silent stigma.

The imagery of course is not Romantic, being what we have called allusive; that is to say, the mountain and the rain spoken of do not really exist, are not even metaphors, but are an approximate expression of certain feelings or a certain human attitude. The comparison with a hill does, however, suggest that there is something majestic about the poet's wickedness and precedents for this idea can be frequently found in Romantic poetry (and even in the early Neruda).

Bousoño can also write in the grand rhetorical manner:

> Sólo la voz se queda que dice para siempre
> el signo doloroso de los sin esperanza

> que tuvieron deseos e incumplidas promesas,
> dulces desasosiegos, efluvios, resonancias,
> transparencias absortas, misteriosos presentes
> y arcangélicos sueños junto a inocentes ansias.[32]

> Only the voice is left now which keeps repeating always
> The one unhappy watchword of those who have no hope left

> But who once had desires and promises they did not
> Fulfill, and sweet disquietudes, effluvia, resonances,
> Engrossing transparencies, presents that were a mystery
> And archangelic dreams, besides innocent longings.

The second line suggests Dante's Hell. The lines following bear a high-sounding list of substantives. The flow of the alexandrine helps the rhetoric and the effect of the whole passage is more like Romantic poetry than like Aleixandre's.

But, at other times, there is a suggestion of Arcadia:

cuando habla la lengua del adolescente sin sombras
escuchamos el sonido de una flauta lejana
que sin tiempo va nombrando las riberas,
los bosques y los ríos, las rocas, las montañas.[33]

When the tongue of the young man speaks without any shadows,
Then we can hear the sound of a flute in the distance
Which, timeless, goes on naming the shores of all the rivers,
The forests and the fountains, the boulders and the mountains.

A sound—the shepherd's pipe—recalls the scenery in which it is traditionally played. At the same time the flute itself does not exist, but is only the impression that the speech of adolescents are said, by the poet, to produce. But the last two lines of the passage could easily belong to some sixteenth-century pastoral poet, such as Garcilaso. This revival of a past style reminds us of the "Neoclassicals."

These echoes from the past are natural enough and probably no poet has ever been completely without them. On the other hand, there have been great poets who have not had Bousoño's technical sureness.

Bousoño, the Poetical Theorist

We have seen that while the influence of Aleixandre is strong in Bousoño's poetry, it is not by any means the only one. He calls Hernández, for instance, "en cierto modo, usando la terminología de Petersen, origen y 'guía' de nuestra generación, como primer miembro de ella"[34] (to a certain extent, using Petersen's terminology, the origin and "guide" of our generation, being the first member of it). If we look up Julius Petersen's definition of "guía," we find that this is an even greater eulogy than it appeared at first. Petersen writes:

> f) *El guía.* Cada época y, si se mira con atención, cada generación, tiene ante sus ojos un determinado ideal de hombre: el Renacimiento, *l'uomo universale,* el Barroco, al cortesano, la Illustración francesa, al *bel esprit,* la inglesa, al *gentleman,* la alemana, al hombre honrado, la época de la Restauración, al desgarrado, la decadencia del XIX al *dandy,* mientras que a fines del siglo, se convierte en consigna el superhombre.[35]

> f) *The guide.* Each period and, if we examine it with attention, each generation has before its eyes a special ideal man; the Renaissance has *l'uomo universale;* the age of Barroque, the

courtier; the *Illustration* in France, the *bel esprit;* in England, the gentleman; in Germany, the man of honor; the period of the *Restauration,* the *roué;* the decadence of the 19th century, the dandy; while, at the end of the century, the Superman becomes a watchword.

In short, Miguel Hernández, the "Neoclassical" goatherd, was the ideal of Bousoño's generation—young men living in towns and some of them frequenting the university Faculty of Philosophy and Letters; "casi todos los jóvenes poetas son universitarios" (almost all the young poets have been to a university), Bousoño affirms, exaggerating.

Bousoño finds that modern man loves, above all, what is "human": " 'Un libro muy humano,' 'un poema muy humano,' 'un hombre muy humano,' son frases que todos decimos."[36] ("A very human book," "a very human poem," " a very human man" are phrases we all use.) This is no doubt a sign of the reaction against the *Deshumanización del arte* in the first third of the present century. The new poetry in Spain has, according to Bousoño, had to *humanizarse.* Even older poets such as Guillén have become more "human," he says.

Bousoño believes that we live in an age which has revolted against Reason. Bousoño says that there has been a final break with the Renaissance (yet it is in the Renaissance itself that he has found early examples of the unreason of modern forms of poetical expression). The revolt against Reason apparently had its early beginnings with the Romantics; at any rate some of them use what Bousoño calls "visiones" to effect an "atribución de cualidades o de funciones irreales a un objeto" (attribution of unreal qualities or functions to an object). He goes on to explain:

> A partir de Bécquer, en cuyas rimas comienza a manifestarse, la visión se instaura en la poesía española, y su abundancia se vuelve característica desde los alrededores de 1923, sobre todo en la escuela de aproximación "supra-realista."[37]

> Starting with Bécquer, in whose rhymes it begins to appear, vision finds its place in Spanish poetry. Its frequency becomes a special feature from about 1923 onwards, above all in the school which comes nearest Surrealism.

We have already seen what Bousoño had to say about this visionary quality in Aleixandre's poetry.[38] We also saw examples of the same kind of *visión* in two English poets before Aleixandre. The Biblical Psalms say that the hills "skipped like lambs," which is also an "atribución de cualidades o de funciones irreales," or allusive image. Blake's prophetic books have images of the same kind; the river Thames is said to be groaning beneath an iron forge, and so on; Blake probably found the original suggestion for such imagery in the Bible. In the same way, Ruskin points out how Scott compares the rocks of the Trossachs to spires, not because they are pointed or towering in form—they are not—but because they have a grandeur which the traditional image of a spire also possesses.[39]

Then again the attribution of feelings to inanimate objects (Ruskin's "pathetic fallacy") is a very old literary device. But, on the whole, when the *generación de la Dictadura* and those after them used allusive imagery or *correspondance* they did it much more constantly and consistently than any writers before (but not more or less than poets in countries other than Spain at the same time). A large part of the novelty of Aleixandre and other modern poets, more or less affected by Surrealism and psycho-analysis, is that the different images are linked in a relationship like those in dreams or like obscure personal symbols. This is in contrast with practically all former literature of the imagination which, even when using dream imagery, strove to make it as clear and as consistent as possible.

Before discussing *visión,* Bousoño explains another characteristic of modern poetry:

> El hecho es éste: a partir de Juan Ramón Jiménez, o por lo menos a partir de su generación, se inaugura, según todas las señales, en la poesía hispánica, una especial técnica, que consiste en una cesión de atributos acaecida en cierto objeto con respecto a sus partes.[40]

> The fact of the matter is that, by all the tokens, from Juan Ramón Jiménez onwards, or at least from his generation onwards, a special technique begins to be used in Spain which consists of an assignment of attributes occurring with regard to a certain object and its relation to its parts.

The two examples Bousoño gives, from Juan Ramón Jiménez's *Platero y yo,* are, first, a phrase in which he speaks of the "barrios desiertos, entornados, y eróticos" (deserted erotic quarters all ajar) of a town, and secondly a reference to "el cielo rápido" (the swift sky) during a thunder-storm. This use of attributes was not unknown to poets in other centuries, though very infrequently used. Milton writes of "blind mouthes,"[41] Marvell of "a green thought,"[42] and

Góngora of "calientes plumas"[43] (warm feathers), but such expressions are almost accidental. The device, however, gradually became common in French poetry after Baudelaire and from France passed to other countries. For instance Mallarmé writes "bleus angélus" and D. H. Lawrence describes a snake that "trailed his yellow-brown slackness soft-bellied down."[44] Such a phrase as this last one or the first one from Jiménez would have been considered bad writing in former centuries. A number of subordinate clauses would have been introduced to avoid such a rapid mixture of different impressions.

Bousoño goes on to say that the device is used even more frequently by Lorca than by Jiménez. (In this, as in other modes of expression, Lorca is far nearer to the Surrealists than Jiménez is.) The passage from *Platero y yo* could be satisfactorily paraphrased, but hardly Lorca's lines: "verde carne, pelo verde,/ con ojos de fría plata."[45] (Her flesh was green, her hair was green,/ And her eyes of cold silver.) The third evidence of a revolt against Reason in the modern age (as shown in its poetry) is the *imagen visionaria*. The example which Bousoño gives of this device is a specially coined poetic phrase: "El pájaro es como un arco iris." (The bird is like a rainbow.) This does not mean that the bird is of many colors, but that to hear and see it gives a feeling of joy similar to that experienced on beholding a rainbow. (This is one aspect of what we have called an "allusive image.") This, he says, is fundamentally different from the old poets' saying that their lady's hair was of gold, because in the latter case there really was a physical likeness between the yellow of the woman's hair and the hue of the gold.[46]

What Bousoño means to say is that the phrase he has coined depends for its effect on the previous associations which the words *arco iris* may have for the reader. The case of the rainbow presents no great obstacles; a reasonably intelligent reader will associate a rainbow with God's promise to Noah, Iris the messenger of the gods, and personal and literary memories in which the rainbow has played a part as a sign that the rain was over and good weather might be expected. Unpleasant associations connected with the rainbow are unlikely. Let us, however, imagine, purely for the sake of argument, that the Chinese regarded the rainbow with superstitious terror or that they had been used to finding it represented as an evil omen in their classical literature. Bousoño's phrase would then acquire a completely opposite meaning for them.

Thus our acceptance of the rainbow as an image depends on convention and tradition in the same way as the comparison of a woman's hair to gold does. Bousoño might have done well to discuss this possible complication. Up to this point, the *Teoría de la expresión poética* does not add too much to the book on Aleixandre. But Bousoño goes further—he wishes to effect a revision of the ideas on style given in the ordinary manuals. Bousoño thinks that the force of poetry consists in its substituting a word or phrase which is unexpected for one which is expected:

> . . . las sustituciones poéticas son el único medio para transmitir *tal como es* una realidad psíquica, en la cual, como hemos dicho antes, se entreverá lo conceptual con lo afectivo y lo sensóreo. Acabamos, pues, de volver un guante del revés: los procedimientos no son para nosotros, como para el pensamiento anterior, expresión *impropia* de contenidos anímicos que pueden ser expresados *propiamente.* Sucede lo opuesto: los procedimientos representan la *única* expresión *propia,* pertinente, y la "lengua" la expresión *impropia,* impertinente, de tales contenidos.[47]

> . . . Poetic substitutes are the only means of transmitting a psychical reality *just as it is.* In this, as we have said before, what is conceptual is intermingled with what is affective and sensory. Thus we have, as it were, turned the glove inside out. For us the procedure is not—as it was to a former way of thinking—an *improper* expression of psychic contents seeking to be expressed *properly.* The opposite takes place; the procedure represents the *only proper* pertinent expression; and "language," the improper, non-pertinent expression of such contents.

Many different examples of "substitution" are studied, apart from those we have already mentioned. He gives excellent analyses of various poems as examples. A whole sonnet by Unamuno on the tragic sense of life develops, as Bousoño shows, from one single image of a tormenting vulture.[48] The section on Antonio Machado is particularly interesting. Bousoño explains how Machado, in an apparently simple description of a countryside or street, can suggest a mood of heavy-heartedness, of solitude, or of awareness that time is passing. He does this, according to Bousoño, by using words which suggest the feeling that he wants to convey to us; thus without ever directly referring to his mood he has made us aware of it. For example, Machado describes a village square by using words like *negro, humean, cipresal,* and *muertas* which give an impression of melancholy.[49]

But we have already referred to this aspect of Machado in Chapter 1 and to Machado's superposition of two periods of time in the sonnet about his father. Bousoño also gives other examples of this kind of superposition. Keats's "Ode to a Grecian Urn" is, as he says, another transposition of the time theme, since Keats contrasts time grown static on the urn with the ordinary passing of mortal life. Bousoño is right to insist that the time theme appears in much great writing in the twentieth century. Indeed he might have made much more of this and shown, as Wyndham Lewis does in *Time and Western Man*, the connection of the literary time theme with the ideas of Bergson and Einstein. He might, at the very least, have mentioned at this point the names of important writers such as Proust and Pirandello, instead of Priestley's *Time and the Conways* and Arthur Miller's *Death of a Salesman*.

In order to examine another type of substitution, Bousoño inspects Jiménez' poem about a child from a poor family wearing a badly-fitting new suit in which he imagines he is as well-dressed as a rich child.[50] This is not a modern device, so that examples are also given from Lope and Quevedo. We might add that such situations are not only to be found incidentally in poetry but are often an essential part of a drama or novel.

Examples are discussed of irony, climax, and reiteration. Bousoño notices how the repetition of a word or phrase several times gives it an added overhead meaning which it did not possess the first time. Similarly, when an unexpected word, phrase, or notion is introduced,

> El desgarrón producido, si no conduce al chiste o al absurdo, conducirá, indefectiblemente, a la poesía.[51]

> The cleft thus produced, if it does not lead to a jest or an absurdity, will unfailingly lead to poetry.

He says that formerly it was nearly always humorists who juggled with words and images in this way, but that now serious poets do so too. He gives Neruda's description of Lorca as an example: "su presencia era mágica y morena" (his presence was magical and brown). This is not altogether convincing, since the *Diccionario de literatura española* quotes, as an example of zeugma; "ludo fatigatumque somno" from Horace's *Odes* III, 4, 11, which is not unlike Neruda's phrase. What is really remarkable about Neruda's passage is that *presencia . . . morena* is really an allusive image, so that

Bousoño seems to be confusing two devices here. It is however true that our appreciation of some modern poetry depends on our not finding images and expressions funny which would formerly have been thought so. This is surely part of the dream atmosphere on which modern poetry sometimes depends; just as we suspend disbelief when an actor appears on the stage impersonating Hamlet or Julius Caesar, so in dreams and in some of modern poetry we must forget the unfitness or illogicality of certain images.

He also gives examples, from the literature of the past, of the use of the psychologically unexpected. He quotes Quevedo's poem on Charles V:

> Retiró a Solimán, temor de Hungría,
> y, por ser retirada mas valiente,
> se retiró a sí mismo el postrer día.[52]

> He made the scourge of Hungary retire.
> And, seeking a retirement even braver,
> He, at the last, retired himself as well.

And:

> "y te dilatas cuanto más te estrechas."[53]

> And, by dilating, closer in you grow.

And:

> "pues falta (y es del Cielo este lenguaje)
> al pobre mucho, y al avaro todo."[54]

> For there is lacking (it is Heaven has said so)
> Much to the poor man, all things to the miser.

Though Bousoño apparently approves of the modern revolt against Reason, it does not seem to bring him any new spiritual values or hopes. We have seen that Aleixandre thinks that existence is "Entre dos oscuridades un relámpago" (a lightning flash between two darknesses). And Bousoño reflects despairingly that a time of political absolutism may be coming to the world in which the phrase "más vale morir de pie que vivir de rodillas" (it is better to die standing than to live kneeling) may have no meaning. He even goes so far as to doubt the absolute value of poetry. He sees change everywhere:

> Llegará día, pues, en que los cipreses no se planten en los tristes recintos, y ese día los lectores . . . no sentirán la palabra "cipresal" poblada del sentido que hoy tiene.[55]

> A day will come on which cypresses will no longer be planted in the precincts of sadness and then readers . . . will no longer feel that the word "cypress-grove" carries the feeling within it which it now does.

This would not really follow, so long as people were familiar with literary references to cypresses. In modern England cypresses are not often found in graveyards and coffins are not made of their wood and yet the line, "And in sad cypress let me be laid," does not seem to have lost its force. Few Englishmen know what an asphodel looks like; some confuse it with a daffodil; but that does not make them insensitive to it when they read of it in ancient Greek poetry. Shakespeare had probably never seen a lion and nobody has ever seen a unicorn, yet Shakespeare uses the one and many poets the other as a symbol of strength. Therefore the total disappearance of cypresses ought not to prevent a well-read person being moved by *el ciprés erguido* in Machado's sonnet, for example. We may even go further and say that the literary associations of the cypress are partly responsible for what people feel on seeing it in a cemetery; otherwise they might not distinguish between it and any other tree they saw there.

Bousoño's closing words are:

> La poesía, en buena parte, surge acaso desde una materia a prueba de siglos. Pero ya es bastante observar la posible carroña en un cuerpo que soñábamos incorruptible: siempre vivaz y fresco siempre, como el rostro de una diosa juvenil.[56]

> The greater part of poetry perhaps arises out of material which is proof against the centuries. But it is rather a bad thing to notice possible corruption in a body we dreamed was incorruptible, always lively and fresh like the face of a youthful goddess.

Thus, in spite of his *símbolos,* his *visiones,* and his *imágenes visionarias,* Bousoño ends his book on a note of despair. Though he tells us what a "human" age we live in, he is not really free of the dehumanized conception of art and letters of which Ortega wrote. On the other hand, there has undoubtedly been a great change in the use of imagery in twentieth-century Spanish poetry (and poetry everywhere). Several critics have written on the imagery of Guillén or Lorca, but Bousoño's field is wider, what he says applies more directly to the poetry of modern Spain. The poets he analyzes so carefully and well in *Teoría de la expresión poética* are just the ones who have exercised the most influence in modern Spain. In the first place, and before all others, Machado, then Juan Ramón Jiménez, Aleixandre, the Dámaso Alonso of *Hijos de la ira* and, among the writers of the Golden Age, particularly Quevedo. Finally, he sees evidences in modern poetry of a revolt against Reason, which he considers characteristic of the present age; this means, really, that he does not see poetry as something separate from modern life. However, his belief in poetry is not unqualified, since he foresees, though with great regret, the possibility of its disappearance in the future.

Bousoño was the writer who showed most clearly that he belonged to the Aleixandre group. But the heritage of *Sombra del paraíso* (and *Hijos de la ira*) was a slow one. It may in fact be said to include most of the poetry which has been written in Spain since 1944.

NOTES TO CHAPTER 4

1. Prologue to Bartolomé Lloréns, *Secreta fuente* (Madrid, 1948), pp. 23-24.
2. (Madrid, 1942).
3. (Madrid, 1944).
4. (Madrid).
5. *Ibid.*, p. 55 ["Las cinco de la tarde"].
6. (Madrid).
7. (Valencia, 1944), and (Santander, 1945).
8. (Madrid, 1947).
9. *Ibid.*, p. 17 ["Flores bajo los muertos"].
10. *Ibid.*, p. 40 ["Has bajado"].
11. (Madrid, 1943).
12. *Antología consultada de la joven poesía española* (Santander, 1951), pp. 125-126.
13. *Poemas del toro,* p. 31 ["Toros en la noche"].
14. (Madrid, 1947).
15. *Ibid.*, p. 7.
16. *Ibid.*, p. 17 ["Los leprosos"].
17. *Canción sobre el asfalto* (Madrid, 1954), p. 60 ["Cancioncilla de amor a mis zapatos"].
18. *Primavera de la muerte* (Madrid, 1946), p. 26.
19. *Ibid.*, p. 29.
20. (Madrid, 1945).
21. *Ibid.*, p. 26 ["La tristeza"].
22. Gustavo Adolfo Béquer, *Rimas y Leyendas* (Madrid, 1940), p. 45.
23. *Subida al amor,* p. 23 ["Salmo desesperado"].
24. Antonio G. de Lama, "Tres poetas nuevos," in *Espadaña* (León), 14, 1944.
25. *Las mil mejores poesías de la lengua castellana* (15th edition; Madrid, n.d.), p. 295.
26. *Subida al amor,* pp. 55-56.
27. *Ibid.*, p. 56.
28. *Ibid.*, p. 54 ["Recuerdo de infancia"].

29. *Ibid.,* p. 59.
30. *Teoría de la expresión poética* (Madrid, 1952), p. 157.
31. *Primavera de la muerte,* p. 43.
32. *Ibid.,* p. 99 ["Melodía sin esperanza"].
33. *Ibid.,* p. 97, from the same poem.
34. *Secreta fuente,* p. 22.
35. Julius Petersen, *Filosofía de la ciencia literaria* (Mexico, 1948), pp. 179-180.
36. *Secreta fuente,* p. 17.
37. *Teoría de la expresión poética,* p. 96.
38. See Chapter 2, Note 68.
39. *Lectures on Architecture and Painting* (London, 1899), p. 50.
40. *Teoría de la expresión poética,* p. 67.
41. *The Poetical Works of John Milton* (Oxford Univ., 1935), p. 41 ["Lycidas"].
42. *The Oxford Book of Seventeenth-Century Verse* (Oxford Univ., 1951), p. 751 ["The Garden"].
43. *Antología general de la literatura española* (Madrid, 1954), 1, p. 693 ["Soledades"].
44. *Birds, Beasts and Flowers* (2nd edition; London, 1931), p. 113 ["Snake"].
45. *Antología general de la literatura española* (Madrid, 1954), 2, p. 826 ["Romance sonámbulo"].
46. *Teoría de la expresión poética,* p. 93.
47. *Ibid.,* p. 51.
48. *Ibid.,* p. 103.
49. *Ibid.,* pp. 107-110.
50. *Ibid.,* pp. 173-177.
51. *Ibid.,* p. 224.
52. *Obras completas. Verso* (Madrid, 1943), p. 375 ["Inscripción de la estatua augusta del César Carlos Quinto en Aranjuez"].
53. *Ibid.,* p. 405 ["A un amigo que retirado de la Corte pasó su edad"].
54. *Ibid.,* p. 392 ["Enseña como no es rico el que tiene mucho caudal"].
55. *Teoría de la expresión poética,* p. 295.
56. *Ibid.,* p. 301.

Poets not Belonging to the Aleixandre Group

Gaos's *Arcángel de mi noche,* though written in the "Neoclassical" style, is a book of poems about the poet's personal unhappiness. The poets we are about to examine in this chapter are still more personal than Gaos. The first two of them used to describe themselves as Neo-Romanticism in the first half of the nineteenth century; they merely they were not "Neoclassical." They had to make this distinction because they had been friends of García Nieto's and intimately associated with *Garcilaso*—members, in fact, of the *Juventud Creadora,* even though they themselves had never written in a completely "Neoclassical" style. Reacting against "Neoclassicism," they argued that Spain had never really had a Romantic movement and that now was the time for one.

They did not of course mean that there had been no Spanish Romanticism in the first half of the nineteenth century; they merely felt that it had not produced enough genuine poetry. Yet, if the poetry of the Spanish Romantics was really a failure, that of the Neo-Romantics was too different from it to supply the lack. In one way, however, they did resemble certain Romantic poets, such as Byron or Alfred de Musset or Espronceda; they were very personal in their writings.

Rafael Montesinos (1920-   )

The poetry of Montesinos is very personal; he writes about his memories, his first love, the girls he was momentarily interested in or, later, his married life. He was a Carlist volunteer in the Civil War at the age of sixteen. He never studied at a university. His first book of poems, *Resurrección* (1942), published when he was twenty-two, shows the influence of Salvador Rueda and of Antonio Machado at his most rhetorical, but contains no poetry of any value. His literary and poetic training, such as it was, was gained later by contact with García Nieto and other poets of the review *Garcilaso.*

He is from Seville. Some of his poems describe his memories of
the Holy Week processions in his native town; in these he was influenced by a poem in Cernuda's *Ocnos*. He is not so directly popular
in his inspiration as the two Andalusians, Lorca and Alberti, in the
Romancero gitano and *Marinero en tierra,* yet some of his poems are
like folk poetry. Here now is an example of Andalusian folk-poetry
from Fernán Caballero's *Cuentos y poesías populares andaluces:*[1]

> ¡Ay! Madre de los Remedios,
> Madre de los afligidos,
> Los trigos se van secando,
> Manda tu santo rocío.

> Oh, Our Lady of the Remedies,
> Mother of all the afflicted,
> The cornfields are growing drier;
> Oh, send your holy dew to us.

And here are four lines by Montesinos showing how the Sevillanos
manifest more devotion towards the statues of the Virgin than towards
those of Christ in their Holy Week processions:

> Ay, María Inmaculada,
> niña guapa sin igual,
> a Dios no le sienta mal
> saberte la preferida.[2]

> Oh, Mary the Immaculate,
> Beautiful girl with no equal,
> God doesn't feel bad about it
> That people prefer you to Him.

This casual, half-humorous tone in writing on a religious theme
would seem very irreverent in anyone who was not from Seville; those
who have watched the people of that town during their Holy Week
processions will, however, understand it.

In Rodríguez Marín's *Cantos populares españoles*[3]—published in
Seville and possibly more widely collected in Andalusia than in other
regions of Spain—we find poems of this kind:

> Tengo en el pecho escritas
> Tus falsedades;
> Tengo de publicarlas,
> Aunque te enfades.
> Pues no creyera
> Que me hubieras vendido
> De tal manera.

In my breast lies written
Your falseness to me.
I must blaze it abroad
Though you get angry.
I never thought
You'd have betrayed me
In such a manner.

This is not unlike the conversational tone and the conscious use of unliterary turns of expression in much of Montesinos's poetry. For instance, he writes:

Mi juventud se fué
a la guerra conmigo.
Yo volví, pero a ella
la mataron a tiros.[4]

My youth went at my side
To the war with me.
I came back, but she
Had been killed by a bullet.

He is expressing his feeling of personal tragedy at having known war so early in life, but the language he uses is of extreme simplicity. Or again he speaks of "mi pobre melancolía / por la que me salvaré"[5] (And my poor melancholy / Which will save my soul at last). These two lines represent a lighthearted, almost careless religious faith similar to that in the four Holy Week lines quoted above.

He is proud of the Moorish origin of his people and himself:

Hombres de hierro oscuro
crucificaron
tu árabe cielo mío
despreocupado.

Lloran junto a tu río
torres y chopos
desde aquel mil doscientos
cuarenta y ocho.[6]

Men clothed in dark iron
Have come to crucify
Your Arab sky of mine,
Carefree and careless.

The towers and the poplars
Weep by your river
Ever since twelve hundred
And forty-eight A.D.

We should not take these lines seriously as a rejection of Christianity. The playful and very slightly decadent inclusion of the historical date of the conquest of Seville by Saint Ferdinand is an example of his lighthearted style.

He is especially a love poet and writes of his sentimental walks in the Retiro Gardens in Madrid, thinking of his absent love. Or, in the London winter, he remembers the South:

> el alma entera se va
> volando al Sur donde está
> mi mediterráneo amor.[7]

> The whole of my soul has gone
> Flying to the South where he finds
> My Mediterranean Love.

But at other times his loves are passing sensual caprices.

Montesinos could only be considered a Romantic insofar as he is rather too concerned with his own personal sorrows or because he has written a poem idealizing the statue to the Fallen Angel in the Retiro Gardens. Otherwise, he is a remarkably simple poet whose only complication consists in a fondness for plays upon conversational phrases and words, a poetic habit he probably learned from Rafael Laffón and Adriano del Valle, two older poets from Seville.

His wife and child are the central figures in *El tiempo en nuestros brazos*.[8] In fact, the child is time in his arms. But the type of verse is much the same as before, and the nostalgic sadness is never absent. He has left the themes of childhood and early loves, which seemed to be essential to his poetry. He writes of his new surroundings as if he had never known any others, and this is because his poetry is part of his life. Yet the bitter taste of death, which is never far away from his most lighthearted poetry, is to be found here when he speaks to his baby son. Also he plays with popular conversational phrases as before:

> Si juego al escondite,
> búscame luego
> en mis palabras: todo
> lo que te dejo.

> Al alimón, mi niño,
> ven y juguemos,
> que la vida y la muerte
> se vuelven juegos.[9]

If I play hide-and-seek with you,
Look for me later
In my words, which are all that
I shall have left you.

Come, my child, we will play at
This game together,
Since both life and death can be
Turned into a game.

From time to time, he has written poems on the social message
of Christianity. Christ spoke in anger to the rich about the camel
and the needle's eye: "Ojo de aguja. / Ni más ni menos."[10] (The
eye of a needle. / No more nor less.) Like the later Alberti, Montesinos has used short verses in a popular Andalusian style to protest against inequality:

Soñador de aceitunas
que será aceite,
los sueños que cosechas
otros los beben.[11]

You, dreamer of olives
Which will be oil,
The dreams which you gather
Are drunk by others.

He calls the olive-gatherer an oliver-dreamer because of that peasant's
hope that there will one day be a just society in which he will have
his fair share.

Yet, however much Montesinos may vary or enlarge the scope of
his subject-matter, he always really writes the same type of poetry.
All his work has a fine consistency.

Salvador Pérez Valiente (1919-   )

Pérez Valiente is as personal a poet as Montesinos, but there is
a suggestion of individual revolt about his poetry which is lacking
in Montesinos and which brings Pérez Valiente nearer to some of
the writers in the Romantic movement. The word he is most fond
of is *angustia*, by which he means, not a feeling of philosophical insufficiency or amorous dissatisfaction, but of financial weakness:

mi madre fregaba la cocina
con un trozo de su colcha de novia.
(Creo en Dios)

Yo, el buen Salvador Pérez,
me quité los zapatos,
contemplé el calcetín que iba rompiéndiose
y me puse a pensar en esas cosas,[12]

And my mother was washing the kitchen floor
With a rag off her wedding counterpane.
(I trust in God)
I, the good Salvador Pérez,
Was sitting there taking my shoes off.
I had a look at my sock, which was going to holes.
And I started to think of things of that sort,

Baudelaire disapproved of the Romantic poet Hégésippe Moreau
complaining of poverty in his poetry. Yet this is the root of Pérez
Valiente's poetry and his feeling of revolt:

Es por el pan por lo que grito,
por sólo el pan y los zapatos,
por respirar, por ir muriéndome
tan duramente solitario.

Hacéis las cárceles, los premios,
lleváis la cuenta de la rosa,
asesináis tan lentamente
que oigo mi sangre gota a gota.[13]

It's for my bread that I am shouting,
Just for my bread and shoes to put on,
That I may breathe and go on dying
In this hard manner and quite lonely.

You make the jails and recompenses
And keep account-books for the roses.
Your murdering is done so slowly
I hear my blood drop by drop falling.

He has translated his personal feelings into something larger; the
literary expression is well cared for. The rhythmic flow is strong
and satisfying. The rose appears, a flower almost too commonplace
for modern poetry, but here set in effective and ironical contrast with
that common, everyday object, an account-book.

Pérez Valiente was a political revolutionary while still very young,
during the Civil War. His present spirit of revolt is not really political,
though it borders on being so, as we can see by the above passage.
There is a considerable influence of Alberti's revolutionary poems,

especially in Pérez Valiente's earlier poems in free verse, but he has more humor than Alberti. This is how he describes his own funeral:

> Tres curas y cuatro grillos
> cantarán la letanía:
> gori, gori, gori, gori ...
> ....
> Y yo, solo. Como antes.
> Como siempre, siempre, ¡ siempre !
> Muerto.[14]

> Three chanting priests and four crickets
> Will be there to sing the litany,
> Tra la, tra la, tra la, tra la.
> ....
> I am alone. As before.
> And as always, always, always!
> But dead.

Here he feels personal grief for his own life, not merely financial *angustia* and not a desire for social revolt.

Ricardo Molina (1917-   )

The only two poets who actually called themselves Neo-Romantics were Pérez Valiente and Montesinos, but especially Pérez Valiente. If we are speaking of personal poets, however, we should also include the Cordobese poet, Ricardo Molina. Molina is a teacher in Córdoba. As his poetry review *Cántico* shows, he takes a lively interest in poetry in other countries and he at one time kept up a correspondence with André Gide. Many intellectuals, both Spanish and foreign, visit him on their way through Córdoba.

Cántico created a school of three Cordobese poets, Ricardo Molina, Pablo García Baena (1923-   ), and Juan Bernier (1913-   ). (We might even add some other names, such as those of Julio Aumente and Vicente Núñez.) Their styles are similar. They believe that to belong to Córdoba and Andalusia implies superiority, they do not express this by writing folk-inspired poetry, however, but rather by describing what they see around them in town and country. The poetry of García Baena, for example, is usually written in long free-verse lines and complicated sentences. Religious themes are frequent, though mixed with a suggestion of sensuality in keeping with a poet who thinks of himself as descended from the Spanish Arabs. These characteristics are less marked in Ricardo Molina, the most important of the three poets and the one whose constant efforts kept *Cántico* alive and gave it the most international tone of any contemporary Spanish poetry review. Nevertheless, religion and sensuality are dominant themes in Molina also. He also likes to record the life around him, practically in the style of a novelist. For instance, in one of his poems he describes the people he has seen in the street, such as that:

> canónigo de Ceuta que pasea aburrido
> su triste obesidad y su larga sotana
> con ojales, botones y filos de escarlata.[15]

> The canon from Ceuta who strolls about enduring
> His sad obesity and lengthy soutane
> With buttonholes and buttons and trimmings all of scarlet.

As an example of his love-poetry, we will quote a passage in which he speaks of himself in his schooldays:

> Mis padres me reñían a la hora del almuerzo.
> Me decían que iba a perder todo el curso,
> pero yo soportaba sus riñas en silencio
> y ellos seguían hablando, amargos, del futuro.

> Yo me decía mientras: "¿Qué importan los amigos,
> qué importa el porvenir, los padres, los estudios,
> si las tardes de mayo son tan claras y bellas
> y te amo, amor mío, más que a nadie en el mundo?

> ¿Qué importan estas cosas si me estás esperando
> en el vasto pinar, al borde del camino,
> y tus ojos son verdes como las hojas verdes
> y tu aliento fragante lo mismo que el tomillo?[16]

> My parents used to scold me when I came in at lunch-time.
> They told me I should never pass my exams that Summer.
> I listened to their scolding and bore it all in silence.
> And so they went on talking bitterly of the future.

> All the while I was thinking: "What do friends matter to me,
> What do the future matter, my parents, or my studies,
> If only these May evenings may be so bright and lovely
> And I, my love, may love you far more than anybody.

> What do all these things matter if you are waiting for me
> In the enormous pinewood by the side of the pathway
> And your eyes are as green as the leaves of the trees are
> And your breath is as fragrant and fresh as the thyme is?

The expressions are almost excessively simple; the May afternoon and eyes green as the leaves are commonplaces, but they are effective poetic rhetoric here. Molina and the poets commented on earlier in this chapter are less intellectual than Aleixandre and his school. The name of Neo-Romantics might have suited them if they had had more sympathy with the real Romantics.

NOTES TO CHAPTER 5

1. *Cuentos y poesías populares andaluces coleccionados* (Sevilla, 1859), p. 203.
2. *Las incredulidades* (Madrid, 1948), p. 24 ["Sine labe concepta"].
3. (1883), 3, p. 103.
4. *Las incredulidades*, pp. 78-79 ["Elegia conjunta"].
5. *Ibid.*, p. 33 ["Canción de mis veinteséis años"].
6. *Ibid.*, p. 83 ["El poeta decide terminar por seguidillas"].
7. *Ibid.*, p. 43 ["A un petirrojo que convertí en ruiseñor"].
8. (Madrid, 1958).
9. *Ibid.*, p. 41 ["Nana triste y esperanzada"].
10. *El polvo de los pies*, in *Cuadernos hispanoamericanos*, 133, January, 1961 (Madrid), p. 31 ["Cancioncilla con ira"].
11. *Ibid.*, p. 32 ["Canción del cogedor de aceitunas"].
12. *Por tercera vez* (Madrid, 1953), pp. 49-50 ["Letanía del abandono"].
13. *Ibid.*, p. 16 ["Homenaje a mi tiempo"].
14. *Cuando ya no hay remedio* (Valladolid, 1947), p. 19 ["Muerte mía"].
15. *Elegías de Sandua* (Madrid, 1948), p. 67 ["Elegía XXVII"].
16. *Ibid.*, p. 32 ["Elegía X"].

6

Surrealist Influence

Surrealism has never flourished in Spain. The movement is eminently French and has its center in Paris and, in any case, needs a strong academic literary tradition to revolt against. The latter is lacking in Spain.

Certain Spanish poets have been through phases which show the influence of the French Surrealist movement following on André Breton's Surrealist manifesto in 1924,[1] yet there has been no real attempt to produce a Spanish Surrealist movement. This is obvious even from the number of the review *Verbo* which is entitled *Antología del surrealismo español.*[2] However, several poets of before and after the Civil War are included in this anthology. In the first part of this chapter we shall examine how far they can be considered to have been or are Surrealists.

To begin with, very few Spanish poets indeed have complied with Breton's fundamental rule for producing what is called "automatic writing": "Écrivez vite sans sujet préconçu, assez vite pour ne pas être tenté de vous relire."[3] (Write quickly, without any preconceived subject-matter, quickly enough not to be tempted to reread what you have written.) Nevertheless, we should be careful not to limit our notion of what is or is not Surrealist to works strictly following the precepts laid down in Breton's manifestoes. Breton as a critical writer has perhaps too much of the intellectual clarity for which the French are particularly remarkable to be a perfect guide for a movement depending so largely on the "Freudian" unconscious. Gómez de la Serna says:

> Breton y Paul Eluard son los presidentes constantes de esa revolución pura, de este estado frenético de búsqueda, de esa crisis de conciencia sin derivativo.
> Cada vez despejan más su campo los promotores, y no vale nada la colección de su revista *Révolution Surréaliste,* porque fuera de lo que dicen los profetas lo otro que llena los textos se

101

vuelve suspecto, ya que a cada nuevo número tiran por la borda a sus antiguos colaboradores y denuncian su moralidad y su literatura. Quizá algún día quede sólo sobre cubierta Breton, aguantando el fuego de todas las escuadras.[4]

Breton and Paul Éluard are the chairmen in perpetuity of this pure revolution, of this frantic state of quest, of this crisis of the conscience deriving from nothing.

The promoters clear the ground more and more. It's no use having a collection of their review *Révolution Surréaliste* because, apart from what the prophets say, the rest of the stuff in the texts is suspect. In each new number they throw their former contributors overboard and inveigh against their morals and their writings. Perhaps one day only Breton will be left on deck withstanding the fire from all the squadrons round.

Gómez de la Serna, writing in 1931, is a good Spanish authority on Surrealism, because some of his own writings show a modified Surrealist influence. Also it is very likely that his prose writings had an influence on the poetry of his contemporaries. Breton, he tells us, acting as the head of the French Surrealist movement, rejected several apparently Surrealist writers on the grounds that they were too concerned with "morality" and "literature." Good French Surrealists were not supposed to believe in either of these. License in private life and drug-taking, for instance, were to be approved of, because they showed a contempt for conventional morality. The noisy and ostentatious eccentricity of Surrealists in public gatherings was another proof of the same attitude. In literature or art, the slightest respect for traditional canons was similarly frowned on.

But in Spain it has always been more difficult to flout the accepted formalities of life than in other European countries, and literature, in its turn, naturally tends to reflect this. Certainly Gómez de la Serna and Alberti, in their public lectures, sometimes behaved in the same sort of way as the French Surrealists; Gómez de la Serna, for instance, would eat what was apparently a candle standing on the table before him. After the Civil War, the formalities were even more strictly observed in Spain than before; and Gómez de la Serna, though an unconditional supporter of the régime, found that when he visited Madrid in 1949 from the Argentine his eccentric lectures failed to impress his audiences.

The most confirmed Surrealists, even Breton himself, admit that certain works written in the past are partially—though never completely—Surrealist. All literature drawn from dreams qualifies from this point of view, especially, one would imagine, a poem like Coleridge's *Kubla Khan,* conceived in a dream-state probably induced by the taking of drugs. Fantastic or nonsense literature, such as the books of Lewis Carroll, also approached Surrealism closely. And a few writers, such as Rimbaud, lived and wrote very like Surrealists, even before the movement came into being.

Surrealists, however, are more likely to admit a writer of the past as a predecessor than an independent contemporary writer as one of their number. More is required of contemporaries. To win the acceptance of the Surrealists, modern artists and writers are expected to behave very much in the same way as a psychiatrist's patient, who must hide nothing from his mental doctor; one image must be allowed to suggest another, as it does in our sleeping visions. Yet surely, even bearing this in mind, many modern works, and particularly poems, could be called Surrealist.

The relationship of modern Spanish poets to Surrealism is mainly of this sort. We have even seen that "Neoclassicism" is not untouched by what we might call the oniric use of imagery. Antonio Machado wrote a long dream poem called "Los complementarios." Surrealist elements can be found in Alberti's *Sobre los ángeles,* Lorca's *Poeta en Nueva York* (and also his *Romancero gitano,* though to a lesser degree) and the early poems of Cernuda. But certainly these poets were not writing in the way Breton recommended, being too conscious of the artistic effect they wished to produce. On the whole, for instance, they avoided those revolting images in which the works of orthodox Surrealists abound. Yet these considerations have not prevented the compilers of the *Antología del surrealismo español* from including Alberti, Lorca, and Cernuda.

The Spanish *creacionistas* were even nearer to Surrealism, though they never revolted against the use of conscious artistry as the Surrealists did. This is not surprising, since the *creacionista* movement began some time before the Surrealist one. As early as 1916, the South American poet, Vicente Huidobro, was "en París propugnando una nueva concepción de la lírica, que denomina *creacionismo*"[5] (in Paris defending a new conception of lyrical poetry which he calls Creationism). That he did this in Paris is a sign that *creacionismo* was as much a French as a Spanish movement and therefore possibly one of the stages which led up to Surrealism. Guillermo de

Torre, in his *Literaturas europeas de vanguardia,*[6] shows that *creacionismo* led up to *ultraisme.* Consequently there are doubts as to whether Huidobro or the Frenchman Pierre Réverdy was the true founder of the school.

The two principal Spanish *creacionistas* were Gerardo Diego and Juan Larrea. In Diego it is particularly clear that the apparent confusion of images obeys certain aesthetic laws of fitness, though no logical ones. He says, in one of his *creacionista* poems: "Déjame pasar la mano por el lomo suavísimo de estos versos que escribo / La eternidad así bajo mis dedos maullará tiernamente."[7] (Let me stroke the very soft back of these verses I am writing / And then eternity will mew tenderly beneath my fingers.) The poet seems quite conscious of the unusualness of his metaphor. This would probably not happen with the images of Juan Larrea, whom the *Antología del surrealismo español* considers the purest Spanish Surrealist. It says of him:

> [Larrea's] poemas que reproducimos en esta Antología parecen escritos según el más riguroso criterio automatista.[8]

> [Larrea's] poems which we give in this Anthology appear to have been written in the most strictly Automatic manner.

Some of Aleixandre's poetry written before the Civil War is at least as near Surrealism as that of the *creacionistas.* We have already seen[9] that he wrote his prose poems *Pasión de la tierra* (1935) under the influence of Freud and using Freudian imagery. Dámaso Alonso denies the influence of Surrealism on Spanish poetry and especially on that of Aleixandre.[10] But, since Aleixandre's first book in what might perhaps be described as the Surrealist manner—*Espadas como labios* (1932)—was published eight years after the first Surrealist Manifesto, a complete lack of obligation to Breton and his school would be difficult to prove.

In Barcelona, after the Civil War, Segalá, Julio Garcés, and Juan Eduardo Cirlot produced a certain amount of poetry which they considered Surrealist; a selection from these poets is included in the *Antología del surrealismo español.* Cirlot experimented in writing "automatic" poetry with a traditional meter and rhyming pattern, though he says himself, in his book on Surrealism:

> André Breton no ha vacilado nunca en calificar de reaccionarias todas las modalidades poéticas que conserven la fidelidad a las normas de la rima, el metro y el tema conductor.[11]

André Breton has never hesitated to label reactionary all poetical manners which keep to the forms of rhyme and meter and have a leading theme.

Camilo José Cela (1916-   ), the novelist, is the only writer whose poetry is quoted in the article on "Superrealismo" [Surrealism] in the *Revista de Occidente's Diccionario de literatura española.*[12] The recitation, in 1949, by Cela of some of his poems certainly produced a public protest from the smart audience of the Sunday morning poetry recitations ("Alforjas para la poesía") at the Teatro de Lara, Madrid.

Joaquín de Entrambasaguas (1904-   ) wrote *Voz de este mundo* in a style similar to that of the Surrealists.[13] The *Antología del surrealismo español* claims Rosales' *La casa encendida* as belonging to the school, but it is plain that Rosales was consciously following a plan in that poem, even though he chose a dream-setting. Apart from these writers, little else has been written in modern Spain which could be seriously considered as Surrealist. We should, however, end this chapter with a short account of the *postista* movement, which is obviously related to Surrealism.

Postismo

In 1944, the ephemeral movement called *postismo* was started. It never gained many followers. It was devised by three writers: Carlos Edmundo de Ory (1923-   ), Eduardo Chicharro (1906-   ), and an Italian called Silvano Sernesi. They were very conscious of Surrealism, but sought an improvement by imitating it with more conscious artistry. The result was slightly similar to *creacionismo,* though *postista* poems were more coherent than those of the *creacionistas.*

The principal *postista* poet is Ory; of him the *Antología del surrealismo español* says:

> Ory suele frecuentar los caminos propiamente surrealistas, aunque llevando consigo algunos inevitables rezagos del prejuicio musical: similicadencias, aliteraciones, palabras de simple valor fónico, etc. Esta parte de su obra es, sin duda, la mejor.[14]

> Ory takes a road which is properly speaking Surrealist, though he carries with him some of the inevitable remains of a musical prejudice—half-cadences, alliterations, words of a merely phonic value, etc. This part of his work is, beyond doubt, the best.

This makes him rather less of a Surrealist than, say, the Alberti of *Sobre los ángeles,* whom he resembles in usually avoiding unpleasant imagery. Yet Chicharro says of Ory that he himself introduced Ory to

> Mundo extraño y riquísimo en cuya entretela se forjaron los genios de Max Ernst, Harp, Picasso y Picabia, Dalí y Breton, y Aragon, y Chagall, y Roux, y muchos otros.[15]

> That strange and very rich world of the stuff of which Max Ernst, Harp, Picasso and Picabia, Dali and Breton, and Aragon, and Chagall, and Roux, and many others were formed.

Ory's work is much simpler than that sounds. At his best, he is often playful, almost child-like, and capable of a charm of expression which is quite his own:

> Estuve en el cine esta mañana
> y allí desayuné. Mañana corro
> hacia un país que no diré, y mañana
> recordaré cómo bebí mi cine.[16]

> This morning I was in the cinema
> And there I had my breakfast. Tomorrow I'll run
> Towards a land I must not name; tomorrow
> I shall remember how I drank my cinema.

The cinema and the breakfast become something quite different and the point is, as in a dream, that we do not know what that something is.

Chicharro, though his defences of *postismo* were too involved and pedantic, acquired something of Ory's light touch when writing his poetry of the *postista* period:

> Carlos yo te escribo trenes
> trinos trece te estremece
> y te envío mecedoras
> a tu casa.
> Que tu casa es una cosa
> que no pasa.
> En el filo sutilísimo te escribo
> del estribo.[17]

> Carlos I write you trains
> Trills thirteen a trembling takes you
> And I am sending you rocking-chairs
> To your flat.
> For your flat is a fact

Which does not happen.
I'm writing to you on the most subtle edge
Of the stirrup.

Clearly, in this passage, Chicharro fails to suggest much beyond the jingling repetitions from which he gains his effect. The sense of there being something beyond the words, which we noticed in the passage from Ory, is absent here.

A single number of a review called *Postismo* was published in January, 1945. It contained a *postist* manifesto and polemics. Subscriptions were collected in advance for further numbers, but the Spanish authorities seem to have feared that the movement might lead to immoral eccentricities such as those of the Surrealists, and so no second number appeared. A single number of *La cerbatana: Revista de la nueva estética* was, however, brought out in the same year by the Postists, as a thinly disguised continuation of the other review and indeed sent out to the subscribers as such.

The *postistas,* in their review, describe Surrealism as "el movimiento más profundo y más completo de nuestro siglo"[18] (the deepest and completest movement in our century), though they themselves claim to add IMAGINATION to the Surrealist program.

In *La cerbatana* several young Spanish writers give their opinions of *postismo,* of which Cela's is the most original:

> Primero, el postismo; luego, la antropofagia. Quizá llegue el día en que nos alimentemos de jóvenes poetas.[19]

> First *postismo*. Then anthropophagy. Perhaps the day will come when we shall feed on young poets.

The public appearances of the Postists were a failure. Ory read extravagant manifestoes at art-exhibitions, but the well-conducted and well-dressed listeners made no comment. The Postists invited friends, by relays, to a studio to hear what they had to say, and punctuated their largely incoherent speeches with puerile shouts, turning out the light when they thought the particular group should go. This tame imitation of Surrealist public behavior had even less effect than the Postists' writings. Soon afterwards, even the Postists themselves had forgotten about their movement.

Unlike Spanish painters, Spanish writers have never really cultivated Surrealism consistently.

NOTES TO CHAPTER 6

1. *Manifeste du surréalisme* (Paris, 1924).
2. José Albi and Joan Fuster, *Verbo* (Alicante), 23-25 (1952).
3. *Manifeste du surréalisme*, p. 2.
4. *Los ismos* (2nd edition; Buenos Aires, 1943), p. 269.
5. *Diccionario de literatura española* (Madrid, 1949), p. 310.
6. (Madrid, 1925).
7. *Biografía incompleta* (Madrid, 1953), p. 61 ["Los hombros de los filósofos"].
8. *Antología del surrealismo español*, p. 179.
9. In chapter 2.
10. *Poetas españoles contemporáneos* (Madrid, 1952), p. 188.
11. *Introducción al surrealismo español* (Madrid, 1953), p. 79.
12. See Note 5.
13. (Madrid, 1946).
14. P. 185.
15. *Ibid.*, p. 186.
16. *Panorama de la poesía moderna española* (Buenos Aires, 1953), p. 471 ["Estuve en el cine"].
17. *Antología del surrealismo español*, p. 145 ["Carta de noche a Carlos"].
18. This quotation is taken from an interview originally broadcast from Radio S.E.U. on November 15th, 1944, and later printed on the second page of the review *Postismo*, published in Madrid, January, 1945. This interview presented the new *postista* school to the public before the review appeared, and was therefore printed under the heading, *Primer anuncio del Postismo al mundo* (*Postismo's* first Announcement to the World).
19. *La cerbatana* (Madrid, n.d.), p. 16.

7

Revolutionary Poetry

In 1951, an *Antología consultada de la joven poesía española* appeared. Nine poets were included: José Hierro, Gabriel Celaya, Eugenio de Nora, Victoriano Crémer, Blas de Otero, Vicente Gaos, Carlos Bousoño, Rafael Morales, and José María Valverde. The first five of these poets are well-known in Spanish literary circles for their left-wing or Marxist sympathies. The remainder have no particular bias, except José María Valverde, who wishes to be known as a Catholic poet and intellectual.

The book, as originally planned, was to have contained ten poets. In order to select these, a large number of Spanish intellectuals (whose names are given in the anthology) were asked to send their choice of the best ten poets who had come to be known after the Civil War. The names which occurred most frequently in the lists were included in the *Anthology*.

That more than half the poets included should be definitely left-wing makes the book partly political, which may have been what the editors intended. In the years immediately after the Civil War, writers who actively supported the régime were in the ascendent, and this unfortunately resulted in certain poets coming to the fore whose political prestige was greater than their poetic gifts. By 1951 the situation was almost reversed. It had become fashionable to admire poets who, though living and working in Spain, were professedly of the left in ideas. The poems they published referred fairly openly to their political ideas and yet passed the censorship; this would not have happened if they had written in prose. There are two reasons for this. First, books of poetry in Spain have only a very small circulation and therefore verse is not examined very searchingly. Secondly, the revival of poetry among the young was felt to be an intellectual advantage to the country which should be encouraged by allowing a relative freedom of expression.

109

The arrival in Spain of smuggled copies of Neruda's latest books of Communist poetry, such as his *Canto general a Chile,*[1] helped to prepare the ground for a school of "social" poetry in Spain. Crémer and Nora published a completely Communist essay of Neruda's in *Espadaña* in 1951. Angela Figuera (1902-   ) at a public reading in 1953 of her latest poems—under the auspices of the government-subsidized review *Poesía española*—declared herself a disciple of Neruda's (and a friend to Gabriel Celaya and Blas de Otero). In fact, many people turned to Otero in the early 1950's as they had turned to Aleixandre in the 1940's. There was also a revival of interest in another left-wing South American poet, the late César Vallejo (1892-1938).

The editors of the *Antología consultada* evidently reckoned on this change of taste both in those who would read their book and in those who would vote the list of poets. Nevertheless, they did not find the result of the voting entirely satisfactory. Awkwardly enough, the tenth poet selected was García Nieto, whom many people in Spain consider the most "right-wing" of all contemporary Spanish writers. He did, however, have far fewer votes than the ninth poet, so that the editors decided to publish a graph showing a line descending precipitously between No. 9 and No. 10. They explained that under the circumstances they did not feel justified in publishing the tenth poet. (They did not mention his name, but García Nieto afterwards commented severely on their behavior in an article.)[2]

There were other limitations to the scope of the Anthology besides the rejection of García Nieto. The editors tell us that "se dejaron fuera de cuestión los poetas conocidos antes de nuestra guerra"[3] (poets who were known before our war have not been included), and for that reason Leopoldo Panero and Carmen Conde (1907-   ) had been omitted. But Panero did not publish a book till 1949, even though he had been fortunate enough to have a poem published in Neruda's review *Caballo verde para la poesía*—one of the most famous poetry periodicals of the time of the Republic.[4] So the real reason for omitting Panero was probably because he was felt to be personally too bound up with the régime. Especially did this seem true as Gabriel Celaya—the most left-wing writer in the book—was not excluded even though he had, before the Civil War, published one book of poetry and received a prize for another.[5]

Gabriel Celaya (1911-   ) (pseudonym of Rafael Múgica)

Part of the plan of the *Antología consultada* was that each of the poets should state his views on poetry and its importance to society in a little preface to the selection from his poems. The only poet who appears to have no doubt about the social usefulness of his own poetry and that of poets like him is Gabriel Celaya:

> La Poesía no es un fin en sí. La Poesía es un instrumento, entre nosotros, para transformar el mundo. No busca una posteridad de admiradores. Busca un porvenir en el que, consumada, dejará de ser lo que hoy es.[6]

> Poetry is not an end in itself. Poetry is an instrument, with us, for changing the world. It does not seek for a posterity of admirers. It seeks for a future in which it, consummated, will cease to be what it is.

Quite clearly he believes that all poetry should have a revolutionary or social aim in view. From this point of view, the poetry now being written by his group in Spain excells that of the poets before the Civil War:

> Nuestros hermanos mayores escribían para 'la inmensa minoría.' Pero hoy estamos ante un nuevo tipo de receptores expectantes.[7]

> Our elder brothers wrote for 'the vast minority.' But nowadays we are faced with a new type of expectant receivers.

That is to say, poets can now reach strata of society that they never reached earlier when their only audience was the bourgeoisie. Thus they can now give forth a revolutionary message. He sees in poetry written, like that of Juan Ramón Jiménez, for an "inmensa minoría" merely a seeking after aesthetic excellence, whereas what interests him is the value of writing for the present time. For this reason, "en el poema debe haber barro, con perdón de los poetas poetísimos"[8] (in a poem, begging the pardon of the very poetical poets, there should be mud). There should be ideas, animal heat, rhetoric, descriptions, plot, and even politics. A poem should be an integral whole. And he says clearly why he thinks all this:

> La Poesía no es neutral. Ningún hombre puede ser hoy neutral. Y un poeta es por de pronto un hombre.[9]

> Poetry is not neutral. No man can be neutral nowadays. And a poet is, to start off with, a man.

This is of course the Marxist argument that everyone is, whether he realizes it or not, working either for or against the eventual revolution of the people. Celaya's practice is consistent with his theories. Especially in the books he has published from 1951 onwards, he has shown himself the most decidedly and consistently revolutionary poet now in Spain.

Between 1935 and 1949, Celaya published ten books of poetry, some of them in his own series of booklets entitled *Norte* which he brought out in San Sebastian between 1947 and 1950. His poems at this period avoided grandiloquence and mingled conversational and poetic language, much as Eliot has done in English poetry.

Las cosas como son (un decir)[10] is an account of his views on personality and existence. He says that his longing to be immortal is a defect and that

> el catolicismo
> —lógica perfecta de tal apetito—
> (¡no se escandalicen!) se preste a mi vicio.[11]

> Catholicism—
> Which is the perfect logic of such an appetite—
> (Don't be shocked!) may lend itself to my shortcoming.

(This quotation, with its two parentheses in one sentence and its prosaic tone, is an example of the style of this book.) Celaya considers *Las cosas como son* his most successful poetic work.[12]

Las cartas boca arriba[13] contains a poem to Neruda, whom Celaya acclaims as the great poet of revolution:

> Los jóvenes obreros,
> los hombres materiales,
> la gloria colectiva del mundo del trabajo
> resuenan en tu pecho cavado por los siglos.
> Los primeros motores, las fuerzas matinales,
> la explotación consciente de una nueva esperanza
> ordenan hoy tu canto.[14]

> The young workers,
> Material men,
> The collective glory of the world of work
> Sound in your hollow breast carved out by the ages.
> And the first motors and the morning forces,
> The conscious exploitation of new hope
> Make up your song today.

This verse is a mixture of rhetoric and allusive imagery. Three nouns govern "resuenan" and three "ordenan," but only the third of each group of three could, in traditional language, be used with its verb (workers do not resound, that is to say, nor motors and forces set in order). In a poem to Blas de Otero, Celaya says bluntly that "we" have not forgiven (the Civil War).

In other poems in the same book he contrasts the poetic world with the real one, always in favor of the latter. He tells a carpenter, for instance, that he, Celaya, is just a carpenter of verse. He reviles his friends for their cultivation of the ego. He has become more rhetorical, but also more certain of himself as a writer.

To combat his own ego or personality becomes his chief concern in *Lo demás es silencio.*[15] This long poem—68 pages of close type —is written in the form of a dramatic dialogue without action. The speakers are the Protagonist, the Chorus, and a Messenger. The Protagonist is the poet himself, with his doubts and hesitations, and the Chorus is the voice of his social conscience and of the People.

At first the poet tries to assert his individualism:

> Aquí estoy con mi boina, mi sombra, mis zapatos,
> mi cuerpo, mi momento, mi idea intransferible,
> y nadie, nadie puede decir lo que yo digo,[16]

> Here am I with my beret, my shadow, and my shoes,
> My body, my instant, my intransferable idea,
> And no one, no one can say what I say,

But the Chorus denies his right to say this, because

> Mientras haya en el mundo tantos infortunados
> buscar la salvación personal es mezquino,
> ¡oh pueblo, tierra tierna!![17]

> While there are in the world so many unhappy people
> It is petty to seek for your personal salvation.
> Oh people, tender ground!

The arrival of a *Mensajero* points out the proletarian moral yet more clearly:

> ¡A la eh!
> Que los trabajadores
> se pongan a una en pie.
> Caminad todos juntos.
> Combatid sin perdones.
> Yo anuncio un evangelio
> que callaban los dioses.[18]

> Hey there!
> Let the workers stand
> Up together.
> Now all go side by side!
> And combat without mercy!
> I'm announcing a gospel
> Which the gods never spoke of.

Only the scansion makes writing of this sort verse. The images are not remarkable. Here, as elsewhere, however, Celaya has rhetorical force. But it is in his few descriptive passages that he comes nearest to feeling in this book:

> Y es tremendo en verano. Y a las tres de la tarde
> que es la hora de morirse sin excusa de hastío,
> . . . .
> A las tres de la tarde, cuando suenan cornetas
> tercamente doradas en un cuartel cerrado,
> a las tres de la tarde, cuando calla el convento
> dejando en el vacío su loca campanita,
> a las tres de la tarde seguir, seguir andando
> por estas calles secas de la ciudad de otro tiempo,[19]

> And it's terrible in Summer. At three in the afternoon,
> The time to die of boredom without any excuses.
> . . . .
> At three in the afternoon, when the cornets are sounding
> All obstinately gilded, inside a closed-up barracks,
> At three in the afternoon, when the convent is silent
> And its mad little bell left untolled in the void there,
> At three in the afternoon, to go on, go on walking
> Down the dry streets of a town that's of another epoch,

Even in this passage, Celaya has not forgotten his political ideas; the town he lives in, with its barracks and convents, belongs to the past. Yet, apart from that, the repetition of the time in the afternoon and the account of the sounds he hears when walking along the streets conjure up feeling in the reader, as descriptive poetry should.

In the prose preface to *Paz y concierto* he says that "El yo no existe"[20] (the ego does not exist). The genius of the true poet, like that of the shoemaker at the corner of the street, consists in expressing what is bigger than himself.

> Nadie es nadie. Nadie es nadie. Hay que decirlo y redecirlo
> hasta sentir cómo en el hombre del pueblo la modestia y la
> dignidad se identifican y cómo, a ras de tierra y sin filosoferías,

nuestra ibérica matriz, rica en aceites, en metales, en espartos, en vinos, en cordilleras vertebrales y ríos decisivos, en sales extendidas y en almendras ricamente espesas, en tormentos geológicos, estilos neolíticos, hombres varios del mar abierto y el mar colonizable, de la meseta y la huerta, de la alta y la baja montaña, la humildad y el orgullo sustancian un único sabor precioso.[21]

No one is anyone. No one is anyone. That is what must be said and repeated until one feels how, as in a man of the people, modesty and dignity are made one and how, at ground level and without any cheap philosophy, our Iberian matrix, rich in oils, metals, espartos, wines, vertebral mountain-ranges and decisive rivers, in wide-spread salts and richly thick almonds, in geological torments, Neolithic styles, different men from the open sea and the colonizable sea, from tableland and plain, from high and low mountains goes to make up, in its humility and pride, one single precious flavor.

This Whitmanesque list of the elements that go to make up Spain has more poetical force, though in prose, than many passages of Celaya written in verse.

The later books of Celaya are written in light, easy rhythms, and are full of jokes and jingles—probably this is one sort of poetic "mud." At times he seems to be parodying Guillén. His world is full of *plenitud* (fullness), too, but it is not *bien hecho* (well made), as Guillén's is (in *Cántico*). This is because Celaya is never likely to forget he is a revolutionary—not even in his love poems, in which he declares his will to go on loving even though

> La policía, Dios,
> la fuerza del dinero,
> las leyes del rebaño
> nos exigen respeto.[22]

> All the police force, God,
> The powerfulness of money,
> The laws made for the herd
> Demand we should respect them.

In fact, the tone of disrespectfulness in Celaya's verses becomes increasingly more marked.

José Hierro (1921-   )

Hierro was the poet who obtained the most votes for the *Antología consultada*. There are frequent indirect references to politics in his poetry, though he writes about love and other emotions as well. There is less revolutionary spirit expressed in his poems than in Celaya's. He says of his work:

> Soy honrado cuando escribo, y presumo pertenecer al grupo de los que no saben decir. . . . Si algún poema mío es leído por casualidad dentro de cien años, no lo será por su valor poético, sino por su valor documental.[23]

> I am an honest fellow when I write and I take it I belong to the group of those who don't know how to express themselves. . . . If any poem of mine is perhaps read in a hundred years' time, it will be not for its poetical but its documentary value.

That is to say, that as neither poet nor reformer has he any deep belief in his own creations. The idea that whatever one writes nowadays has no real value seems to occur very often to modern Spanish writers, and not only revolutionary ones.[24] Fortunately other people do not agree with Hierro in his slighting opinion of his own work and even periodicals in France have spoken well of him *(Cahiers du Sud, Esprit, Arts, Seghers)*.

In 1947, he won the Adonais Prize for poetry with *Alegría*.[25] The influence of Guillén is quite strongly marked in this book, though Hierro mingles a sense of tragedy with his expression of joy, in a manner unlike that poet.

As an example of Hierro's likeness to and differences from Guillén we can take a passage from a later book *(Quinta del 42)*.[26] It is a description of life in prison:

> (Grifos
> al amanecer. Espaldas
> desnudas. Ojos heridos
> por el alba fría.) Todo
> es aquí sencillo,
> terriblemente sencillo.[27]

> (Taps
> At daybreak. Half-naked
> Bodies. And eyes wounded
> By the cold dawn.) Everything
> Here is very simple,
> Terribly simple.

The lines are wholly uninvolved, and it is suitable that the word "sencillo" should be repeated here on two consecutive lines. Hierro is telling us of his personal memories rather than trying to evoke a mood. The apparently straight-forward descriptive phrases do, however, suggest sadness. The men are washing at dawn because they are prisoners. Their eyes are "wounded," though it is only by the morning light. Guillén's method is less direct. Here are some lines from Guillén in the same meter and a not dissimilar style:

> (Un brusco
> Surtidor impone al viento
> Su irresistible exabrupto.)
>
> ¡Maravilla de regalo:
> Ser y aparecer—pedrusco,
> Hoja en la rama, calandria,
> Oreo sobre murmullo,
> Amistad por alameda,
> La perspectiva de Junio!²⁸

> (A sudden
> Jet of water flings upwards
> Its irresistible rejoinder.)
>
> Marvel given as a present—
> Being and appearing—rough boulder,
> Leaf on the branch, sky-lark,
> A breath of air on a murmur,
> Friendship along an avenue,
> The month of June's perspective.

Guillén is allusively accumulating sense-impressions which he wishes to be as far as possible devoid of emotional overtones—above all, of sad ones. We have already seen that, even on the few occasions when Guillén is inescapably led to express sadness, he does so in a very tranquil manner. Therefore, even if he had had the same prison experiences as Hierro, he would not have been likely to express them in the same way.

Hierro has a good sense of rhythm:

> Ya nadie sabía qué hacer, qué palabra
> decir. No quisimos romper el silencio.
> Entraba la luz, nos llegaba la luz.
> Pero nadie sabía qué hacer, qué palabra
> decir. Cada uno miraba sus manos,
> cada uno tenía sus manos mojadas de sombra.²⁹

> Now nobody knew what to do, nor what words he should say.
> No one wanted to be the first who should break the silence.
> And the light entered in, the light came upon us.

But nobody knew what to do, nor what words he should say.
Each one of us was having a look at his hands;
And each one of us had his hands wet with shadows.

Here only the enjambement (not retained in the translation) reminds us of Guillén. The rhetorical repetitions are unlike that poet. So is the idea of a damp shadow, though it is in the usual tradition of modern poetry, which mixes sense-impressions so freely. Yet it has become almost a commonplace in Spanish literary circles to say that Hierro imitates Guillén. Hierro himself does not care for Guillén's poetry, and denies undergoing his influence, but it is fairly clear that he has done so.

We can perceive this if we consider what has made Hierro's poetry, though apparently so like that of many other young Spanish poets, more popular (relatively) than theirs. His political references have something to do with it, but the main reason is probably the directness of his poetry, its avoidance of literary, mythological, or novelistic atmosphere.

The growing acceptance in Spain of Hierro as the foremost living Spanish poet is due to these qualities, which he and Guillén both possess. Neither depends on previous poets or symbolisms for his effects. There is a minimum of tradition in their individual talents. The tradition is there, of course, because otherwise chaos, not poetry, would have been produced, but it is not readily to be observed.

This is how Hierro reviles a poet whom he calls an "aesthete":

Lo has olvidado todo porque lo sabes todo.
Te crees dueño, no hermano menor de cuanto nombras,
Y olvidas las raíces (*Mi Obra*—dices—), olvidas
que vida y muerte son tu obra.[30]

You've forgotten about everything just because you know
     everything.
You think you're owner, not younger brother, of what you
     speak of,
And you forget about the roots. ("My work," you say.) And
You forget that living and dying are your work.

Because he has forgotten the roots, the aesthete is less than what he speaks of, that is to say, he is lacking in social consciousness. He is also, perhaps for that very reason, deficient in poetic intuition, and Hierro has said that "El poeta ha oído una llamada misteriosa"[31] (the poet has heard a mysterious call).

Victoriano Crémer (1909-   )

Two other left-wing poets included in the *Antología consultada* are Victoriano Crémer and Eugenio de Nora. Apart from their books of poems, these two poets won notice for themselves by publishing in León from 1944 to 1950 a poetry review called *Espadaña*. *Espadaña* launched the first public attacks on García Nieto and the poets of *Garcilaso;* Father Lama was mainly responsible for these.[32]

Crémer is a manual worker and his views tend to be Anarchist rather than Marxist. In his statement about poetry, printed in the *Antología consultada,* he is more dissatisfied than Hierro, since he finds not only his own but all poetry fundamentally useless:

1. No vale engañarse. La Poesía es un extraño culto, sostenido por gentes de muy dudosa eficacia vital.

2. Evitar a los poetas en el concierto de la República, es una conclusión filosófica de primera magnitud, y un acierto.

3. Esgrimirse sobre un canto rodado al sol del estío por el placentero afán de lanzar gorgoritos rítmicamente, mientras el hombre a secas trabaja, sufre y muere, es un delito.[33]

1. It's no good deceiving oneself. Poetry is a strange cult maintained by people whose vital effectiveness is very doubtful.

2. To avoid having poets in the plan of the Republic is a philosophical conclusion of the first magnitude and absolutely right.

3. To play at foils on a rolling stone in the Summer out of a pleasing longing to throw forth rhythmic trills, while undistinguished Man works, suffers, and dies, is a criminal offense.

But this is not a final and definite opinion, since he writes in his answers to the questionnaire that his aim as a poet is "Comunicarse con los hombres" (to communicate with men).

Espadaña first appeared in 1944, the year when Aleixandre published *Sombra del paraíso,* and Dámaso Alonso, *Hijos de la ira.* Crémer himself published a book at this time, *Tacto sonoro.*[34] The book was not so striking or original as it was said to be in the account given of it in *Espadaña.* Some of the poems were too like Lorca and in general Crémer did not seem quite sure of himself as a poet.

In *Caminos de mi sangre,*[35] the language has become more personal and violent. When his thoughts turn to God, he feels a physical

horror of himself, like Dámaso Alonso in *Hijos de la ira.* He calls
God a *mastín* (mastiff) and says he is afraid of Him and His love.
The idea is surely taken from *The Hound of Heaven,* of which
Muñoz Rojas published a translation in *Cruz y Raya*[36] before the
Civil War, but Crémer's poem lacks the tenderness and sincere re-
ligious spirit of Thompson's. In a love poem called "La loba blanca"[37]
(The White Wolf) Crémer says that his beloved delights in tearing
and rending in the manner of that beast.

At times he carries his rough, harsh imagery too far and uses
expressions which border on the ridiculous. His social poetry is sometimes as unsubtle and ineffective as Rafael Morales' poems about
lepers and madmen. At his best, he has a rollicking revolutionary
violence which makes him one of Victor Hugo's numerous spiritual
grandchildren:

> Yo no cambio mi flor soñada y virgen,
> ni mi nerviosa agilidad de espina
> por un vientre redondo ni unos ojos
> de mirada de harina.
>
> Yo me salvo en mi mundo, desterrado
> de un azar amarillo de panteras
> donde el aire es silbido y brotan dientes
> y lenguas como hogueras.[38]
>
> I will not change my dreamed-of virgin blossom
> Nor my nervous agility like the hawthorne
> For a rounded belly or a pair of eyes
> Which look at things doughily.
>
> I save myself in my world, and I am exiled
> Away from the yellow hazard of the panthers
> Where the air is a whisper and teeth are sprouting
> And tongues like raging flames.

The imagery is effective, though not consistent. In the first of
these verses Crémer's enemies are fat, listless, and rich, and in the
second they are wild beasts inhabiting a kind of Inferno full of snakes
and flames. Yet the fat rich men and the panthers are both monsters
and are contrasted with the beautiful things of Nature—which sym-
bolize the poor—flowers or hawthorns. Crémer knows how to find
poetical beauty in what is ugly, as a descendent of Hugo should.

Crémer was perhaps the first poet after the Civil War to publish
poetry written in a politically revolutionary spirit. In the passage

just quoted he attacks the complacently rich. Another of his poems
in the same book is the "Fábula a B.D." (Buenaventura Durruti),
the Anarchist killed by Communists during the Civil War. The exact
political implications of the poem are not clear, but death is the
dominant theme.

After *Caminos de mi sangre,* Crémer has published other books of
similar poems. Favorite images of his are mountains and the bull
of Spain—since he loves the grandly rhetorical. As a man of the
people, he shows an imaginative sympathy with the poor.[39] Neruda
does not seem to have influenced his way of writing.

Eugenio de Nora (1924-   )

Like his friend and fellow-editor Crémer, Eugenio de Nora is a
man of the people, "de familia de labradores"[40] (of a peasant family).
His political views are Marxist. From 1942 to 1946, he studied Law
and Letters at Madrid University. He is now lector in Spanish at
Berne University, Switzerland, where he went in 1949.

Nora says that "Mi poesía surge cuando ella quiere; yo la busco,
pero no la invento."[41] (My poetry springs forth when it wants to.
I seek it out, but I do not invent it.) He does not think of its usefulness when he writes it, though he is by no means opposed to poetry's
serving political ends.[42]

In early days he derived pleasure from feeling he belonged to a
group of young poets:

> Yo era uno más y sentía en común con todos. Mis amigos se
> llamaban Crémer o Valverde, Eloy Terrón o Blas de Otero, Bar-
> tolo Lloréns o Rodrigo Carvajal, Antonio de Lama y Leopoldo
> Panero.[43]

> I was one of them and felt in common with all of them. My
> friends were called Crémer or Valverde, Eloy Terrón or Blas
> de Otero, Bartolo Lloréns or Rodrigo Carvajal, Antonio de Lama
> and Leopoldo Panero.

That is to say, incidentally, that some of his friends had had revolutionary political ideas while others were Catholics; one, Father Lama,
is a priest.

But, nowadays, Nora feels dissatisfaction with himself and with
his contemporaries. The reasons for this do not really seem to be
political. His criteria of greatness are to be found:

en la Biblia y el Romancero, en Dante y en San Juan de la Cruz, en Quevedo y en Eluard, en Walt Whitman o en Juan Ramón Jiménez. . . .[44]

in the Bible and the Spanish Ballads, in Dante and Saint John of the Cross, in Quevedo and in Éluard, in Walt Whitman or in Juan Ramón Jiménez. . . .

Thus the highest kind of poetry may be written by Catholics or by Communists, by those who believe in democracy, and by those who stand for Pure Poetry and the "inmensa minoría" (vast minority). Yet all good poetry, he adds, is social—by which he must mean having an effect on society and forming part of it. That is why Nora attacks Ortega y Gasset, the writer who defended "form" against "human interest" in his *Deshumanización del arte*. The classic, according to Nora, has a general appeal and is not written for a "minority" however "immense." But, at the present time,

nos educamos y vivimos en una cultura lánguida, apocada, medio muerta de desnutrición y asfixia. No pienso en España, sino en Europa entera. Para salir de este ambiente haría falta ser un bárbaro; yo no lo he sido lo suficiente.[45]

we are brought up and live in the midst of a languishing, diminished culture, half dead of malnutrition and asphyxia. I am not thinking of Spain, but the whole of Europe. To get out of this atmosphere a man would have to be a barbarian. I haven't been enough of one.

He also denies real greatness to any of the poetry written in Spain from Unamuno onwards:

Sin duda yo he admirado profundamente, y admiro, y debo mucho, a Machado y Unamuno, a Juan Ramón, a todo el grupo que cronológicamente abre Salinas y cierra Luis Cernuda, y me he formado en la amistad y la camaradería generosa de algunos de ellos, Dámaso y Aleixandre ante todo, y estos mismos lazos se funden en verdadera fraternidad con amigos aún más cercanos, desde Leopoldo Panero a los más jóvenes que yo. . . . por eso mismo: todos (o los más conscientes) sabemos, como en el poema de Dámaso, que vamos en el mismo tren, pero que ese tren no lleva a ningún sitio.[46]

Doubtless I have deeply admired and still admire and owe much to Machado and Unamuno, Juan Ramón and all the group which begins chronologically with Salinas and ends with Luis Cernuda. I received my training from the friendship and comradeship of some of them, Dámaso Alonso and Aleixandre above all. These same ties are soldered into true brotherhood in the case of yet nearer friends, from Leopoldo Panero to those who are younger than I. . . . That's just why. We all know (or the most conscious of us do) that, as in Dámaso Alonso's poem, we are all in the same train, but that the train will not take us anywhere.

This feeling of uselessness probably comes from Nora's conviction that he lives in a society which no longer really believes in itself and cannot, therefore, produce writers who appeal directly to humanity. Yet we have seen that he finds great poetry in Juan Ramón Jiménez, whose essential value as a writer he here denies, together with that of the other contemporary poets. This surely shows Nora's own state of uncertainty, which he shares with all the other revolutionary poets of the *Antología consultada* except Celaya.

In spite of *Espadaña's* attacks on "Neoclassicism," Nora's early poems are fairly "Neoclassical" in style: "el mundo es breve / para tu voz y para mi destino."[47] (The world is little / To hold your voice and hold my destiny.) We have already noticed that "voz" is a key-word for many "Neoclassicals" and "destino" here merely forms a complement to it.

> Yo, muchacho aldeano, regresando
> por mis años de fresca y verde senda,
> traigo, para tu tiempo, la alegría
> de aquella inagotable primavera.[48]

> I, a boy from the village, travelling back
> Across my years, along their fresh green pathway,
> Bring, to adorn your time, the joyfulness
> Of all that Spring-time which was inexhaustible.

"Inagotable" is an emphatic word which clashes with the "Neoclassicism" of these lines, giving them meaning. When Nora wrote this he was, whether he knew it or not, preparing himself to write quite a different kind of poetry. Soon afterwards he was expressing his revolutionary feelings in free verse:

> Pero aquel incidente nunca habrá concluído.
> ¡Sabedlo bien, hombres de los anillos!
> ¡Nadie está libre de la sangre que ha vertido!
> Podemos todos circular, podemos
> escupir, o callar, o remedar suspiros.
> ¡Podéis clavar las puertas, las ventanas del cielo,
> cuando pidiendo un rifle pase descalzo un niño!
> ¡Todo ha de ser inútil![49]

But that incident will never be finished.
Let me tell you that, you men with the rings.
No one is free of the blood which he has shed!
We can go about our business, we can all
Spit, or be silent, or pretend we're sighing.
You can bolt up the doors and the windows of Heaven
When a bare-footed boy goes by begging for a rifle.
It will all be quite useless.

The influence of Alberti's Communist poems is clear. Here is a passage from one of these:

Es más,
estáis de acuerdo con los asesinos,
con los jueces,
con los legajos turbios de los ministerios,
con esa bala que de pronto puede hacernos morder el sabor de
   las piedras
o esas celdas oscuras de humedad y de oprobio
donde los cuerpos más útiles se refuerzan o mueren.
Estáis,
estáis de acuerdo,
aunque a veces algunos de vosotros pretendáis ignorarlo.[50]

Moreover,
You are in agreement with the murderers,
With the judges,
With the turbid bundles of papers in the ministries,
With that bullet which may suddenly make us taste the stones
Or those dark cells of damp and infamy,
Where the most useful bodies grow stronger or die.
You are,
You are in agreement,
Though sometimes some of you try not to know it.

The two passages are alike, except that Nora is attacking those who advise indifference *(hombres de los anillos)*, whereas Alberti is speaking of oppression by the state. But the tone is remarkably similar, with, however, one important difference: Alberti writes in the second person plural and Nora in the first person plural. Alberti's *estáis* makes what he says immediately objective; he is the good man denouncing bad men. Nora is one of the oppressed even though *podéis* follows shortly afterwards. This may be due to the altered circumstances for the Spanish revolutionary since Alberti's time. But the result is that Nora's poem is more personal, though no doubt less effective as political propaganda, than Alberti's.

In such passages, Nora draws nearer to the language of prose.
Here are some lines in which he attacks the poets themselves in the
name of the sufferings of the poor:

Cierto que gentes más oscuras,
los que a veces trabajan, y otras veces
se pasan con su hambre, los que viven
y duermen
en cualquier parte—en los derribos
deshabitados, en las alcantarillas, en los interminables
trenes de mercancías . . . y un etcétera
inverosímil . . .—; vamos a ver, poeta:
sitios todos en que tu "amante vida"
lleva máscara sucia
de polvo y pelo al rape, ellos
acaso no comprenden
ese nombre hostil: "patria."[51]

Certainly obscurer people
Who sometimes work and other times
Put up with hunger, who live
And sleep
Anywhere, in the deserted
Rubble, in gutters, in the interminable
Goods-trains, etc. to the
Most unbelievable point. Think of that, poet.
Those are all places in which the "life you love"
Wears a dirty mask
Of dust and hair cropped short, so that perhaps
They cannot understand
The hostile name of Fatherland.

This is more human than Alberti, who was powerful in reviling
political enemies but less understanding about the poor:

Siervos,
viejos criados de mi infancia vinícola y pesquera,
con grandes portalones de bodegas abiertas a la playa,
amigos,
perros fieles,
jardineros,
cocheros,
pobres arrumbadores,
. . . os llamo camaradas.[52]

Serfs,
Old servants of my wine-growing, fishing childhood,
With the great doors of cellars opening on to the beach,

Friends,
Faithful dogs,
Gardeners,
Coachmen,
Poor cellar-hands,
I call you comrades.

Alberti is still what Unamuno called, in the time of the Republic, one of the "señoritos de la Revolución."[53] Nora, in the above passage, feels he is one of the people; this conflicts with what is usually thought poetic—and we must remember that Nora started very nearly as a "Neoclassical," so perhaps the *poeta* is partly himself. The *nombre hostil: patria* is the Spain within which Nora himself is living and not suffering as the really poor suffer. In a poem of this sort we can see the reason why Nora feels that his poetry and that of his contemporaries is insufficient. (The name of Alberti was not included among Nora's list of names of Spanish poets in the passage quoted earlier, but there is no valid reason for thinking that he excepts Alberti from his general criticism of 20th-century Spanish poets.)

The book in which these lines occur is called *España, pasión de vida* (Spain, a Life's Passion), surely a reflection of the name of César Vallejo's book on the Civil War *España, aparta de mí ese cáliz* (Spain, take this Chalice from Me). Nora even names this poet in one of his poems, calling him "tierno César Vallejo" (tender César Vallejo).[54]

Nora often writes in abstract terms and is then difficult to follow. But when he is revolutionary we have seen that he expresses himself strongly. He was twelve years old when the Civil War started and his home was in Nationalist territory:

Cumplidos hombres
de doce años *entonces* . . . Nos mataron
al muchacho.[55]

Grown-up men
Of twelve years old *at that time* . . . As to the boy,
They killed him.

That is what Nora, as a revolutionary, feels about the world in which he lives and what the poems we have quoted above express.

Ramón de Garciasol (1913-   )
(pseudonym of Miguel Alonso)

Ramón de Garciasol was not included in the *Antología consultada,* but he has been mentioned on the Paris radio as one of the members of the revolutionary or "social" group of Spanish poets. He writes on the same themes as others of the school, though not exclusively, for some of his poems are religious and addressed to God. He is not a poet of the mud, as Celaya claims to be, since he uses the topical poetic images—"roses," "light," "stars"—even when inciting to revolt.

In his "Quejas a Rubén Darío," he complains that the earlier poets were not fighters:

> El mundo tiene hoy alma y el alma es pura llama,
> y en los pulsos del hombre hay soles inspirados.
> En vuestro pobre tiempo se moría en la cama
> y se iba ante la muerte con los ojos vendados.[56]

> The world now has a spirit, the soul is a flame burning,
> In the pulse of a man there's a sun's inspiration.
> In the poor days you lived in, it was a bed men died in;
> They went into the presence of death with their eyes blindfold.

The first two lines remind us of Rubén Darío. The last two show us by their prosaic phrases *en la cama* and *ojos vendados* that the world is no longer the one Darío inhabited. Nevertheless, this is rhetorical writing inspired by Darío and of a kind quite different from that of the previous poets we have commented on in this chapter. We may therefore suspect that the "social" poets do not form a school; they are merely a number of independent writers who happen to have similar political ideas.

Garciasol's book *Defensa del hombre*[57] won an *accesit* (an honorable mention) in the Adonais Prize Competition for 1949. It is mostly in traditional meter and uses poetic rhetoric freely. The poet (having been on the losing side in the Civil War) feels useless to his fellow-man, but tries to defend himself for feeling as he does:

> un futuro . . . os prometo
> por el dolor sin retórica
> que ya todos conocemos,
> por las balas, que han hablado
> a nuestros años moceros
> hondas palabras de amor,
> por los vivos y los muertos.[58]

I promise you . . . a future
For the sorrow without rhetoric
Which we all know already,
For the bullets which have spoken
To the years of our boyhood
Their profoundest words of love,
For the living and the dead.

As before, the old rhetoric is used in this passage to express a way of feeling, new in the sense that it is proper to the poet's own time.

Blas de Otero (1916-   )

The revolutionary theme is kept more in the background in the earlier poetry of Blas de Otero, who at first sight seems a "Neo-classical" sonneteer affected with a religious pessimism similar to that of the last sonnets of Antero de Quental. Otero, besides, does not seem to have very definite views on the political usefulness of poetry, since he writes in the *Antología consultada:*

> Creo en la poesía social, a condición de que el poeta (el hombre) sienta estos temas con la misma sinceridad y la misma fuerza que los tradicionales.[59]

> I believe in social poetry so long as the poet (the man) feels these themes with the same sincerity and the same force as the traditional ones.

And he answers our question, "What are you trying to do in your poetry?" by the single word, "Conforme" (that depends).

He only became known after 1950. The fashion for the sonnet was almost over at that time, but he could write in that form with feeling and art:

> De tierra y mar, de fuego y sombra pura,
> esta rosa redonda, reclinada
> en el espacio, rosa volteada
> por las manos de Dios, . . .
> . . . .
> Pero viene un mal viento, un golpe frío
> de las manos de Dios, y nos derriba.
> Y el hombre, que era un árbol, ya es un río.
>
> Un río echado, sin rumor, vacío,
> mientras la Tierra sigue a la deriva,
> oh Capitán, mi Capitán, Dios mío![60]

Of land and sea, of fire and of pure shadow
This round rose is composed which is reclining
In space itself, the rose which God is twining
In His hands.
. . . .
But a bad wind comes up, a chilly blow
Given us by God's hand, which throws us down.
And man, who was a tree, is now a river.

A river lying without a murmur, empty,
While the earth drives on, floating willy-nilly.
Oh, God of mine, oh Captain, oh my Captain.

(The last line is, incidentally, an echo of Whitman's famous line on the death of Lincoln. A similar echo can be found in one of Nora's poems.)[61] The sonnet is not unlike some of Gaos' in *Arcángel de mi noche,* but the artistry is both more traditional and more perfect, and one would say that the religious feeling was deeper. If this is so, he hardly qualifies as a "Neoclassical," who should have achieved a serene balance not disturbed by conflicts; yet undoubtedly the simple imagery of "river," "tree," "rose," added to the sonnet form, makes this poem "Neoclassical" in most ways.

If the religious feeling in Otero's poetry is greater than in Gaos', so is the religious rebellion: "Si eres Dios, yo soy tan mío / como tú. Y a soberbio, yo te gano."[62] (If you are God, I am as much my own / As You are. And, in being proud, I win.) Phrases of this kind, and his political references, lost him the Adonais Prize in 1950, for which he was the most favored candidate. For all his nearness to "Neoclassicism," his views are not to be mistaken, when he expresses them. Of religion he writes: "¿a qué vidrieras, crucifijos / y todo lo demás?"[63] (Why the stained-glass windows, crucifixes, / And all the rest?) And this is how he addresses Nora, whose ideas we already know:

Tú y yo, cogidos de la muerte, alegres,
vamos subiendo por las mismas flores:
un manto rojo, en pleamar, el tuyo;
un manto verde, como el mar, el monte.[64]

You and I, caught by death, will go on happily
Making our upward pathway through the flowers;
Your cloak is red, when the tide's at its fullest;
A cloak of green, like the sea, is the mountain.

The imagery is allusive and practically "Neoclassical," but the sentiments are plain. Blas de Otero, in style, is yet another kind of poet who is at the same time a revolutionary in politics.

All the poets discussed in this chapter have read their poems from time to time in State-subsidized centers, such as the Ateneo in Madrid, and many others. We have seen that they are quite open about their views. These do not include a frank support of Russia or the official Communist party; that, indeed, would be impossible in modern Spain. Yet, even in England, most people would consider their political opinions extreme.

NOTES TO CHAPTER 7

1. (Mexico, 1950).
2. *Indice* (October 15th, 1952).
3. *Antología consultada de la joven poesía española* (Santander, 1951), p. 11.
4. Five members published in Madrid (1935-1936). Printed by Altolaguirre and Concha Méndez.
5. *Marea del silencio* (Zarauz, 1935), and *La soledad cerrada* [Lyceum Prize, 1936] (San Sebastián, 1947).
6. *Antología consultada,* p. 44.
7. *Ibid.,* p. 46.
8. *Ibid.,* p. 44.
9. *Ibid.*
10. (Santander, 1949).
11. *Ibid.,* p. 23.
12. Opinion expressed in private conversation.
13. (Madrid, 1951).
14. *Ibid.,* p. 63.
15. (San Sebastián, 1952).
16. *Ibid.,* p. 15.
17. *Ibid.,* p. 22.
18. *Ibid.,* p. 54.
19. *Ibid.,* pp. 42-43.
20. (Madrid, 1952), p. 10.
21. *Ibid.,* p. 9.
22. *De claro en claro* (Madrid, 1956), p. 43 ["La puta verdad"].
23. *Antología consultada,* p. 105.
24. See p. 000, p. 00 and most of the poets in this chapter.
25. (Madrid).
26. (Madrid, 1952).
27. *Ibid.,* p. 29 ["Reportaje"].
28. *Cántico* (Mexico, 1945), p. 366 ["La vida real"].
29. *Alegría,* p. 24 ["Interior"].
30. *Quinta del 42,* p. 14 ["Para un esteta"].
31. *Antología consultada.* p. 100.
32. Especially in the early numbers published in 1944.
33. *Antología consultada,* p. 63.
34. (León, 1944).
35. (Madrid, 1947).

36. (Madrid), (June, 1934), pp. 89-96.
37. *Caminos de mi sangre,* pp. 33-36.
38. *Ibid.,* p. 39 ["Canción del obstinado"].
39. See the prose introduction to *La espada y la pared* (San Sebastián, 1949), pp. 7-10.
40. *España, pasión de vida* (Barcelona, 1953).
41. *Ibid.,* p. 7.
42. *Ibid.*
43. *Ibid.*
44. *Antología consultada,* p. 150.
45. *Ibid.,* p. 153
46. *Ibid.,* p. 154.
47. *Cantos al destino* (Madrid, 1945), p. 41 ["Canto al demonio de la sangre"].
48. *Siempre* (Madrid, 1953), p. 32 ["Carmen de la riqueza"].
49. *Antología consultada,* p. 164 ["Lo que yo pienso sobre ello"].
50. *Poesía española antología contemporáneos* (Madrid, 1934), p. 472 ["De un momento a otro"].
51. *España, pasión de vida,* p. 22 ["España"].
52. *Poesía española antología contemporáneos,* p. 473 ["De un momento a otro"].
53. In *Ahora,* (March 29th, 1935) ["Cabilismo y caciquismo"].
54. *España, pasión de vida,* p. 32 ["Futuro envejecido"].
55. *Ibid.,* p. 32.
56. Sainz de Robles, *Historia y antología de la poesía española* (2nd edition; Madrid, 1951), p. 1165.
57. (Madrid, 1950).
58. *Ibid.,* p. 30 ["Del hombre que voy haciendo"].
59. P. 180.
60. *Angel fieramente humano* (Madrid, 1950), p. 65 ["La tierra"].
61. "Tú sabes, capitán, que el mundo es breve" (You know, my captain, that the world is brief). (*Cantos al destino,* p. 41.) Though both Blas de Otero and Nora probably had Whitman's famous line in mind, the thought expressed in the two poems is, in every other way, different.
62. *Panorama de la poesía española* (Buenos Aires, 1953), p. 472.
63. *Redoble de conciencia* (Barcelona, 1951), p. 20 ["Basta"].
64. *Angel fieramente humano,* p. 52 ["A Eugenio de Nora"].

8

Religious Poetry

Catholicism is nearly always implicit in the art and poetry of Spain. It certainly is so in Spanish poetry written since 1939, even sometimes when written by exiles: Alberti's "Un hilo-azul-de-la-Virgen"[1] and a number of Cernuda's poems, especially "Atardecer en la catedral,"[2] show this. Revolutionaries in Spain, as we have just seen, write poems on man's relationship to God. And yet, few modern Spanish poets could be called in any full sense religious or Catholic poets. Vivanco and García Nieto, though they publicly declare themselves Catholic writers, are far less concerned with the artistic expression of their faith than the principal religious poets of England or France would be. They are Catholic poets at times, as Verlaine was, though their religious poems have not at all the same quality as his.

Several reasons may be suggested for the lack of any very definite poetic achievement in contemporary Catholic poetry in Spain. The first may be that, in so consistently Catholic a society, certain religious themes do not in themselves possess the same power of impact as in other countries. The force would be felt more where Catholics are either a minority or, as in France for example, opposed by an extremely active group. Their presentation in Spain demands a perfection which tends to make writers fearful of their powers of expression not being equal to the task. Secondly, religious poetry as such may also possibly lead an author unwittingly into unorthodoxy, unless he is a priest or a trained theologian. For that reason, also, he may prefer some other class of writing.

When the *Times Literary Supplement*[3] observed that there was hardly any real religious poetry in modern Spain (referring actually to the younger writers), Radio Nacional indignantly quoted José María Pemán as an example of the fine Catholic poetry written there. Pemán is certainly a poet with a delicate sense of the technical beauties of rhythm and verse, indeed with the same sensibility in this

132

direction as other Andalusian poets such as Lorca, Alberti, and Montesinos. His versification is simple and traditional and his imagery clear and satisfying. But he is not a poet of the deep inner life and therefore not really a religious poet of the kind we are seeking for in this chapter. He has been very successful in the theater as a dramatic poet and this gives him an exterior approach in much of his writing, even when not for the stage. Thus, much of his lyric poetry has a dramatic quality. For instance, his "Poema de los conquistadores" produces a lively effect on a Spanish audience when spoken. I have heard this very enthusiastically applauded when Pemán recited it:

> Y se viste de lutos el día.
> Y se mustia de pena la esposa.
> Y el uno: ¡Abrid paso a mi luz victoriosa!
> Y el otro: ¡Adelante, que la tierra es mía!
> Y nosotros, tercos: ¡Por amor: la rosa
> la rosa, la rosa . . . y el Ave María.[4]

> And the daylight is burdened with mourning.
> And the wife grows all withered with sorrow.
> And one says: "Make way for my light of victory."
> Another: "All the earth is mine. Forward!"
> And we, in our stubbornness, say: "The rose for loving,
> The rose, the rose and the Ave Maria."

Material success is contrasted to an attachment to spiritual values. The repetition of the word "rosa" three times is largely responsible for the emotive power of the passage. Such a device achieves its fullest effect when read aloud. This effectiveness is the secret of Pemán's great success on the stage, in poetry, and as one of the most accomplished public speakers in present-day Spain.

José María Valverde (1926-   )

The most consistently Catholic of the young poets in Spain is José María Valverde. He began as one of the poets of *Garcilaso* in 1943, when only seventeen. He was considered a prodigy whose weak health made people think that he would die very young. He often chose death as his theme. He was always a Catholic poet, but he was perhaps not thought of at that time as a particularly representative one. Valverde's first book *Hombre de Dios*[5] was published while he was a student at the Faculty of Letters in Madrid. Dámaso Alonso, in a Preface, takes the term "religious poetry" in a very wide sense:

Toda poesía es religiosa . . . Si se vierte hacia las grandes in-
cógnitas que fustigan el corazón del hombre, a la gran puerta
llaman. Así va la poesía de todos los tiempos a la busca de Dios.[6]

All poetry is religious . . . If it turns to the great unknown quan-
tities which lash at the heart of man, it calls at the great gate.
Thus the poetry of all ages goes out in search of God.

What perhaps distinguished Valverde most clearly from other poets
appearing in *Garcilaso* was his earnestness. When he wrote of death
he spoke of the little things of life which he would be forced to leave.
In one poem he asked God to "drink" him—an expression also to be
found in Bousoño and which caused unfavorable comment as too
theatrical; we may suspect some influence of Dámaso Alonso's *Hijos
de la ira.*

By 1949, the year of Valverde's second book, *La espera,*[7] his style
was further from the *Garcilaso* school of "Neoclassicism." The statements of religious faith are straightforward. In his poem "El tonto,"[8]
for instance, he speaks of himself as a *tonto* (fool) and of God as
good-naturedly roaring with laughter at him. He is *torpe* (awkward) ;
he is a *pajarito que se enreda entre sus propias patas* (little bird get-
ting mixed up with his own feet). Here again there is some influence
of *Hijos de la ira.* It is interesting to see how often the religious poetry
of Valverde recalls that book.

On the other hand, the poem entitled "Para el tiempo de Navidad"[9]
is like Milton's Nativity Ode, though it is unlikely that Valverde
has read that poem. Valverde uses quite "metaphysical" images such
as the following :

La eternidad fluía
gota a gota en su pulso, a la manera
mortal, en tanto hacía
jornales de faena carpintera.[10]

Eternity was flowing
Drop by drop in His pulses, in the manner
Of mortals, whilst He did
Day-labor at His work as carpenter.

The "Primer poema de amor" speaks simply and religiously of love;
it is part of the author's life as a Christian. In this Valverde is different from nearly all his contemporaries, whose love-poetry is on
a plane other than that of their religious poems. Valverde's insistence

on death now ended. His physical health improved at this time, and he made a happy marriage with Vivanco's sister-in-law.

"Cuatro elegías" is a long-winded attempt at political poetry. The poet—with a pessimism which events up to now have fortunately not justified—laments the state of Europe in 1944 and 1945. Europe, he says, is finished and Communism is a matter of months. Here are some lines from one of these Elegies:

> Este es el tiempo triste de nacer con recuerdos.
> Cuando yo vine al mundo, habían muerto cosas
> que he crecido esperando. Y yo no lo sabía,
> las suponía cerca, tal vez tras de mi casa,
> tal vez tras de esos montes a donde van los pájaros.[11]

> This is the sad time to be born with memories.
> When I came to the world, there were things that had died
> Which I grew up expecting. I didn't know about it,
> I supposed they were near me, at the back of my house or
> Perhaps behind those mountains to which the birds are flying.

This is one of the most successful passages poetically, though it is so near prose that the first four lines could be printed straight on as one sentence in a well-phrased essay; the last line, however, uses poetical rhetoric of too easy a sort.

Valverde's mature poetry is the logical development of his early work. He still uses traditional verse-forms as his most natural means of expression, though a tractor or an airplane may be sometimes mentioned in them. Married life becomes a central theme in his religious verse, so that he mingles personal poems on this theme with others illustrating the life of Our Lord. There is, too, a fair variety in subject-matter. He may write of his children or the ruins of Rome or the dawn breaking over Madrid, as the workmen catch their tramcars. He is always serious. He almost certainly represents the highest point yet reached by religious poetry in contemporary Spain.

Poetry by members of the religious orders

Some of the poetry by members of the religious orders, or by priests, has a curious resmblance to Valverde's later writing. Father Jorge Blajot, S.J. has studied in England and shows a knowledge of the poetry of Hopkins and Eliot. Father José Luis Martín Descalzo, a secular priest, writes poems that are simple and direct, and uses day-to-day imagery. The Carmelite Order has more poetic tradition than others and it published a review called *Elica*.[12] Three Carmelite poets should be mentioned here. The first is Fray Casto del Niño Jesús; his former name was Julio Maruri, and he was one of the best-known of the Santander group. Fray Augusto de la Inmaculada is an uneven writer, capable of absurdities of expression which mar his work. Some of this extravagance may be derived from Dámaso Alonso's *Hijos de la ira,* that source of so much modern Spanish religious poetry, as we have seen. He also imitates Lorca. His best poems are those describing the performance of his religious duties in the setting of a little Northern village. The finest Carmelite poet is Fray Angel María del Sagrado Corazón.

Fray Angel María del Sagrado Corazón

Fray Angel was ordained very young, but in his boyhood he had been a friend of Rafael Morales in their native Talavera. Morales influenced him poetically.

Three of his poems are especially interesting. The first two are sonnets, "Los ancianos" and "La mala casa." The images flow on into one another in "Los ancianos." The old are like waves washing on to the shore *con paz y mansedumbre* (with peace and the quietness of the old). We are told of eternity advancing like a river. The head of an old man is a sky without a sun. This poem is effective because it makes us see the old men by apparently describing other things.[13]

"La mala casa" is about a mysterious house, never really identified, on the outskirts of a city. A *mala casa* (bad house) might be a brothel, and we should not assume that this idea is absent. Perhaps the house is Fray Angel's body in the days before he was a priest since, though it is *mala,* it recalls ideas of purity.

> La casa está para parar el viento,
> para esperar el beso de la helada.

> La casa está vacía. Dentro, nada,
> blanca de cal, cual limpio nacimiento.[14]

> The house is there so as to stop the wind,
> And it is waiting for the kiss of frost.

> The house is empty. Inside it, there is nothing,
> White with its wash, like a clean Christmas crib.

An object—a house—becomes a living person; Antonio Machado, as we saw, also gave human life to things. Though the house is empty, a light shines in the bedroom, making it seem like the snows of January. The house also suggests imprisonment *(encarcelada)* and a wounded she-wolf lying alone. All this metaphorical richness gives strength to the poem.

These two poems, probably the finest written by a priest in modern Spain, are not actually on religious themes. In a free-verse poem called "Tránsito," this poet speaks of the conflict and contrast between his former worldly name of Antonio—Antonio had many friends—and his present "good" name, Angel María. The names become personified:

> ¿Por qué te aturde ya el salir si Antonio no te espera?
> ¿Si Angel María es el amigo bueno
> que te ha crecido el alma,[15]

> Why are you embarrassed about going out if Antonio is not
>   waiting for you?
> If your good friend is Angel María
> Who has made your soul grow strong?

This poem is rather loose in structure compared to the admirable precision of the two sonnets.

José Luis Prado (1919-   )

So far in this chapter we have examined writers who set out to be religious poets. Others may be so, without really intending it. This is the case with José Luis Prado, one of the early group of *Garcilaso* poets or *Juventud Creadora*. Religion appears constantly in his poems, much as it does in Unamuno. He has also written love-poems and others.

Though few, Prado's religious poems ring truer than even Valverde's. The finest of his early poems[16] speaks of his sin of pride, which made him depend on himself and not on God for strength. His parents had died without his being with them, though sons always desire to be present at the death of their parents, perhaps because they were not there at their coming. His best and firmest friend (José García Nieto), "Ya no me da la misma mano que antes me dió"[17] (does not give me his hand in the way he did before). He had been extremely in love once in his life and God had denied him his beloved.

In a series of sonnets—which he, in private conversation, says that he considers unorthodox—to each day of the Creation of the World, he writes:

Dios era Uno. Amándose en sosiego
Uno quiso ser más, Uno quería
saber sabor de su sabiduría:
era exquisita y blandamente ciego.[18]

Loving Himself in quietness, God was One.
One wanted to be more than One. One wanted
To know about the savour of His sapience.
He was so excellently, softly blind.

The poetical effectiveness of this passage is bound up with its repetitions. The unorthodox idea is that of a limitation on God which makes God seek an adventure of the spirit.

In the "Introducción" to his book *Testigo de excepción*[19] he says candidly that he is a person of no importance possessing the "nobleza triste del español hidalgo" (sad nobleness of the Spanish gentleman) and conscious of, though humble about, man's position in the scheme of life: "Debo decir mi nombre. Yo soy José Luis Prado."[20] (I must tell you my name. I am José Luis Prado.) The best three lines of his love-poetry are the closing *terceto* of his *"Nocturno Número 2 (Chopin)"*:

Hubo una vez un ciervo y una cierva.
Moraron en el bosque. Y aun perdura
la huella del amor sobre la hierba.[21]

A stag and doe were, once upon a time,
Living within a wood. There still persists
The track of their swift love among the grasses.

This animal metaphor to express human love has a fine simplicity very characteristic of the poet.

More recently, he has written three long poems. They are monologues. The first, *Oratorio del Guadarrama*,[22] is addressed to his small son during the summer holidays in the mountains near Madrid. The thoughtful seriousness of the author is reflected in the regular meter of the verse.

His poetry is still occupied with the great problems of man's life which he treats with remarkable directness. He is simple where most writers are complicated and involved—in expressing his relationship to his wife in his second monologue, *Respuesta a Carmen,*[23] or in his third monologue beside his mother's tomb, *Miserere en la tumba de R. N.*[24]

Respuesta a Carmen and *Miserere* are written throughout in a completely personal idiom and, except for some passages in the first, in unrhyming hendecasyllables. The prolonged contemplation of death in *Miserere* leads him to some strange fantasies, such as the idea that he could disinter his mother. Then he would make a flute to play on with one of her bones and with another a cigarette-holder, to remind him of how he used to smoke by her bedside. This would, however, he goes on to say, be useless. What he is conveying with this not very pleasant sequence of images is that no possible human effort can draw the dead nearer to us for

> el humo
> de mi meditación, canalizado
> en tu hueso, no más penetraría
> en su materia que en la de un pedazo
> de marfil de un anónimo elefante
> nunca visto.[25]

> The smoke
> Of my imaginings, although its channel
> Was through your bone, would penetrate no more
> Into its substance than into some piece
> Of ivory from some nameless elephant
> Which I had never seen.

The deliberate use of several words of an almost unwieldy length, together with the *enjambements* they cause, creates an atmosphere of rather monstrous abruptness and bareness. On the other hand, the unrhyming eleven-syllable lines are exactly right for a long meditative poem. (The metre is, in fact, the equivalent of English blank verse.) It is interesting to compare it with the published fragments of a similar poem by Panero, in the same lines, called *La estancia vacía.*[26] But nothing can relieve the pessimism of Prado's poem, especially not the final prayer in it, which pleads for the admission of the validity of philosophic doubt. Yet Prado still has the will to be a religious poet, as we can see in the dedication of the poem:

> Al Rvdo. Padre Luis Izquierdo, S.J., que un día me dijo: "Si no tiene fe, diga, de todos modos, estas palabras: 'Tú que me has creado, ten piedad de mi,' en espera de que se cumplan."[26]

> To the Reverend Father Luis Izquierdo, S.J., who said to me one day: "If you have not got faith, say, at any rate, these words: 'Thou who hast created me, have pity on me,' hoping that they may be fulfilled."

The lack of an inspiring body of religious poetry in modern Spain is perhaps due to the same feeling of insufficiency which troubles the revolutionary poets. Poets writing after the Civil War, whatever their ideas may be, feel that they have come too late, that they have missed the great age of literature which ended in 1936.

NOTES TO CHAPTER 8

1. *Poesía (1925-1944)* (2nd edition; Buenos Aires, 1946), pp. 287-288.
2. *La realidad y el deseo* (Mexico, 1940), pp. 217-220.
3. August 29th, 1952.
4. *Poesía española actual* (Madrid, 1946), p. 231.
5. (Madrid, 1945).
6. *Ibid.*, p. X.
7. (Madrid).
8. *Ibid.*, pp. 85-86.
9. *Ibid.*, pp. 93-94.
10. *Ibid.*, p. 93.
11. *Ibid.*, p. 37.
12. (Burgos, 1950-1952).
13. In *Elica*, 2 (March, 1951), p. 30.
14. *Ibid.*
15. In *Elica*, 5 (March, 1952), p. 83.
16. In *Garcilaso*, 17 (September, 1944).
17. *Ibid.*
18. *Testigo de excepción* (Madrid, 1953), p. 20.
19. Pp. 15-16.
20. *Ibid.*, p. 16.
21. In *Garcilaso*, 6 (October, 1943).
22. (Madrid, 1956).
23. (Madrid, 1958).
24. (Sevilla, 1960).
25. *Ibid.*, p. 43.
26. Published in *Escorial* (Madrid, 1944).

9

Some Representative Poems Explained

Up to now, we have been speaking of the main trends of contemporary Spanish poetry. Particular attention has been given to some few poets. Others could have been chosen also or in their place, but the general picture would have been the same. We could only arrive at this, indeed, by being strictly, and often arbitrarily, selective. And, in this chapter, we intend to go over the same ground again, this time much more quickly and by the method of taking nine representative poems by different authors, and discussing them almost line by line.

We begin with Miguel Hernández. Nearly all readers of Spanish poetry, however they may otherwise disagree, are at one in thinking him the greatest Spanish poet born since 1910. His output was not very great. His *Obra escogida* consists of about two hundred pages of poems—and those omitted from that book would not fill more than twenty to twenty-five more—and two plays in verse; but they are very varied in style. They include a Catholic *auto sacramental,* in the style of Calderón, many poems in the style of the Spanish Renaissance poets, revolutionary verses intended for a more popular audience, and his sad, but most mature, poems written in prison, blending his two former styles. The poem we quote here is taken from among these last. Though the vocabulary is mainly that of poetry rather than of prose, the main imagery is taken from the task of a manual worker.

Miguel Hernández

Sepultura de la imaginación

Un albañil quería . . . No le faltaba aliento.
Un albañil quería, piedra tras piedra, muro
tras muro, levantar una imagen al viento
desencadenador en el futuro.

141

Quería un edificio capaz de lo más leve.
No le faltaba aliento. ¡Cuánto aquel ser quería!
Piedras de plumas, mares de pájaros los mueve
una imaginación al mediodía.

Reía. Trabajaba. Cantaba. De sus brazos,
con un poder más alto que el ala de los truenos,
iban brotando muros lo mismo que aletazos.
Pero los aletazos duran menos.

Al fin, era la piedra su agente. Y la montaña
tiene valor de vuelo si es totalmente activa.
Piedra por piedra es peso y hunde cuanto acompaña
aunque esto sea un mundo de ansia viva.

Un albañil quería . . . Pero la piedra cobra
su torva densidad brutal en un momento.
Aquel hombre labraba su cárcel. Y en su obra
fueron precipitados él y el viento.[1]

Tomb of the Imagination

A bricklayer was hoping (he had the breath to do it),
A bricklayer was hoping, stone after stone, wall after
Wall, to raise up an image formed in the wind's own likeness;
The wind is the unchainer in the future.

He would set up a building apt for the greatest lightness.
He had the breath to do it. How much that being was hoping!
Stones made out of feathers, seas made of birds can be moved by
Imagination when it faces Southwards.

He went on laughing, working and singing. And his arms had
A power that was higher than the wing of the thunder,
So that walls sprouted from them as if they had been wing-strokes,
Except for one thing—wing-strokes are less lasting.

The stone became his agent in the end, and the mountain
Has the virtue of soaring if it's totally active.
Stone after stone is weight and it sinks all things around it,
Even a world of anxiousness for living.

The bricklayer was hoping . . . But then the stone recovered
Its savage brutal denseness, all in a single moment.
That man carved his imprisonment. Into his handiwork
He and the wind were both thrown headlong downwards.

The poem suggests that the writer feels his life has been a failure.
The building turns out to be the bricklayer's own prison; at the same
time, it is the symbol of a society or, rather, a social happiness which

Hernández had hoped to achieve by espousing the revolutionary cause. The wind referred to is a mental or spiritual atmosphere. The poem can be read in a non-personal sense as symbolizing the people of Spain after the defeat of the Republic.

Let us now examine it more closely, line by line.

"Un albañil quería . . . No le faltaba aliento." *Aliento* introduces the "air" *motif* so common in Hernández, two of whose titles are *El labrador de más aire* (The Countryman with the greatest Air) and *Viento del pueblo* (Wind of the People).

"Un albañil quería, piedra tras piedra, muro / tras muro." This enjambement, coming as it does at the beginning of the poem, frees it from a possible monotony of tone noticeable when Hernández writes in long lines.

"levantar una imagen al viento." The very building is to be the image of the wind. "Air" or "wind" for Hernández means the vitality of life, particularly of popular life. An image of the wind would therefore mean an ideal life for the people.

"desencadenador en el futuro." This hendecasyllabic line at the end of the verse avoids the danger of the alexandrines becoming monotonous—a very real one in modern Spanish poetry. The use of the long word *desencadenador* is telling. Within the word *desencadenador* another is hidden—*cadena* (chain). A poet's life affects his choice of words; Miguel Hernández is a poet of liberty against imprisonment and against chains, the poet of the wind. The tragedy of his own imprisonment, that prelude to his death, adds a deeper force still to the word *desencadenador*. And yet this was probably not the principal meaning that the poet was thinking of. Let us see what the Dictionary of the Spanish Royal Academy of Language says:

Desencadenar. tr. Quitar la cadena al que está con ella amarrado. 2. fig. Romper o desunir el vínculo de las cosas inmateriales. 3. r. fig. Dícese de algunas cosas que, por el ímpetu y violencia con que obran, rompen o estallan, parece como que han quedado libres de todo freno que las pudiera contener. *DESENCA-DENARSE las pasiones, el viento, una tempestad.*[2]

Desencadenar. tr. To take away the chain from the person bound with it. 2. fig. To break or disunite the link of immaterial things. 3. r. fig. Said of things which, because of the impetus and violence with which they work, break and burst, seem to have become free of every check which might restrain them. *Desencadenarse used of passions, the wind, a storm.*

The example of the use of *desencadenarse* with *el viento* shows us what Hernández is thinking of principally, though a great poet instinctively uses all the possible meanings of a word at the same time because of his sensitivity to language.

"Quería un edificio capaz de lo más leve." He uses *edificio,* not *casa. Edificio* reminds us of modern cities and buildings which can be of public utility. *Leve* is usually a poetical, not an everyday, word. The contrast with *edificio* suggests the inner conflict of the ideal with the real.

"No le faltaba aliento. ¡Cuánto aquel ser quería!" He sees himself from outside, as an isolated being.

"Piedras de plumas, mares de pájaros los mueve." One image or idea leads on to another. *Aliento—ala—aletazo—pájaros—plumas.* The *edificio* is, on the one hand, built of stone and, on the other, composed of all these airy elements, for it is the idea of wind which suggests wings.

"una imaginación al mediodía." The imagination can freely interchange stones and feathers. The word *mediodía* has great poetic force. The South, for a European, means warmth of climate, more beautiful natural surroundings and probably a greater wealth of artistic and ancient historical associations. Yet even the Chilean poet Neruda writes: "Todo de ti me aleja, como del mediodía." (Everything takes me from you, as from the South.)[3]

"Reía. Trabajaba. Cantaba. De sus brazos." This line is very simple, the working day of a bricklayer.

"con un poder más alto que el ala de los truenos." That is to say that the arms of a man, of a worker in modern times, can achieve more than a god—Jupiter the Thunderer—in the old times. There is an implied reference to Jupiter's eagle.

"iban brotando muros lo mismo que aletazos." The simultaneous idea of air and stone is continued.

"Pero los aletazos duran menos." The airy hope is less lasting than the brute material out of which the poet has been building. This gives him a deep feeling of failure.

"Al fin, era la piedra su agente. Y la montaña / tiene valor de vuelo si es totalmente activa." The greatest possible accumulation of stone is a mountain, commonly a symbol of what is supremely static. But if the stones of the social edifice which the bricklayer wants to build are air, then a mountain—a complete new world or social system—can be active, can be airy also, or at least can have *valor de vuelo*. *Agente* is a good word because it makes a contrast with the complicated double metaphor in the rest of the poem; it is, above all, a more practical word.

"Piedra por piedra es peso." But, though the mountain may be active and possess *valor de vuelo,* though the whole social ideal may be a thing of lightness, of joy, of life, the individual effort does not share in that airiness; the poet has built in single stones, not in air. *Peso* is another good word, apt, because of its everyday uses, for expressing a feeling of despondent sadness; the alliteration helps.

"y hunde cuanto acompaña / aunque esto sea un mundo de ansia viva." This world of living aspirations is the winged desire to build a joyful house of air, a desire which is in itself great enough to constitute a world—but that world may be defeated by hardness. *Ansia* is a good abstract word interpolated between the wind images.

"Un albañil quería . . . Pero la piedra cobra / su torva densidad brutal en un momento." Density is the great enemy of airiness; the literary adjective *torva* and the commonly used and forceful everyday adjective *brutal* are placed before and after, in order to mark the evilness of density.

"Aquel hombre labraba su cárcel." The sudden simplicity of this statement in a poem which has been so full of complicated metaphors brings us back to the actual situation of the man writing the poem, who is in prison.

"Y en su obra / fueron precipitados él y el viento." The liberator has enclosed himself and his airy hope in the prison which is the actual *work* he has achieved.

Viento is the key-word of this poem. The usual associations of wind, such as velocity, inconstancy, and playfulness are set aside for one of force. As an earlier example of Hernández's "air" metaphors here is a passage from *El labrador de más aire.* In that play, the image of wind is constantly used by the other characters to describe the vital force in the hero, Juan. Encarnación says:

> Su aire alborotó un molino
> como un fuerte ventarrón,
> y ante el airoso empujón,
> en la llanura desierta

sentí cerrarse una puerta
y abrirse mi corazón.
                    (Act I)[4]

His air set a mill in motion
As a gust of wind would do,
And, feeling that breezy pushing
Over the deserted tableland,
I heard a door quickly shutting
And my heart within me opening.

Miguel Hernández was the leading poet of the left at the time of the Civil War, with the possible exception of Rafael Alberti. The young poet of the Nationalists was Dionisio Ridruejo. They, nevertheless, belong to the same age in Spanish poetry, and are men of the same generation who have read and been influenced by the same Spanish poets. Possibly Ridruejo carried "Neoclassicism" rather further than Hernández but, if he did, it is a matter of degree only. Hernández came from the peasantry, as Burns did, but his debt to the poetic literature of the past is much more obvious than that of the Scottish poet. Taking that into account, he expresses himself more directly and gives the impression of being less traditional than Ridruejo. That is the only poetic difference between much of Hernández' and Ridruejo's writings. Both use images and phrases which belong to the Renaissance; both use them in a way that really belongs to the present time.

If *viento* is the key-word of the poem of Hernández' which we have been discussing, the word *piedra,* representing the second half of Hernández' double metaphor, is very important, too. *Piedra* is the key word of the following sonnet by Ridruejo (and *aire* appears in the first line).

Dionisio Ridruejo

Primer soneto *(Sonetos a la piedra)*

A ti, yunque del aire, pensativa
de las altas y puras soledades;
a ti, duro tambor de tempestades,
armadura de siglos: piedra altiva.

A ti, en líneas y números cautiva,
vertical ambición de eternidades;
a ti, rostro sin voz de las edades
desnudo de cinceles, piedra viva.

A ti, cuando tu parto de la aurora,
cuando a eternos laureles elevada,
cuando fría en la sombra del secreto,

cuando libre en la forma triunfadora,
que canten en tu carne reposada
los catorce martillos del soneto.[5]

For you, air's anvil, thoughtful and alone
Among the purest heights of loneliness;
For you, the hard drum of the tempest's stress,
The framework of the centuries, proud stone.

For you, whom lines and numbers make their own,
Vertical aim of everlastingness;
For you, the face of all the ages—less
A voice, if bare of chisels—living stone.

For you, when you were given birth at dawn,
When endless laurels honor you, their lord,
When you lie cold within the secret's shade,

When you are free in your triumphant form,
Your flesh at rest achieves song in the chord
The sonnet's fourteen hammer-strokes have made.

The stone is at first in its natural surroundings on the mountain-side. Then it is spoken of from one aspect after another until the fourteen hammer-strokes of the sonnet sing it into artistic form.

"A ti, yunque del aire." The stone in its natural shape is only beaten upon by the winds.

"pensativa / de las altas y puras soledades." The high, pure solitude of the mountains induces to thought, therefore the stone itself is thinking.

"a ti, duro tambor de tempestades." "D," "t," "t," and the roll of the words makes this line onomatopoeic. We do not only have the image of high rocks; we also hear them being drummed on by the storm.

"armadura de siglos." The poet uses the word in the third meaning given by the Academy Dictionary, *esqueleto* (skeleton).[6] The rocks are the bones of the centuries over which the earth is constructed.

"piedra altiva." These two words sum up the idea of the stone given by lines three and four, and even by the first quatrain. The notion of height has been implicit in all the images, and now the height has become a noble pride.

"A ti, en líneas y números cautiva." The poem might here begin
to become obscure if we were troubled about its exact meaning, instead of letting ourselves be carried along by its strong rhythm and
the fine implications of its well-placed words. It is in passages of
this sort that modern Spanish "Neoclassicism" can at times be nearer
to Surrealism than to the poetry of the Renaissance. If we look down
to the end of the sonnet, we shall see that the stone in question is a
type of the sonnet-form itself which, presented as the poet presents
it, is also of stone. We notice that this way of regarding it comes
more naturally to sonneteers such as Ridruejo and García Nieto than
to those of the seventeenth century. The latter, even at their most
formal, were primarily concerned with conveying some thought or
emotion about love or the spiritual life—except, possibly, in their
lightest works. But here we find that the form of the poem has become one of the writer's gravest concerns.

"vertical ambición de eternidades." The line before is now linked
to the idea of greatness by *ambición* and *eternidades*. But the most
important word is *vertical,* a geometrical adjective as cold as these
sonnets of Ridruejo's are.

"a ti, rostro sin voz de las edades." *Edades* is the rhetorical or
poetic word for time. *Voz* is, as we have seen in Chapter 3,[7] a word
very often used by "Neoclassicals," but it is here used unneoclassically,
with its normal meaning of a sound issuing from a mouth.

"desnudo de cinceles: piedra viva." The chisel, by clothing the
stone, makes it less living. This is the opposite of what one would
have expected.

"A ti, cuando tu parto de la aurora." This is an example of the
use of words for their associative value; they have no clear meaning
and do not evoke any definite visual image. The old poets such as
Góngora might complicate their imagery and their expressions; but
if these are not confusing, you can always understand what they are
saying. Modern Neoclassicals suggest things without actually implying them.

"cuando a eternos laureles elevada." The birth of stone is when
it receives form from man (either as sculpture or as a building). If
the work produced is a fine one, we may say it has won eternal
laurels. Laurels are, of course, a traditional synonym for fame. This
line might almost belong to an early seventeenth-century poet.

"cuando fría en la sombra del secreto." The mysteriousness of *sombra del secreto* in relation to *fría* creates a physical sensation, even if no visual image accompanies it. The meaning presumably is, "when the stone is still metaphorically under the shadow of the as yet un-achieved form which will later be given to it *(secreto)*."

"cuando libre en la forma triunfadora." The meaning of this line appears to be the same as that of the "eternal laurels" one. The point, however, is that it ends rhetorically and effectively on *triun-fadora*. We are now ready for the two concluding lines.

"que canten en tu carne reposada / los catorce martillos del soneto." Obviously these last two lines would have clenched the poem better as a rhyming couplet, in the Shakespearian manner. The phrasing, though not the rhyming-scheme, of this poem makes up three groups of four lines ending in these final two. Spanish practice has obliged Ridruejo to follow the Italian and not the English model in his rhymes. Indeed, the Spanish language is probably not suited to the Shakespearian type of sonnet.

This gives point to the whole sonnet. The stone is the material for artistic creation, and it here becomes poetry.

We now come to a sonnet by García Nieto which is, if possible, even more "Neoclassical" than Ridruejo's.

José García Nieto
"A cantar dulce y a morirme luego."
—Góngora.

No sé si soy así ni si me llamo
así como me llaman diariamente;
sé que de amor me lleno dulcemente
y en voz a borbotones me derramo.

Lluvia sin ocasión, huerto sin amo
donde el fruto se cae sobradamente
y donde miel y tierra, juntamente,
suben a mi garganta, tramo a tramo.

Suben y ya no sé dónde coincide
mi angustia con mi júbilo, ordenando
esta razón sonora y sucesiva.

Y estoy condecorado, aunque lo olvide,
por un antiguo nombre en que cantando
voy a mi soledad definitiva.[8]

"Singing in dulcet manner and dying after."

—Góngora.

Am I like this and named (I do not know)
As people always name me every day?
I know that love fills me in a sweet way
And my voice bubbles forth to overflow.

Rain without cause, orchard of which there's no
Owner, where fruit falls without stop or stay
So that the honey and the earth there may,
Flight after flight, up to my gullet go.

Go up, but I do not know at what set
Point all my joys and anguish coincide
In sense's loud, successive ordinance,

And I am honored, though I may forget,
By an old name with which, while singing, I'd
Travel on t'wards definite solitude.

Explicit meaning has less place here than in our last example. The whole poem hardly says more than the quotation from Góngora at the head of it.

"No sé si soy así ni si me llamo / así como me llaman diariamente." Short words repeat the same sounds in the first line. The meaning is that the poet does not know if he is the being whom others see in his daily life.

"sé que de amor me lleno dulcemente." Here we have the word *dulce;* Father Lama in *Espadaña*[9] complained that this was used much too frequently by García Nieto and other contemporary Spanish poets. (The word is also in the quotation from Góngora at the head of the poem.) The love spoken of may be a specific emotion for someone in particular or a general feeling of tenderness proper to a poet.

"y en voz a borbotones me derramo." "Hablar uno a borbotones" means "Hablar acelerada y apresuradamente, queriendo decirlo todo de una vez"[10] (to speak rapidly and hurrriedly, wanting to say everything at once). This phrase might be used derrogatively of a writer who failed to express himself clearly. But probably what is intended here is quite the contrary. The line would seem to refer to a facility for writing in verse similar to that of Ovid and Pope.[11] If this is what he claims, it is not without considerable justification. An examination of all García Nieto's work would show that he is a quite exceptional technician of verse. His constant insistence on using accepted verse-forms is probably due mainly to his remarkable proficiency at them.

"Lluvia sin ocasión." The voice becomes rain which falls for no real reason.

"huerto sin amo / donde el fruto se cae sobradamente." At the same time, the poet is the orchard in which the rain of his poetry falls. The orchard is also irresponsible, like the rain, because both the rain and the orchard are the poet himself, and he is lacking in a sense of true responsibility when he writes.

"y donde miel y tierra, juntamente, / suben a mi garganta, tramo a tramo." An excess of fruit falls from the trees of the orchard. The sweetness (honey) of this fruit overflows, plot by plot, into the poet's throat again. This means that, of the fullness of his overflowing poetry, new poems are born. The whole verse is of course very involved, but he is in fact telling us that the writing of poetry is something that is almost too easy for him, the poet. Since Neoclassicism implied that the formal beauty of the poetry was more important than its sense, this passage illustrates very aptly how the poet regarded his work.

"Suben y ya no sé dónde coincide / mi angustia con mi júbilo, ordenando / esta razón sonora y sucesiva." The point of all this is more in the pleasure of the sibilant sounds of the last line than in the very slight meaning, which is that his poetry as a whole and this sonnet in particular flow from the poet's anguish and joy.

"Y estoy condecorado, aunque lo olvide." The prosaic word *condecorado* is effective here, as it is in Alberti's "A un capitán de navío," when he says "fuiste condecorado por un golpe de mar";[12] as we have seen,[13] García Nieto copied this passage of Alberti in "Cantar de tierra," when he spoke of his friend being "con la Cruz del Sur condecorado"; repetitions of words and effects are almost inevitable if the vocabulary of poetry becomes voluntarily limited, as it does with "Neoclassicism." The meaning of the line above is that the poet has received some special mark of favor from Providence which separates his poetic self from his everyday existence. This is true, even though he may forget it.

"por un antiguo nombre en que cantando." He means his own name under which he sings.

"voy a mi soledad definitiva." That is to say, to man's essential solitude and also to death—"a cantar dulce y a morirme luego."

Ridruejo's first poems were published before the Civil War. García Nieto's first printed poems were written during it. Rafael Morales, younger than either of them,[14] brought out his first book, *Poemas del toro,* one of the sonnets of which we are about to discuss, in 1943. In the *Antología consultada,*[15] he denies that he is a "Neoclassical."[16] Considering when he wrote the *Poemas del toro,* this statement would really need some qualification. However, he is certainly right in one sense; he is a clear writer who, having felt an emotion, seeks to express it without the Petrarchan impersonality of the "Neoclassicals."

Rafael Morales

El toro

Es la noble cabeza negra pena,
que en dos furias se encuentra rematada,
donde suena un rumor de sangre airada
y hay un oscuro llanto que no suena.

En su piel poderosa se serena
su tormentosa fuerza enamorada,
que en los amentes[17] huesos va encerrada
para tronar volando por la arena.

Encerrada en la sorda calavera,
la tempestad se agita enfebrecida,
hecha pasión que el músculo no altera:

es un ala tenaz y enardecida,
es un ansia cercada, prisionera,
por las astas buscando la salida.[18]

The Bull

Out of this noble head black pain has found
Its only limit in two shoots of rage;
In it there sounds the blood he can't assuage,
And there's a dark lament which does not sound.

Loving, tormented strength is calmed and bound
Within his powerful skin, whose equipage
Is all the force his mindless bones encage—
To thunder rushing on the bullfight ground.

Enclosed within the skull the storm all senseless
Dashes round madly like a feverish thing
Of passion, though the muscle's motionless:

It's a tenacious and a burning wing,
It's a beseiged, imprisoned anxiousness
That through the horns seeks for an opening.

This is the first poem of the *Poemas del toro*. It might be called its title-poem. The idea of writing this book must have come from two sonnets by Miguel Hernández, poems 17 and 23 of *El rayo que no cesa*,[19] written in the same "Neoclassical" idiom. The approach is, however, different. Hernández is comparing himself to the bull, whereas Morales is objectively trying to understand how the bull must feel.

"Es la noble cabeza negra pena." The head is compared to something abstract, *negra pena*. And yet this expression is very vivid; it is used in Andalusian popular poetry and therefore suitable to a book called *Poemas del toro,* for Andalusia is a great bullfighting center. We cannot consider *negra pena* "Neoclassical" because of this vividness.

"que en dos furias se encuentra rematada." The horns have become an abstract feeling—fury. But, as before, the words are not only abstract; they also suggest a visual image of the bull's brutal attack. *Rematada* is one of those words which, not being in themselves poetical, have a telling effect if used in the right place in a poem.

"donde suena un rumor de sangre airada." This line is "Neoclassical," since it seeks after a general effect, paying little heed to the meaning or the visual impression; it is not clear what the *rumor* referred to is, whether it is the bull's blood, which we could not hear in any case, or his bellow.

"y hay un oscuro llanto que no suena." *Llanto* here means "lamentation" or, more properly, "weeping." (Lorca's "Llanto por Ignacio Sánchez Mejías" is usually translated into English as "Lament," which is too weak and hackneyed for a title, especially as Lorca himself did in fact weep on hearing of the great bullfighter's death.)[20] Perhaps Morales also suggests the tragic limitations of strength, especially of sensual potency, of which the bull is one of the great symbols. *Que no suena,* because people do not know of, or do not realize this unhappiness. The bull is humanized by hinting more than the statement actually contains.

"En su piel poderosa se serena / su tormentosa fuerza enamorada." *Tormentosa* recalls the sea in tempest, this sea being the bull's blood.

Enamorada implies some higher kind of love in the bull, but also equates human love with its sensual manifestations.

"que en los amentes huesos va encerrada / para tronar volando por la arena." The force in the demented bones expresses itself in the bull's charging. This is a good mixture of sense-impressions. Incidentally, the word *amentes* (without a mind, and therefore demented) is so unusual that many editions print the word "amantes"; indeed, even the Academy Dictionary labels *amente* as *anticuado* (antiquated or archaic).

"Encerrada en la sorda calavera." The word *encerrada* is repeated. The poem depends on the idea of an enclosed, restricted force which both humanizes the bull and makes him a counterpart of man. *Sorda* has several meanings, but the most appropriate here is the figurative one of "insensible"; applied to *calavera,* it signifies an unheeding strength, that which the bull uses when he charges without noticing at what or how.

"la tempestad se agita enfebrecida." This is the idea of a storm in the blood again. But the fever of the blood is fastened within the fury of the bone.

"hecha pasión que al músculo no altera." The muscles, being part of the bony structure, are not perturbed by the fever of the blood.

"es un ala tenaz y enardecida." *Ala* is used "Neoclassically" for its associations with flying, such as being spread out to the wind and able to endure in flight—and therefore speedy and forceful. We find the word, for instance, at the very beginning of *El rayo que no cesa:*

> Un carnívoro cuchillo
> de ala dulce y homicida
> sostiene un vuelo y un brillo
> alrededor de mi vida.[21]

> The wing, sweet and homicidal,
> Of a carniverous knife
> Sustains its flight and its brilliance
> Around the whole of my life.

But much of Hernández' "Neoclassical" vocabulary (*costado* and so on) is not used by Morales.

Enardecida brings back ideas of blood and fever.

"es un ansia cercada, prisionera." The notion of imprisonment within the body is fundamental to the poem.

"por las astas buscando la salida." The last line is the concise climax of the whole sonnet and what the reader remembers most clearly afterwards. *La salida* is freedom for a feverish, sensual sea in torment. In this case, the Petrarchan sonnet has the advantage of the Shakespearian one, because the latter must put into the final couplet what the former can keep until the last line.

We now move quite away from "Neoclassicism." Montesinos, although only a year younger than Morales, knew the same people, and contributed very frequently to García Nieto's poetry review *Garcilaso*. However, he did not begin to attract much notice until three years after the *Poemas del toro,* by which time "Neoclassicism" was no longer the dominant poetic fashion. Having been, as it were, trained in the *Garcilaso* school of García Nieto, he generally adheres to traditional forms. Yet he adheres more to those of the last half of the nineteenth century and of the more "popular" poetry of Jiménez and Alberti than to those of the Renaissance.

Rafael Montesinos

Yo estoy solo en la tarde . . .

> Tot l'estiu l'he enyorada dintre el cor
> i ara l'han vista els ulls . . .
>
> —Maragall.

Yo estoy solo en la tarde. Miro lejos,
desesperadamente lejos. Quedan
por el aire las últimas palabras
de los enamorados que se alejan.

Las nubes saben dónde van, mi sombra
nunca sabrá dónde el amor la lleva.
¿Oyes pasar las nubes, dime, oyes
resbalar por el césped mi tristeza?

Nadie sabe que amo. Nadie sabe
que si llegó el amor, trajo su pena.
Yo estoy solo en la tarde y miro lejos.
No sé de dónde vienes a mis venas.

Te me vas de las manos, no del alma.
Nos separan montañas, vientos, fechas.
El amor, cuando menos lo pensamos,
se nos viste de ausencia.

Estoy en soledad. Miro a lo lejos
oscurecer la tarde y mi tristeza.
Estoy pensando en ti y estoy pensando
que acaso en soledad también me piensas.[22]

I am alone at evening . . .

All summer I longed for her in my heart
And now my eyes have seen her.

—Maragall.

I am alone at evening. I gaze further,
Far, desperately far away. The last words
Of lovers that are leaving this spot linger
Upon the breeze which wafts away behind them.

The clouds know where it is they're going. My shadow
Will never know whither my love will bear it.
Do you hear the clouds passing, tell me, do you
Hear how my sadness sweeps across the grasses?

No one knows that I love. And no one knows
That, when love came, it brought its sorrows with it.
I am alone at evening. I gaze further.
How did you come to where my heart's blood's flowing?

You are out of hand's reach, not out of soul's reach.
By mountains, winds and dates we two are parted.
And even love, when we were least expecting,
Has become clothed with absence.

I am alone. And I see, gazing further,
How the evening grows darker, and my sadness.
I am thinking of you, and I am thinking
Perhaps you, too, alone, are thinking of me.

He quotes Maragall because his beloved, who was Catalan, had
spoken to him of that poet.

As with many of the Romantic poets, he makes his personal feelings the center of everything; "Yo," he begins with the first person
singular, "estoy solo en la tarde." This is a clever device because,
by the act of reading, we are made to share his solitude with him.

"Miro lejos, / desesperadamente lejos." The twice-repeated word
lejos gives the *motif* of absence.

"Quedan / por el aire las últimas palabras / de los enamorados
que se alejan." We have seen how Bousoño notes that Machado,

when describing a countryside or village, was really revealing his own mood while looking at it.[23] The same thing is true of Montesinos in the Retiro Gardens. The lovers *se alejan,* become *lejos;* their words as they walk out of earshot are for him *últimas* because he is reminded of the last words his beloved has said to him.

"Las nubes saben dónde van, mi sombra / nunca sabrá dónde el amor la lleva." The clouds have a more definite sense of purpose than the poet (or his shadow); they know where they are going because they are travelling towards where the poet's love is. *Saben dónde van* is quite colloquial; it is like saying *they know where they're going all right.*

"¿Oyes pasar las nubes, dime, oyes / resbalar por el césped mi tristeza?" She will see these same clouds, and the wind will bear her something of the sound of his voice. External Nature becomes the agent of his personal feelings.

"Nadie sabe que amo. Nadie sabe / que si llegó el amor, trajo su pena." This develops what we have called the "device" of the poet's solitude. This statement that nobody knows that he loves, though true at the time of writing, ceases to be so on publication. And we can hardly assume, as in the case of a private letter, that the possibility of publication was entirely absent from the poet's consciousness. Nevertheless, a sensation of solitude and intimacy is given by these lines.

"Yo estoy solo en la tarde y miro lejos." Again the reader shares his solitude. Repetition adds still more force to this.

"No sé de dónde vienes a mis venas." The use of *venas* for blood, passion, tenderness is "Neoclassical."

"Te me vas de las manos, no del alma." A colloquial phrase, "te me vas de las manos," is placed in an unusual juxtaposition to *alma.* A stronger accent than before falls on the first syllable of the line, marking a change of tone, for the poet is now speaking of mutual love, not only of his own feeling of solitude and nostalgia.

"Nos separan montañas, vientos, fechas." The idea of geographical separation is contrasted with *fechas.* As the poet is absent from his love, the dates *(fechas)* of her letters are earlier than the dates when he reads them. This is another form of separation.

"El amor, cuando menos lo pensamos, / se nos viste de ausencia." The language is simple and leads up to the word *ausencia,* which is the theme of the poem.

"Estoy en soledad. Miro a lo lejos." This is a third repetition, but so subtly introduced that the reader may hardly notice the poet's insistence, particularly because this time *miro* has a complement or object in the following line: "oscurecer la tarde y mi tristeza." Night-fall becomes the expression of his mood. *Tarde* and *tristeza* are one; this is a development of the Machado system.

"Estoy pensando en ti y estoy pensando / que acaso en soledad también me piensas." The repetition of *estoy pensando* is to emphasize the hope in the last line. The solitude at last becomes a point of union with the beloved.

After Montesinos we are going to take some examples of more recent developments in Spanish poetry. We can see that Caballero Bonald (1926-   ), the first of these newer poets, has no traces of "Neoclassicism." On the other hand, he has assimilated Vicente Aleixandre and, especially, Dámaso Alonso,[24] besides some Surrealism and possibly some contemporary French poetry as well.

José Manuel Caballero Bonald

Espera

Y tú me dices
que tienes los pechos vencidos de esperarme,
que te duelen los ojos de tenerlos vacíos de mi cuerpo,
que has perdido hasta el tacto de tus manos
de palpar esta ausencia por el aire,
que olvidas el tamaño caliente de mi boca.

Y tú me lo dices que sabes
que me hice sangre en las palabras de repetir tu nombre,
de lastimar mis labios pronunciándote,
de darle, pronunciándote, a mi vida
una nueva manera de encadenarte en besos
desde la ausencia en la que tú me gritas
que me estás esperando.

Y tú me los dices que estás tan hecha
a esta sustancia de mi carne ociosa,
que apenas si tu sombra se delata,
que apenas si eres cierta,
pues somos ya una espera inacabable
en esta oscuridad que tu distancia pone
entre tu cuerpo y el mío.[25]

Waiting

And you tell me
That your breasts are subdued by waiting for me,
That your eyes ache because you have them empty of my body,
That you have lost even the sense of touch in your hands
Through a feeling for this absence in the distance,
That you forget the warm size of my mouth.

And you tell me you know
That I made my words bleed repeating your name,
By hurting my lips pronouncing you,
By finding for my life, pronouncing you,
A new manner of chaining you in kisses
From out of the absence in which you shout to me
That you are waiting for me.

And you tell me that you are now so molded
To the substance of my flesh standing idle
That even your shadow hardly betrays its presence,
That you are hardly real
Because we have become unending, waiting
Within this darkness that your distance puts
Between your body and mine.

"Y tú me dices." The repetition of these words is very important in the poem. All three verses begin the same—with a "lo" added in verse two and a "los" in verse three—which gives a form to the poem.

"que tienes los pechos vencidos de esperarme." The *pechos vencidos* is the first of a number of references to the body. The body is the expression of the mind, as it is in some of the poems in Aleixandre's *Historia del corazón*. Practically speaking, for Aleixandre and Caballero Bonald, but especially for the latter, the body and the mind are one. The insistence on the body and certain disagreeable images connected with it—above all, connected with the eyes—is one of the most characteristic features of Surrealist poetry. It is even, though less obtrusively, present in the work of such a poet as Dylan Thomas. From this point of view Caballero Bonald's poem belongs very clearly to the present age, and not just to the poetry of Spain. The breasts are conquered by the lapse of time and the coming of age.

"que te duelen los ojos de tenerlos vacíos de mi cuerpo, / que has perdido hasta el tacto de tus manos / de palpar esta ausencia por el aire." The enumeration of the effects of absence on the different parts of the body continues; they are slightly unreal, but must be understood allusively. For instance: "una tristeza que era como un ciempiés monstruoso que le colgara de la mejilla" (a sadness which was like a monstrous centipede hanging from her cheek) in *Mujer con alcuza* is an example of Dámaso Alonso's using expressions of this sort.[26]

"que olvidas el tamaño caliente de mi boca." The concluding phrase of this verse takes its image from another angle. It is not now a part of the beloved's body which is remembering him. She has forgotten a part of him. This change should be noticed, because it is paralleled in the other two verses.

"Y tú me lo dices que sabes / que me hice sangre en las palabras de repetir tu nombre." The phrases now refer to the physical effects of absence on the poet himslf, as related by his beloved. The *sangre* is of course not real blood; the feelings of the poet have been wounded by absence. This same image of the speaking of a name producing pain and blood on the lips is used at greater length in another poem by Caballero Bonald called "Nombre entregado."[27]

"de lastimar mis labios pronunciándote." We should notice that both the lips and the words have been hurt.

"de darle, pronunciándote, a mi vida / una nueva manera de en-cadenarte en besos." The effect now spreads to the whole existence of the poet. This time he is not wounded and does not feel pain, but has the imaginary pleasure of kissing, even if this is linked to the cruelty of binding her in metaphorical chains.

"desde la ausencia en la que tú me gritas / que me estás esperando." As in the first verse, a new twist is given at the end. This last line speaks of the beloved instead of the poet's feelings.

"Y tú me los dices que estás tan hecha / a esta ausencia de mi carne ociosa." The flesh is *ociosa,* something apparently unnecessary, through which love is obliged to seek expression, yet to it the poet and his beloved are firmly bound. It is interesting to observe that Caballero Bonald has used the phrase *mi carne dichosa* in translating "Hymnes à la Présence solitaire" by René Ménard.[28] This may be a minor proof of the influence of French poetry on Caballero Bonald's.

"que apenas si tu sombra se delata." As to *sombra,* we have seen a similar use of this word by Montesinos. Here even a shadow be-comes physical and is wasted by the material and emotional strain of absence. Even so, his use of the word *sombra* is his nearest ap-proach to "Neoclassicism." We find the word again in another poem of his, "Los hombres sucesivos," also in conjunction with *apenas;* "apenas / si puede mi palabra ser la sombra de mí" (that my word can hardly be the shadow of myself).[29]

"que apenas si eres cierta." In this verse only two, instead of three, effects of absence are related.

"pues somos ya una espera inacabable / en esta oscuridad que tu distancia pone / entre tu cuerpo y el mío." The twist at the end of the poem sums up the whole. The poet at last speaks for both the lovers—as we saw Montesinos do, though in a different way. The image is allusive; so are most of those throughout the poem. Absence does not really put a darkness between two lovers, but their feelings may be like the absence of light. The absence is not really going to be endless; it only appears so now to the lovers.

Let us now take a second example of a possible new trend in poetry. Crespo (1926-   ) is a poet of the same age as Caballero Bonald and no doubt stands for a similar concept of poetry. Both poets are seeking a personal imagery but Caballero Bonald's is more fleshly and Crespo's vaguer and almost apocalyptic. The poem analyzed is an example of his restless, insistent imagery.

He turns to Dámaso Alonso, because Alonso is the poet behind so much in the gradual change of poetical values which seems to be taking place in Spain. When *Hijos de la ira* first appeared, no one in Spain realized how deep the new attitude towards poetry which that book represented would sink into the Spanish poetical consciousness.

Angel Crespo

A Dámaso Alonso

Arrancado de cuajo, tropezando
voy contra muros, contra heladas aguas,
veo acercarse a un viento en el que flotan
monedas que rehuso. Yo, tan pobre
que no puedo comprar ni mi desprecio,
por esquivar al aire me lastimo.
Pero ¿acaso soy yo quien hace nada
se hurtó del aire? ¿Acaso no soy otro?
Si hace un instante estaba frente al viento,
¿soy junto a ti también o me he perdido?

Si yo-viento me era, ¿puedo acaso
yo-Dámaso volver al que antes fuera?
¿O he de dejar al sueño que reúna
lo que he sido a través de cada instante?

Porque vamos saltando como verdes
ranas sobre la orilla, tú lo has dicho,
y cada salto va dejando un muerto
sobre la humedecida superficie.
Mírame, pues, jugar. Sobre esa hoja
yerto he quedado con el pecho hendido,
al pie de aquellas cañas parecía
que tan sólo dormido iba a quedarme,
y ahora, desde esta muerte, me pregunto
si al instante en el río debo hundirme.
Pero sobre esta piedra, a la que el agua
lame segura de vencer, contemplo
la procesión que por la opuesta orilla
encabeza una niña que no sabe
si sumergirse, al fin, en la corriente;
y aunque la llamas madre, ella no pesa
el tiempo que ha pasado hasta que el hijo
la hizo volver de su camino largo.
Va detrás la mujer que nadie sabe
adónde va, con su cacharro a cuestas,
y, aunque la orilla es verde, va pisando
las ramas secas. Tras de sí una larga
oquedad de silencio deja abierta
y la veo perderse entre los árboles,
ante su rostro de óleos acedos.
¿Quiénes vienen detrás? ¿De qué tejados
se descolgaron, desde qué tinieblas
se han apedreado, sobre cuáles dalias
han dejado hace poco tanto cieno?
Sin embargo, en sus ojos brillan astros,
pequeños en verdad, mas que prometen
algo más que sus bocas entreabiertas.
¿Mas acaso son ellos los de entonces?
El gozo de mirar, las alabanzas
a la luz que desciende, yo adivino
en unos cuantos. En las manos llevan
hojas de vid, y olivo y aun espejos,
y algunos de ellos, con los pies desnudos,
entran sin protestar en la corriente.
Mas ¿qué hacemos tú y yo? Si Dios me empuja,
dime tú qué palabra he de mentirle,
pues todavía tengo la esperanza
de que quiera engañarse con nosotros.

Porque vamos también por la otra orilla
verificando el paso, haciendo nuestro
su caminar, pisándoles las huellas.
Si Dios tira de todos, si conmueve
la recua de un tirón, ¿con qué palabras,
si no es con nuestros nombres, y en qué instante,
si el infinito número que fuimos
será recuperado de repente,
nos hemos de entregar? "Legión me llamo
porque muchos han sido," mi palabra
ésta será. "Mi número incontable
a tu incontable número reúno."
Pero antes dime, Dámaso, si al viento
puedo llamarle Dios, pues ya se acerca
y creo que esta vez estamos solos.[30]

To Dámaso Alonso

I, torn up by the roots, go staggering
Against the walls, against the frozen waters,
I see a wind draw near in which there float
Coins I refuse. Though I am even so poor
That I cannot afford to scorn myself,
I hurt myself so as to dodge the wind.
But can I be the man who fled the wind
No time at all ago? And not some other?
If, only an instant past, I faced the wind,
Am I with you as well, or am I lost?
If I-the-wind was I, why, then, how can
I-Dámaso return to what I was?
Or must I leave the dream to draw together
That which I have been through each separate instant?

We leap around as though we are green frogs
Upon a bank—and it was you who said it—
And every leap has left a corpse behind
On that flat strand soaked in humidity.
So, watch me playing. I lie upon that fallen
Leaf with my chest all hollow and all broken.
When I was by those reeds it seemed to me
That I should just remain at that spot sleeping,
And now, from the place of this death, I ask myself
If I should dive into the river this instant.
But here upon this stone, washed by the water
That is so sure of conquering it, I watch
A line of people on the other bank
Led by a girl who never can decide
If she should plunge, at last, into that current;

And, though you call her mother, she takes no heed of
The time that has gone by now since her son
Made her come back from her long pilgrimage.
Behind her walks the woman, about whom no one
Knows where she's going to, carrying her jar,
And, though the bank is green, yet she goes treading
Upon dry branches. After her, she leaves
A prolonged hollowness of silence open
And I see her go out of sight among the trees,
Before her face shining with bitter oils.
Who are these coming after? From what roofs
Have they dropped down, from what shades have they thrown
Stones at each other, on what dahlias
Have they, so short a while since, scattered mud?
There are stars shining in their eyes for all that;
Those stars there may be small, but yet they promise
More than their mouths do as they gape half open.
But yet are they, by chance, the ones there were then?
I can divine, in just a few of them,
Pleasure in gazing and the praise of light
As it descends. They carry in their hands
Vine leaves, and olive, even looking-glasses,
And there are some of them who wade barefooted
Into the flowing river, unprotesting.
But what must you and I do? If God thrusts me,
Tell me the word with which to lie to Him;
I have not yet lost hope that He may be
Still trying to deceive Himself about us.
For we, too, walk along the other bank,
Finding our path along, making their way
Ours, since we follow along in their footsteps.
If God plucks all men to Him, if He moves
The mass in one great pull, then, with what words
Unless we say our names and at what moment
Shall we surrender, if the infinite number
That we have been will be recuperated
Suddenly, in a moment. "My name is Legion,
Because they have been many." These shall be
The words I'll say. "I will unite again
My countless number with your countless number."
Only, before that, Dámaso, tell me whether
I can call the wind God; it's coming nearer
And this time I believe we are alone.

The poem, though written in a very personal imagery, obviously
contains some references to certain poems of Dámaso Alonso. The
first part is a variation on a poem in *Hijos de la ira* called "El alma

era lo mismo que una ranita verde" (The Soul was just like a little green Frog).[31] Alonso's poem begins:

El alma era lo mismo
que una ranita verde,
largas horas sentada sobre el borde
de un rumoroso
Misisipí.
Desea el agua, y duda. La desea
porque es el elemento para que fué criada,
pero teme
el bramador empuje del caudal,[32]

The soul was just like
A little green frog
Seated for many hours upon the verge
Of some murmuring
Mississippi.
It wants the water and hesitates. It wants it
Because it is the element for which it was created
But it's afraid of
The bellowing rush of the stream,

In Alonso's poem we have the setting for the beginning of Crespo's —a river, a bank, and man compared to a frog. The river is the element of the soul and finally death and eternity. All this is so in Crespo's poem too, and therefore he calls on "Dámaso" to witness the imagery he is using. We might find it strange and disrespectful for a younger poet to address an older one in this way, but the use of a Christian name is less of a mark of familiarity in Spanish than in English and besides the very word "Dámaso" is a quotation, since Alonso frequently addresses himself by that name in his poems.

Examples of this use of "Dámaso" may help to clarify Crespo's poem. In *Oscura noticia*[33] we find an early poem written as a prologue for his *Poemas puros*.[34] In this poem the twenty-year-old poet says:

¡Alégreteme, Dámaso,
porque pronto vendrá la primavera,
y tienes veinte años![35]

I must see you gay, Dámaso,
Because, in a short time, the Spring is coming
And you are twenty years old!

The references to his own name in *Hijos de la ira* contrast with this first one. The majority of the poems in this book were, as the poet continually tells us, written when he was forty-five years old. This age he seems to regard as a frontier between one part of life and another, just as Dante thought of thirty-five as halfway through the path of our life. The poet has been through terrible spiritual experiences, which he relates in metaphors, and some critics have thought the ordeals he speaks of are those of Spain, rather than an individual. He is "este Dámaso frenético"[36] (this frantic Dámaso) and compares himself to every repulsive object he can think of, to show his baseness in the sight of God. "Ah, pobre Dámaso, / tú, el más miserable, tú, el último de los seres."[37] (Ah, poor Dámaso, / You, the most miserable, you the last of beings.) [An anonymous sonnet in the humorous column of *Garcilaso* gave a poetical portrait of Alonso ending with the line: "Alégreteme, Dámaso frenético."[38] (I must see you gay, frantic Dámaso.)]

In *Hombre y Dios* he takes himself as an example of free will:

> Yo me esculpo, hombre libre. Paro, ando,
> hablo, callo, me río, pongo ceño,
>
> yo, Dámaso, cual Dámaso. Pequeño
> agente, yo, del Dios enorme,[39]
>
> I, a free man, chisle myself; stop, go,
> Speak, keep my silence, laugh, and knit my brow,
>
> I, Dámaso, as Dámaso. A little
> Agent, I, of the enormous God.

In this last poem, there is a juxtaposition of "I" and "Dámaso," as in Crespo's work we are about to examine. We can thus measure the force of this "I" and this "Dámaso" when we find them overflowing into the poems of younger writers, translated, as it were, into symbols of man's whole relation to God and the universe. This is of course the test of a poem's real validity—when it transcends the personal values of its writer. Thus, what appears to be the egotism of Unamuno, his longing for personal survival in this world, his habit of speaking of anything he approves of as "my"—for instance, "mi España inmortal"[40] (my immortal Spain)—all this has made others delight in identifying themselves with Unamuno's "yo" and "mi." Indeed, the "yo" of Alonso is almost a prolongation of Unamuno's "yo," as we can see from *Oscura noticia* being dedicated to "dos muertos queridos, Miguel de Unamuno y Antonio Machado"[41] (two beloved dead, Miguel de Unamuno and Antonio Machado), and containing a poem addressed to "mi don Miguel de Unamuno" and full of quotations from Unamuno.[42]

Another poet, José Gerardo Manrique de Lara (1922-   ) has written a gloss or variation on another poem of Alonso's, which forcibly excites comparison with the present poem of Crespo's. The work by Alonso that Manrique de Lara has used is "A un río le llamaban Carlos"[43] (Charles River, Cambridge, Massachusetts), and contains these words, which head Manrique de Lara's poem as a quotation :

> por qué anhelas, hacia qué resbalas, para qué vives.
> Dímelo, río,
> y dime, di, por qué te llaman Carlos.[44]

> What do you aspire after, what do you glide towards, what do you live for.
> Tell it me, river,
> And tell me, tell, why they have called you Charles.

The fact that the river is called by a common Christian name humanizes it for Alonso. He can speak to it as if it were a person.

We already know how powerfully rivers affect the poet Alonso. In this case, the Charles River represents sadness: "El río Carlos es una tristeza gris."[45] (The Charles River is a grey sadness.) As he sits by it, the sadness finally becomes a part of himself. The river ceases to be "Charles" and merges into "Dámaso."

> Ha debido de pasar mucho tiempo, amigos míos, mucho tiempo desde que yo me senté aquí en la orilla, a orillas
> de esta tristeza, de este
> río al que le llamaban Dámaso, digo, Carlos.[46]

> A long time must have passed, my friends, a long time
> Since I first sat down here on the bank, on the banks
> Of this sadness, of this
> River which they call Dámaso, I mean, Charles.

To this Manrique de Lara replies by calling his poem "A un hombre le llamaban río"[47] (they called a man a river) and it is an address to Dámaso Alonso who is "río Dámaso" (Dámaso River), a "cauce vestido / con ropaje de hombre" (a flow dressed in man's garments). Alonso, with his "tierna miopía" (soft short-sightedness)— of which he speaks in the prologue to *Hombre y Dios*[48]—has been the source of feeling in many others, a river of emotions, the poet who inspires others.

Sensible al paso
de todas las lágrimas del mundo,
has descubierto ahora
que Dámaso bien pudiera
ser nombre de río.[49]

Sensitive to the passing
Of all the tears that there are in the world,
In the end you've discovered
That Dámaso very well could
Be the name of a river.

Thus the manner in which Crespo and Manrique de Lara address Alonso show that he is the prophet of their poetry. With the years, the poetic influence of Dámaso Alonso makes itself more and more felt, superseding that of Lorca, Alberti, Aleixandre and others.

Crespo's poem (p. 161) begins: "Arrancado de cuajo." This forceful expression, with its connection with the weaning of a child, starts the poem on a note of loneliness and probably of revolt.

"tropezando / voy contra muros, contra heladas aguas." This gives us an idea of the poet's unprotected and uncertain state.

"veo acercarse a un viento en el que flotan / monedas que rehuso." Though this wind with money might be bringing him the solution to his difficulties, he refuses what he is offered. He is a rebel.

"Yo, tan pobre / que no puedo comprar ni mi desprecio, / por esquivar al aire me lastimo." In spite of his poverty, he will not accept the money, even though he hurts himself avoiding it.

"Pero ¿acaso soy yo quien hace nada / se hurtó del aire? ¿Acaso no soy otro?" This fading of the identity of the speaker is part of the essential core of the poem. The speaker and the wind and the time at which the poem is happening all melt inexplicably into each other, just as the poet writing (Crespo) and the poet addressed (Dámaso Alonso) can sometimes hardly be distinguished.

"Si hace un instante estaba frente al viento, / ¿soy junto a ti también o me he perdido?" The three alternatives underline the uncertainty of the situation. He may be facing the wind or exist beside Dámaso Alonso—*soy*, not *estoy*— or he may be lost.

"Si yo-viento me era." They say that imaginative writers are really each of their characters in turn. So Crespo is the wind he has spoken of, his own creation and yet an image of man's Creator.

"¿puedo acaso / yo-Dámaso volver al que antes fuera?" In what sense can Crespo be "Dámaso"? In so far, surely, as a great poet, Dámaso Alonso, becomes those who read him and whom he affects. At the same time, another explanation might be that, in the first lines, the "I" who is speaking is an interpretation of Dámaso Alonso's "I."

"¿O he de dejar al sueño que reúna / lo que he sido a través de cada instante?" Poetry since the days of Freud and the Surrealists has been more clearly united to dreams than before. If the true explanation of a poem must be found in the unconscious, it follows that it can only achieve its ends out of sight of rational processes. We can only understand it by falling into a kind of sleep. The various facets or instants may then add up to something we can never understand with our conscious minds.

"Porque vamos saltando como verdes / ranas sobre la orilla, tú lo has dicho." Actually, the frog in Alonso's poem is represented as sitting on the bank, though in another of his poems, "La Madre," he describes a line of green frogs which jump into the water.[50] The leaping will be developed by Crespo at some length in what may either be a symbol or a fantasy.

"y cada salto va dejando un muerto / sobre la humedecida superficie." This is a development of the fantasy of the frog which is justified by Alonso's poem. The corpse which is left behind at each leap is presumably something of great value to the leaper and part of him. The dampness of the surface makes the image of the bank rather more sinister.

"Mírame, pues, jugar. Sobre esa hoja / yerto he quedado con el pecho hendido." The bitter irony of the game is that it destroys the player, whose chest has caved in as a result of it.

"al pie de aquellas cañas parecía / que tan sólo dormido iba a quedarme." Sleep after play has taken the form of death, though this is one of the poet's many deaths.

"y ahora, desde esta muerte, me pregunto / si al instante en el río debo hundirme." Should he, like Alonso's frog, now let himself be borne along by the great river of eternity?

"Pero sobre esta piedra, a la que el agua / lame segura de vencer." Water, which in all ages has been the great poetic symbol of love (and death), is washing at his resting-place, a stone.

"contemplo / la procesión que por la opuesta orilla." Across the
river of love and death, he watches the behavior of mortals who are
in the world with him. The mortals he sees are also, as we shall see,
principally taken from the poems of Dámaso Alonso.

"encabeza una niña que no sabe / si sumergirse, al fin, en la corriente." This is a reference to Alonso's poem, "La Madre." In this
poem, the river is the passing of time and memory. Alonso addresses
his mother:

> Oh, sí, tú eres para mí eso: una candorosa niña.
>
> Y verás que es verdad si te sumerges en esas lentas aguas, en
>   esas aguas poderosas,
> que te han traído a esta ribera desolada.
> Sumérgete, nada a contracorriente, cierra los ojos,
> y cuando llegues, espera allí a tu hijo.
> Porque yo también voy a sumergirme en mi niñez antigua,
> pero las aguas que tengo que remontar hasta casi la fuente,
> son mucho más poderosas, son aguas turbias, como teñidas
>   de sangre.[51]

> Oh, yes, that is what you are for me—an innocent girl.
>
> And you'll see that it's true if you plunge into these slow waters,
>   these powerful waters
> Which have brought you to this desolate shore.
> Plunge in, swim against the stream, and shut your eyes,
> And, when you have arrived, wait for your son there.
> For I, too, am going to plunge into my past childhood,
> But the waters I must go back through, right almost to the source,
> Are far more powerful, they are turbid and, as it were, blood-
>   stained waters."

We have already seen[52] how the image of the frog recurs in "La
Madre."

The proof that Crespo was thinking of "La Madre" comes in the
next two lines of his poem: "y aunque la llamas madre, ella no pesa /
el tiempo que ha pasado hasta que el hijo / la hizo volver de su
camino largo." The son calling the mother back to her childhood is
the theme of Alonso's poem just quoted.

"Va detrás la mujer que nadie sabe / adónde va, con su cacharro
a cuestas." This is a reference to yet another of the poems in *Hijos de
la ira:* "Mujer con alcuza."[53] The *cacharro* the woman is carrying is
the *alcuza* (jar) borne, in Alonso's poem, by a poor old woman who
has lost all her family and friends and is left quite alone.

"y, aunque la orilla es verde, va pisando / las ramas secas." The woman with the pot or jar is treading on dry boughs because of the last line of Alonso's poem to her which speaks of her "tristes ramas desnudas, donde ya ni se posan los pájaros"[54] (bare, sad boughs, on which not even the birds perch now).

"Tras de sí una larga / oquedad de silencio deja abierta." The silence of the birdless boughs follows this woman.

"y la veo perderse entre los árboles." The wood, like the river, is a recurring image in *Hijos de la ira*. It signifies the dark passage of time.

"ante su rostro de óleos acedos." The woman's face is anointed with death, with "ese aceite suave / de olor empalagosamente dulce, que es la muerte"[55] (that soft oil / With a cloyingly sweet scent, which is death).

"¿Quiénes vienen detrás? ¿De qué tejados / se descolgaron, desde qué tinieblas / se han apedreado." This is humanity, men seen as apes, dropping from their roofs and pelting each other with stones. One may suspect here an indirect allusion to the Yahoos in *Gulliver's Travels*.

"sobre cuáles dalias / han dejado hace poco tanto cieno?" The ape-men have splashed the beautiful flowers with mud.

"Sin embargo, en sus ojos brillan astros, / pequeños en verdad, mas que prometen / algo más que sus bocas entreabiertas." The small stars which shine in the eyes of the ape-men show something more divine in them than their gaping mouths would have led us to suppose.

"¿Mas acaso son ellos los de entonces?" The same doubt as to whether there is continuity of being within time assails the poet as in the seventh line of the poem, when he asked if he himself was the same as at the beginning.

"El gozo de mirar, las alabanzas / a la luz que desciende, yo adivino / en unos cuantos." Some of the men know how to appreciate the joys of sight (*Gozos de la vista,* the name of Alonso's latest and, as yet, only partially published book) and praise it.

"En las manos llevan / hojas de vid, y olivo y aun espejos." The vine-leaves some of the men are carrying signify, probably, inspiration. Those who bear the olive-branches must be the peace-makers. The men carrying looking-glasses may be taken to be devoted to truth, to holding their mirrors up to Nature.

"y algunos de ellos, con los pies desnudos, / entran sin protestar en la corriente." Some are so familiar with the idea of eternity that they walk into the waters.

"Mas ¿qué hacemos tú y yo?" We return to the poet and Dámaso Alonso, whom he is addressing.

"Si Dios me empuja, / dime tú qué palabra he de mentirle." The poet feels that he cannot tell the truth to God and asks Dámaso Alonso what lie God will accept. This is perhaps a reference to Alonso's dialogue with God, justifying himself, in the last poem of *Hijos de la ira.*[56]

"pues todavía tengo la esperanza / de que quiera engañarse con nosotros." He hopes that God will mercifully accept this deceit.

"Porque vamos también por la otra orilla, / verificando el paso, haciendo nuestro / su caminar, pisándoles las huellas." The poet and Dámaso Alonso are also on the other side of the river, following the ape-men.

"Si Dios tira de todos, si conmueve / la recua de un tirón." It is God Who is in command of the mass of men, those destructive creatures we have just seen.

"¿con qué palabras, / si no es con nuestros nombres, y en qué instante, / si el infinito número que fuimos / será recuperado de repente, / nos hemos de entregar?" God will only hear the individual who has a name. The infinite mass of men is of no account to Him as a mass.

" 'Legión me llamo / porque muchos han sido.' " These are substantially the words of the unclean spirit in St. Mark's Gospel,[57] when Our Lord was going to send him out of a man. Crespo, however, uses the third person plural instead of the first person plural. This change of person must be intentional, so as to compare humanity in the mass to devils, continuing his thought immediately above.

"mi palabra / ésta será." Thus, to some extent, the poet identifies himself with the devils.

" 'Mi número incontable / a tu incontable número reúno.' " If the poet's name is Legion, he can be added to the uncountable number.

"Pero antes dime, Dámaso, si al viento / puedo llamarle Dios, pues ya se acerca." We now return to the wind of the third line of the poem. The solution of accepting the money floating in the

wind had perhaps been offered him by God. It may help to understand the Legion passage if we recall that Our Lord is represented as
the wind in one of Dámaso Alonso's early poems: "Porque El era
sólo el viento / que mueve y pasa y no mira."[58] (For He was only
the wind / Which moves and passes, not looking.)

"y creo que esta vez estamos solos." Now that the others have
gone, the younger poet asks the older one for true guidance.

A much less complicated poem, by José Augustín Goytisolo (1928-
) is of interest because it shows the reaction of some of the
younger poets to the poetic movements whose history we have given
in earlier chapters. It would be wrong, however, to assume from
reading this poem that the poetry of Goytisolo or his friends "Jaime
Ferrán, Carlos Barral, Alfonso Costafreda, Lorenzo Gomis and
Jaime Gil de Biedma,"[59] all from Barcelona, is essentially different
from what was written before. All that we could say would be that
none of them is primarily concerned with form nor aims at being
a religious poet. Whether or not they are, as Goytisolo puts it, "lost
in the tumult of the streets," some of their poetry certainly describes
directly what they have felt in everyday life. Most of them frankly
prefer free verse to traditional forms.

José Augustín Goytisolo

Los celestiales

"No todo el que dice: Señor, Señor,
   entrará en el reino . . ."

(Mat., 7: 21)

Después y por encima de la pared caída,
de los vidrios caídos, de la puerta arrasada,
cuando se alejó el eco de las detonaciones
y el humo y sus olores abandonaron la ciudad,
después, cuando el orgullo se refugió en las cuevas,
mordiéndose los puños para no decir nada,
arriba, en los paseos, en las calles con ruina
que el sol acariciaba con sus manos de amigo,
asomaron los poetas, gente de orden, por supuesto.

Es la hora, dijeron, de cantar los asuntos
maravillosamente insustanciales, es decir,
el momento de olvidarnos de todo lo ocurrido

y componer hermosos versos, vacíos, sí, pero sonoros,
melodiosos como el laúd,
que adormezcan, que transfiguren,
que apacigüen los ánimos, ¡qué barbaridad!

Ante tan sabia solución
se reunieron, pues, los poetas, y en la asamblea
de un café, a votación, sin más preámbulo,
fue Garcilaso desenterrado, llevado en andas, paseado
como reliquia, por las aldeas y revistas,
y entronizado en la capital. El verso melodioso,
la palabra feliz, todos los restos,
fueron comida suculenta, festín de la comunidad.

Y el viento fue condecorado, y se habló
de marineros, de lluvia, de azahares,
y una vez más, la soledad y el campo, como antaño,
y el cauce tembloroso de los ríos,
y todas las grandes maravillas,
fueron, en suma, convocadas.

Esto duró algún tiempo, hasta que, poco
a poco, las reservas se fueron agotando.
Los poetas, rendidos de cansancio, se dedicaron
a lanzarse sonetos, mutuamente,
de mesa a mesa, en el café. Y un día,
entre el fragor de los poemas, alguien dijo: Escuchad,
fuera las cosas no han cambiado, nosotros
hemos hecho una meritoria labor, pero no basta.
Los trinos y el aroma de nuestras elegías,
no han calmado las iras, el azote de Dios.

De las mesas creció un murmullo
rumoroso como el océano, y los poetas exclamaron:
Es cierto, es cierto, olvidamos a Dios, somos
ciegos mortales, perros heridos por su fuerza,
por su justicia, cantémosle ya.

Y así el buen Dios sustituyó
al viejo padre Garcilaso, y fue llamado
dulce tirano, amigo, mesías
lejanísimo, sátrapa fiel, amante, guerrillero,
gran parido, asidero de mi sangre, y los Oh, Tú,
y los Señor, Señor, se elevaron altísimos, empujados
por los golpes de pecho en el papel,
por el dolor de tantos corazones valientes.

Y así perduran en la actualidad.

Ésta es la historia, caballeros,
de los poetas celestiales, historia clara

y verdadera, y cuyo ejemplo no han seguido
los poetas locos, que, perdidos
en el tumulto callejero, cantan al hombre,
satirizan o aman el reino de los hombres,
tan pasajero, tan falaz, y en su locura
lanzan gritos, pidiendo paz, pidiendo patria,
pidiendo aire verdadero.[60]

The Heavenly Ones

> "Not everyone who says Lord, Lord, will
> enter into the Kingdom."
>
> (Matthew 7, 21)

Afterwards, stepping over the fallen wall,
The fallen windowpanes, and wrenched-out door,
When the echo of the explosions died away
And the smoke and the smell of smoke floated away from the city,
Afterwards, when pride took refuge in basement cellars,
Biting its fists in order to say nothing,
Up in the avenues, in the ruined streets that
The sun was caressing with its friendly hands,
The poets came out, being true, law-abiding people.

It is time, they said, for us to sing of matters
That are marvellously insubstantial, that is to say,
This the moment to forget all that has happened,
And compose beautiful verses, certainly empty, but sonorous,
And full of melody, like the sound of a lute,
Able to lull to sleep, able to transfigure,
Able to calm men's souls. What a business this has been!

Having found this wise solution,
The poets then came together and, forming a group,
In a café, they took a vote and, without more ado,
Garcilaso was disinterred, carried on a litter, walked around with,
As a relic, to the villages and reviews,
And enthroned in the capital. The verse was full of melody,
The words were just the right ones, all the remains
Made a succulent meal, a banquet for the community.

And the wind received a medal, and there was talk
Of sailors, of the rain, of orange-blossom,
And, once more, solitude and the country, as before,
And the trembling course of rivers,
And all the supreme marvels
Were, in fact, called together.

And this went on for some time, until little
By little, the reserves began to run dry.
The poets, overcome with tiredness, occupied themselves
With throwing off sonnets to one another
From table to table, in the café. And one day,
Among the clatter of poems, someone said: "Listen,
Things have not changed outside there; we ourselves
Have done a deserving task, but it's not enough.
The trills and the aroma of our elegies
Were not able to calm the wrath and the lash of God.

A murmur arose from the tables,
Full of voices like the ocean. The poets exclaimed:
"It's true. It's true. We've forgotten God. We are
Blind mortals, dogs that His strength, His justice
Have wounded. Let us sing to Him now."

Thus the Good God took the place of
Old father Garcilaso, and He was called
Sweet tyrant, friend, the very far
Messiah, the faithful satrap, the lover, the warrior,
The great one brought forth, support of my blood, and the
    Oh, Thous,
And the Lord, Lords were cast up very loudly, pushed on
By beatings of the breast on paper,
And by the sorrow of so many valiant hearts.

And so they carry on, up to the present day.

That is the story, gentlemen,
Of the heavenly poets. It is a clear story
And a true one. Its example has not been followed
By those mad poets who, lost
In the tumult of the streets, sang of mankind
And satirized or loved the kingdom of men,
Which is so fleeting and deceitful. In their madness
They let forth cries, asking for peace, a fatherland,
And genuine fresh air.

The lines from the Gospels at the head of Goytisolo's poem are
frequently quoted by writers wishing to accuse each other of hypo-
crisy.

"Después y por encima de la pared caída." The poem starts with
después, a word to which the poet wishes to give a funereal tone. He
obviously regards the end of the Civil War as a tragedy. The scene
is Madrid at the time of the Nationalist entry into it, which marked
the end of the Civil War in March, 1939. The city was naturally still

full of ruins, though the writer does not only refer to them, but to the state of moral collapse as well.

"de los vidrios caídos, de la puerta arrasada, / cuando se alejó el eco de las detonaciones / y el humo y sus olores abandonaron la ciudad." War was no longer present in the city. Notice the use of the prosaic word, *detonaciones.*

"después." The accusing word is repeated.

"cuando el orgullo se refugió en las cuevas, / mordiéndose los puños para no decir nada." Two things are suggested here about the "proud" who had been on the Republican side in the Civil War; first, that they were hiding in basements; secondly, that others were in prison, determined not to betray their companions, even under torture. Their heroic behavior is meant to contrast with that of the poets who are going to be the subject of the poem.

"arriba." Up above and not down in the cellars, like the "proud."

"en los paseos, en las calles con ruina / que el sol acariciaba con sus manos de amigo, / asomaron los poetas, gente de orden, por supuesto." The sun, it seems, is kind to the ruins. The fine weather brings the poets out. They are the friends of law and order, that is to say, of the new régime after the Civil War.

"Es la hora, dijeron, de cantar los asuntos / maravillosamente insustanciales." Things that matter, religion and politics, must no longer be the subject of poetry.

"es decir, / el momento de olvidarnos de todo lo ocurrido." The Civil War and the events which led up to it must now be forgotten.

"y componer hermosos versos, vacíos, sí, pero sonoros, / melodiosos como el laúd." The importance of the verses lies in their sound, not their meaning.

"que adormezcan, que transfiguren, / que apacigüen los ánimos." The verses are also intended to draw people's attention away from politics.

"¡qué barbaridad!" A flat expression, something like "how dreadful!," which represents the ineffectual, feeble protest of these poets, when commenting among themselves on the tragedy Spain has just been through.

"Ante tan sabia solución / se reunieron, pues, los poetas." The poets spoken of must be those who founded the review *Garcilaso,* such as García Nieto, Rafael Romero Moliner, Garcés and the Prados.

"y en la asamblea / de un café." The café referred to is the Café Gijón, where the newly formed *Juventud Creadora* used to meet daily.

"a votación, sin más preámbulo, /fue Garcilaso desenterrado." The review *Garcilaso* was founded in 1943. The name was chosen because the figure of Garcilaso de la Vega, the soldier poet, seemed an inspiring one for the Spain of those days.

"llevado en andas, paseado / como reliquia, por las aldeas y re- vistas." Poetry recitals were given in the provinces, where new poetry reviews, imitating *Garcilaso,* were founded.

"y entronizado en la capital." Garcilaso, the poet, was enthroned in Madrid because *Garcilaso,* the review, was published there.

"El verso melodioso, / la palabra feliz, todos los restos, / fueron comida suculenta, festín de la comunidad." Garcilaso is a poet of the past with no message for people of today. All that is left of him is his harmoniousness and his apt use of language. The new poets lapped these up and made full use, in their own poems, of the tech- nical lessons to be learned from Garcilaso and other poets of his age. The reference to good eating and rejoicings is probably a re- minder of how the poets of *Garcilaso* organized dinners in taverns in each others' honor. (But in this they were in no way different from other Spanish men of letters.)

"Y el viento fue condecorado." This does not seem to be an actual quotation, but a phrase parodying the use of key-words by García Nieto and the "Neoclassicals." Earlier in this book we commented on the line: "y con la Cruz del Sur condecorado."[61] *Condecorado* is used frequently enough by García Nieto to be more or less a key-word, in the sense explained in Chapter 2. As to *viento,* it is often a key- word. Goytisolo may be thinking of a poem by García Nieto called "Ofrecimiento del viento," though the word *condecorado* is not actu- ally used in it.

"y se habló / de marineros." This is, of course, a reference to the marked influence of Alberti's *Marinero en tierra*[62] on poetry of the *Garcilaso* school. One of García Nieto's sonnets begins: "Grumete en tierra, son mis travesías / de sueño a sueño, amor."[63] (A cabin-boy on land, my crossings are / From dream to dream, my love.)

"de lluvia." *Lluvia* is a favorite key-word with the "Neoclassi- cals." There is an example to hand in García Nieto's poem analyzed earlier in this chapter: "lluvia sin ocasión."

"de azahares." It is hardly necessary to look for a particular use of this word, which is the name of one of the most beautiful and certainly the most highly-scented blossoms to be found in Spain, besides being a beautiful word of Arabic origin and therefore evoking the legendary days of the Moors. Goytisolo's objection to the word must mean that he does not think poets should be writing about flowers at all.

"y una vez más, la soledad y el campo, como antaño." Here the reference is aimed directly at García Nieto, the title of whose book *Del campo y soledad*[64] is taken from a line of Garcilaso: "Tratar del campo y soledad que amaste."[65] (To speak of the country and solitude that you loved.) This book was published in 1946, and Goytisolo probably thinks of it as an attempt to revive the influence of Garcilaso de la Vega after it was beginning to decline.

"y el cauce tembloroso de los ríos." This is probably not a direct quotation. *Cauce* and *río* were both "Neoclassical" key-words, and *tembloroso* is a suitable adjective for a parody of "Neoclassical" poetry.

"y todas las grandes maravillas, / fueron, en suma, convocadas." The wonders of Nature appear in the poetry of the *Garcilaso* school instead of the world of men.

"Esto duró algún tiempo, hasta que, poco / a poco, las reservas se fueron agotando." The limited resources of "Neoclassical" poetry began to run out.

"Los poetas, rendidos de cansancio, se dedicaron / a lanzarse sonetos, mutuamente, / de mesa a mesa, en el café." This is supposed to show the lack of breadth in the "Neoclassical" school. Their sphere was just the café where they used to meet. A mutual admiration society had been formed. Clearly these lines are an unfair comment on certain poems which the *Garcilaso* poets (like poets in any school) addressed to each other.

"Y un día, / entre el fragor de los poemas, alguien dijo: Escuchad." Exactly who it was who first drew the poets' attention to the possibility of writing religious poetry is far from clear.

"fuera las cosas no han cambiado, nosotros / hemos hecho una meritoria labor, pero no basta." Possibly the supposed poet who is calling for his companions' attention has read *Sombra del paraíso* and *Hijos de la ira,* and feels that Spanish poetry must continue its course from the poets before 1936, through Aleixandre and Alonso, onwards. "Neoclassicism" cannot be a definite halting-place.

"Los trinos y el aroma de nuestras elegías, / no han calmado las iras, el azote de Dios." Here the reference to *Hijos de la ira* is quite plain. The suggestion is that Alonso's book has a deep, political message hidden within it—the point of view of certain left-wing critics.

"De las mesas creció un murmullo / rumoroso como el océano, y los poetas exclamaron." A change has come to the poets who had formerly made up the *Garcilaso* group.

"Es cierto, es cierto, olvidamos a Dios, somos / ciegos mortales, perros heridos por su fuerza, / por su justicia." This is a result of the message of humility in the face of God's power, given in *Hijos de la ira.*

"cantémosle ya." The immediate effect of *Sombra del paraíso* and *Hijos de la ira* was to herald in a number of religious poems. The foremost figures in this revival of religious poems were José María Valverde and Carlos Bousoño (though the latter only wrote a limited number of them).

"Y así el buen Dios sustituyó / al viejo padre Garcilaso." The poets were deserting the *Garcilaso* school.

"y fue llamado / dulce tirano, amigo, mesías / lejanísimo, sátrapa fiel, amante, guerrillero, / gran parido, asidero de mi sangre." As with the "Neoclassicals," these phrases parody a certain manner of writing. They are not necessarily to be found in specific poems.

"y los Oh, Tú / y los Señor, Señor." We are referred to the text at the head of the poem.

"se elevaron altísimos, empujados / por los golpes de pecho en el papel." The suggestion is that the beating of the breast was a purely literary pose, not prompted by any sincere repentance.

"por el dolor de tantos corazones valientes." This is, of course, irony, meaning that there was no real spiritual adventure behind the new religious poetry.

"Y así perduran en la actualidad." The present time spoken of must be about 1958, when the poem was first published.[66]

"Ésta es la historia, caballeros, / de los poetas celestiales, historia clara / y verdadera." The poets were Olympians, above the cares of this world.

"y cuyo ejemplo no han seguido / los poetas locos, que, perdidos / en el tumulto callejero, cantan al hombre." The mad, but truly inspired, poets are men in the street, singing of mankind, presumably with a corresponding interest in politics.

"satirizan o aman el reino de los hombres." Such poets disapprove or approve of certain forms of government. They are not above such things.

"tan pasajero, tan falaz." The fact that the world is ephemeral and deceptive does not make them want to withdraw from it.

"y en su locura / lanzan gritos, pidiendo paz, pidiendo patria, / pidiendo aire verdadero." One might suspect a reference to Blas de Otero, who wrote a book of poems called *Pido la paz y la palabra*.[67] That the poets seek for a fatherland and fresh air is intended to be a proof of their realistic sense of humanity.

To think that Spanish poetry has recently undergone any appreciable change would, however, be a mistake. The work of an even younger poet, Carlos Sahagún (1938-   ), shows this. He was born the year before our poetic period opens and shows clearly how strongly influenced he has been by all the poets we have discussed. He is the youngest of a group of poets following those in Chapter 7. We should mention José Angel Valente (1929-   ), Eladio Cabañero (1930-   ), Mario Angel Marrodán (1930-   ), Claudio Rodríguez (1934-   ), and the lively and colloquial Gloria Fuertes (1918-   ).

Carlos Sahagún

Manantial

Y golpeé las puertas de la tierra,
y sin remedio entré a la vida. Como
al reloj de la torre aquella, dieron
cuerda a mi corazón, y era mi empuje
incontenible, y era mi alegría
yerba verde pisada por un caballo al trote.

Parece que fué ayer, que no era el año
mil novecientos treinta y ocho. Bosques
en llamas, altas
palmeras encendidas, hombres muertos,
hermanos muertos con la frente muerta,
me rodeaban, lo recuerdo todo.

Era un pueblo al alcance de mi mano,
perdido en un rincón, una cabeza
de alfiler en la carne de la patria.
Y la patria sangraba.

Me vendaron los ojos, me decían:
"Es mentira el dolor, el hambre, todo.
No pienses más, olvida. Duerme, duerme."[68]

Fountain-Head

And I beat on the doors of the earth,
And there was nothing for it but to enter life, just like
The clock of that tower they wound up
My heart, and the thrust of me
Could not be held in, and the joy in me was
Green grass that is trampled by a trotting horse.

It seems as if it were yesterday, as if it were not
The year nineteen hundred and thirty-eight, the woods
In flames, tall
Palm-trees lit up, men dead,
Brothers dead with their foreheads dead,
Were all around me. I remember everything.

It was a village within the reach of my hand,
Lost in a corner, a pin's
Head in the flesh of the fatherland,
And the fatherland was bleeding.

They blindfolded my eyes. They said to me:
"Sorrow and hunger and everything are lies.
Do not think any more. Forget. Fall asleep. Fall asleep."

"Y." In spite of Fray Luis de León's poem beginning: "Y dejas, pastor santo"[69] (And dost thou leave, holy shepherd), *y* is very seldom the opening word of poems before the twentieth century. Sahagún may perhaps have been thinking of certain chapters of the Old Testament which begin with *y*. Indeed the whole line has a Biblical sound. The wide circulation in recent years of Spanish translations of the Bible, especially that of Nácar-Colunga, may have had some influence here. In that translation we find that Chapter 30 of *Job* begins: "Y ahora se burlan de mí los más mozos que yo"[70] (And now? Now I am a laughing-stock, even to younger men) (Monsignor Ronald A. Knox), and Chapter II of *Isaias:* "Y brotará una vara del tronco de Jesé"[71] (And there shall come forth a rod out of the root of Jesse) (Douay Version). A Biblical explanation is not, however, conclusive, since Spanish poets, from Antonio Machado onwards, have often opened poems with *y*.

"golpeé las puertas de la tierra, / y sin remedio entré en la vida." The poet was like a spring bursting from the earth. Yet there was something terrible about this. It was *sin remedio*.

"como / al reloj de la torre aquella, dieron / cuerda a mi corazón." What clock in what tower is not specified. The poet is using a personal imagery to which we may or may not, as we please, find the clue. Anyhow, the poet's heart and the clock in the tower are both wound up by people and circumstances. Perhaps winding up his heart for life was unfair and unjust. Yet he immediately contradicts this implication.

"y era mi empuje / incontenible." We must allow for the possibility that *mi empuje* refers to some large force which transcends the self. But at least the form is a personal one.

"y era mi alegría." Sahagún's *alegría* has borrowed something from Hierro's. In Hierro's book *Alegría*,[72] the word means not exactly the spirit of revolution, but at least an irrepressible inner force which may well lead to revolution, just as, on a personal plane, it leads to love and high spirits.

"yerba verde pisada por un caballo al trote." We may suppose that it is the green grass of infancy over which the force of the poet's childhood is trotting.

"Parece que fué ayer, que no era el año / mil novecientos treinta y ocho." The year of Sahagún's birth was during the Civil War. Dates, though apparently prosaic, are sometimes used effectively in modern Spanish poetry. This same year, 1938, appears in Hierro's "Paseo."[73] We noticed previously how Montesinos used the date of the conquest of Seville by St. Ferdinand.[74]

"Bosques / en llamas, altas / palmeras encendidas, hombres muertos, / hermanos muertos con la frente muerta, / me rodeaban, lo recuerdo todo." Sahagún says that he remembers the things going on around him during the Civil War: the burning trees, the dead in the war. (He was a newly-born child then.)

"Era un pueblo al alcance de mi mano, / perdido en un rincón, una cabeza / de alfiler en la carne de la patria. / Y la patria sangraba."

The idea is probably that of the little flags on pins which people stick on maps in wartime to show the position of the front at the moment. Sahagún's village was Onil, near Alicante. There was probably no actual fighting there, but that would not prevent him thinking about it in this way. There were many incidents behind the lines and fears of incidents.

"Me vendaron los ojos, me decían: / 'Es mentira el dolor, el hambre, todo. / No pienses más, olvida. Duerme, duerme.' " He is told to be indifferent, though we can see that he does not in fact feel so.

From these examples we see something of the general character of modern Spanish poetry and the kind of language it uses. The various manners of writing really complement each other.

NOTES TO CHAPTER 9

1. *Obra escogida* (Madrid, 1952), pp. 242-243.
2. *Diccionario de la lengua española* (Madrid. 1939), p. 436.
3. *Veinte poemas de amor y una canción desesperada* (3rd edition; Buenos Aires, 1949), p. 94 ["Niña morena y ágil . . ."].
4. *Obra escogida*, p. 420.
5. *En once años* (Madrid, 1950), p. 191.
6. *Diccionario de la lengua española,* p. 557.
7. See page 53.
8. *Poesía* (Madrid, 1944), p. 21.
9. 3 (September, 1944).
10. *Diccionario de la lengua española,* p. 189.
11. "As yet a child, nor yet a fool to fame, I lisp'd in numbers, for the numbers came"; Alexander Pope, *Epistle to Dr. Arbuthnot* (see Robert Shafer *From Beowulf to Thomas Hardy,* [Washington, 1944], p. 900).
12. *Poesía española actual* (Madrid, 1946), p. 345. See also Chapter 3, note 27.
13. See Chapter 3, p. 62.
14. Born 1919, and therefore five years younger than García Nieto and seven years younger than Ridruejo.
15. (Santander, 1952).
16. *Ibid.,* p. 127.
17. The first edition (1943), and some others read *amantes.* We have followed the later reading *amentes* from César González-Ruano's *Antología de poetas españoles contemporáneos* (Barcelona, 1946), p. 821.
18. *Poemas del toro* (Madrid, 1943), p. 23 (with one emendation, as explained in note 17).
19. *Obra escogida,* p. 127 and p. 130.
20. This incident was related by Germán Bleiberg, who was with Lorca when the news of the bullfighter's death arrived, Bleiberg being one of the actors in Lorca's travelling company, *La Barraca.*
21. *Obra escogida,* p. 117.
22. *Las incredulidades* (Madrid, 1948), pp. 41-42.
23. See Chapter 4, note 49.

24. One of Caballero Bonald's poems, "La belleza," in *Las adivinaciones* ([Madrid, 1952], pp. 37-38) seems almost to imitate the tone of Dámaso Alonso's later poetry.
25. *Las adivinaciones,* pp. 58-59.
26. *Hijos de la ira* (Madrid, 1944), p. 56.
27. *Las adivinaciones,* pp. 45-48.
28. In *Poesía española* (Madrid), 6 (June, 1952).
29. *Las adivinaciones,* p. 30.
30. *Antología de poesía española 1958-1959* (Madrid, 1959), pp. 73-75.
31. *Hijos de la ira,* pp. 101-103.
32. *Ibid.,* p. 101.
33. (Madrid, 1944).
34. *Poemas puros. Poemillos de la ciudad* (Madrid, 1921).
35. *Oscura noticia,* p. 40 [Prólogo inédito a los "Poemas puros"].
36. *Hijos de la ira,* p. 74 ["Monstruos"].
37. *Ibid.,* p. 149 ["Dedicatoria final (Las alas)"].
38. *Garcilaso* (Madrid), 14 (June, 1944).
39. (Málaga, 1955), pp. 49-50.
40. *Andanzas y visiones españolas* (Madrid, 1955), p. 261.
41. *Oscura noticia,* p. 8.
42. *Ibid.,* pp. 47-51 ["A don Miguel de Unamuno"].
43. *Hombre y Dios,* pp. 69-73.
44. *Ibid.,* p. 69.
45. *Ibid.,* p. 71.
46. *Ibid.,* p. 73.
47. *Río Esperanza* (Madrid, 1960), pp. 85-86.
48. Pp. 11-12 ["Mi tierna miopía"].
49. *Río Esperanza,* p. 86.
50. *Hijos de la ira,* p. 82.
51. *Ibid.,* pp. 79-80.
52. See Note 50.
53. Pp. 53-62.
54. *Ibid.,* p. 62.
55. *Ibid.,* p. 22 ["En el día de los difuntos"].
56. *Ibid.,* pp. 149-158 ["Dedicatoria final (Las alas)"].
57. 5:9.
58. *Poesía española antología (contemporáneos)* (Madrid, 1934), p. 369 ["Ejemplos"].
59. On the cover of José Augustín Goytisolo, *El retorno* (Madrid, 1955).
60. *Veinte años de poesía española (1939-1959)* (Barcelona, 1960), pp. 375-377.
61. See page 62.
62. (Madrid, 1925).
63. *Primer libro de poemas* (Madrid, 1951), p. 100.
64. (Madrid, 1946).
65. *Ibid.,* p. 9.
66. *Salmos al viento* (Barcelona, 1958).
67. (Santander, 1955).
68. *Profecías del agua* (Madrid, 1958), pp. 17-18. (Only the beginning of this poem is given, not the whole of it, as with the other examples in this chapter.)
69. *Poesías originales* (Cambridge, 1925), p. 28 ["En la Ascensión"].
70. *Sagrada Biblia* (Madrid, 1944), p. 840.
71. *Ibid.,* p. 598.
72. (Madrid, 1947).
73. *Ibid.,* p. 91.
74. See Chapter 5, Note 6.

10

Translations and Foreign Influences

We have already seen[1] how Dámaso Alonso denies the influence of Surrealism on the Spanish poetry of his generation. It might be as well, for the purposes of this chapter, to quote exactly what he says:

> Es evidente que los elementos oníricos son lo que da trasmundo y misterio a la poesía de Federico desde sus primeras canciones, mucho antes de todo superrealismo. Cuando Vicente Aleixandre, entre 1928 y 1929, escribe su *Pasión de la tierra,* del *surréalisme* francés lo ignora todo. Con este libro y con *Sobre los ángeles,* de Alberti, ha comenzado una nueva era poética.[2]

> Ni hay conexión transmitiva tampoco entre el superrealismo francés y *Sobre los ángeles* de Alberti.[3]

> It is evident that it is the dream world that gives a mysterious other-world quality to the poetry of García Lorca. This was present in his earliest poems, long before there was any Surrealism. When Vicente Aleixandre, between 1928 and 1929, writes his *Pasión de la tierra,* he knows nothing about French Surrealism. With this book and with Alberti's *Sobre los ángeles* a new era of poetry has begun.

> Nor did French Surrealism have any influence on Alberti's *Sobre los ángeles.*

The testimony of Dámaso Alonso is of the greatest importance here, because, at the time when the books he mentioned were being written, he was living in daily contact with the poets of his generation. What he says is very valuable evidence indeed, though we must admit the possibility of subsequent evidence against this statement from writings or reported conversation of these poets which have not yet been published.

This, however, does not seem likely. Poetry in all countries is less open to foreign influences than other branches of literature, and this is perhaps even truer of Spain than of most countries. The present chapter will, we think, offer some proof of this.

Before the Civil War, Juan Ramón Jiménez translated Blake[4] and Tagore in collaboration with his wife. Guillén and Salinas were both admirers of Valéry, whom Guillén translated.[5] Salinas and Alberti translated some of Supervielle together. Cernuda translated some poems by Hölderlin. Muñoz Rojas translated Thompson's *The Hound of Heaven*.[6]

Dámaso Alonso, Salinas, Cernuda, Guillén, and Muñoz Rojas have worked at universities in England, the United States, and other places abroad. Juan Ramón Jiménez lectured at Puerto Rico. Panero lived for some months in Cambridge. They all gained an extensive knowledge of the poetry written in the languages of the countries they visited. It did not, however, have any very appreciable effect on their own work.

After these preliminary examples, we must now examine the translated poetry appearing in Spain since 1939. But first it might be as well to glance through the answers to the fourth query of our questionnaire in the next chapter. Question 4 reads: "What foreign poets do you consider important?"

Only Ricardo Molina claims that foreign poetry is as important for him as that of his own country. Crémer, Pérez Valiente, and Montesinos have avoided answering the question; Montesinos only mentions Rubén Darío—and this is perhaps not as preposterous as it sounds at first, since Darío was far more deeply affected by French poetry than any of the poets in Spain writing after him have been. Pérez Valiente makes a similar joke, speaking of León Felipe. Hierro only refers to French poets. Others, such as García Nieto, name poets they know in translation. One suspects that the only really valid example of an acknowledged influence of foreign poets is that of Éluard and Aragon on Celaya.

As to poems translated into Spanish since 1939, the largest number are from the French. This is natural, because of the special prestige of French literature and the likeness of the two languages.

José Luis Cano has put nineteen years' hard and admirable work into bringing out the series of poetry booklets called *Adonais* after Shelley's poem to Keats. About a hundred and ninety of these have already appeared, including nearly all the poets writing in Spain today and a number of foreign poets in translation. Some twelve of the booklets are translated from the French. Nevertheless, only two living French-speaking poets, Saint-John Perse and Vandercammen, have been given a separate volume. An anthology of French religious poetry[7] contains eleven living poets, six of whom were born after 1900. To these we might add René Ménard, one of whose poems has been translated by Caballero Bonald in *Poesía española.* Another type of poet, Éluard, has had fifteen poems translated by Gabriel Celaya.[8]

The translators of the French poets in *Adonais* are not among the best-known contemporary Spanish poets—except for Gaos, who translated Rimbaud. The standard is irregular.

The second book to be published in the *Adonais* series, after the *Poemas del toro,* was a selection from Péguy by Vicente Pola.[9] It will be noticed that Péguy's name appears quite frequently in our questionnaire. No. 8 in *Adonais* is Rodenbach, rather freely rendered by Dampierre.[10] No. 12 is a translation of some of Verlaine by Luis Guarner, but he has really only produced a book of pleasant little poems with the same images and themes as the original. "Llora en mi corazón / cual llueve en la ciudad."[11] (There is weeping in my heart, / Just as there is rain in the city.)

Vicente Gaos is more successful with Rimbaud in No. 31.[12] At least he gives Rimbaud a clear style in Spanish though, like most of the translators, he chooses free verse for poems which have a traditional form in the original. In his foreword, he attacks Dampierre for not doing this.

Rodríguez Alcalde's *Antología de la poesía francesa religiosa,* No. 37,[13] is uninspiring, though it manages to show the greater richness of religious poetry in France than in Spain. The anthologist speaks of the "libertad lírica" (lyrical liberty) with which Emmanuel "interpreta algunos misterios de la Religión"[14] (interprets some of the mysteries of Religion), which borders on heterodoxy. This would apply to other poets in the book and marks a contrast between French and Spanish Catholic poets, though we have seen a suggestion of this in José Luis Prado.[15]

Curiously enough, the only traceable influence of these poems on Spanish ones can be found in the similarity of the dialogue form of Milosz' "Confession de Lemuel" to that of Celaya's *Lo demás es silencio,* in spite of the difference in subject-matter and ideas.

Rodríguez Alcalde, in No. 51,[16] makes at least one of Supervielle's poems sound like Lorca.

Jean Moréas, No. 67,[17] translated by Paulina Crusat, compares unfavorably with previous renderings of that poet by Juan Ramón Jiménez and Díez-Canedo.

Nos. 108-109 of the series is the Five Great Odes of Claudel,[18] poems in prose, like *Anabasis* by Saint-John Perse, No. 144.[19] It seems a pity that two of the books by French poets still living when the *Adonais* series began should be in prose. Juan Ortega Costa's translations from Valéry, No. 127,[20] partly make up for this. This writer, who has lived for many years in French-speaking countries, has so assimilated the spirit of French poetry that he can now make careful and excellent translations of its most restrained and characteristic poets such as Valéry and Racine. He is also very successful with Apollinaire, No. 177.[21] No. 134 is the *Cancionero* of the 16th century poetess Louise Labé,[22] in a spirited translation, with something of the Renaissance about it, by Ester de Andréis. But all these books are different from what the poets are writing in present-day Spain.

Curiously enough, modern English poetry is better represented. *Adonais* includes nine English poets and four American ones. Though *Garcilaso* in Madrid translated only Kipling from England and Theodore Storm from Germany, *Entregas de Poesía* printed poems by Stephen Spender as early as 1944. This was in spite of his support of the other side in the Civil War.[23] Santa Marina has made an excellent translation of Chesterton's *Lepanto*,[24] and Dámaso Alonso has done what could be done to put some poems of Hopkins's into Spanish.[25]

The translations in *Adonais* are again unequal, though the general standard is higher than with the French. Walt Whitman, translated by Concha Zardoya for No. 15[26]—and for the Editorial Aguilar— loses most of his force. The same may be said for María Alfaro's selection from Byron, No. 18,[27] and for Santiago Magariños' translations from Longfellow, No. 24.[28] Both of these books might equally well have come from the last century.

No. 26 is more interesting, being a volume of Eliot, with translations by Panero, Dámaso Alonso, Muñoz Rojas, and José Luis Cano.[29] This was practically an introduction to Eliot for contemporary Spain, though earlier translations of *The Waste Land* had appeared before the Civil War. In spite of the care and skill of Muñoz Rojas and Dámaso Alonso, Eliot is not adequately presented. The exact meaning is given, but we miss the quality of Eliot's style with its mixture of modern expressions with literary ones and images. This fundamental contrast does not show in Spanish. Valverde, in the review *Alcalá,* is only slightly more successful. However, he must be conscious of certain idiomatic peculiarities in Eliot's style, seeing that he expresses the opinion that Eliot is an American rather than an English poet.[30]

Clemencia Miró's translations from Keats are No. 28 of the *Adonais* series.[31] They fail to give any real idea of the original. Vicente Gaos' translation of Shelley's *Adonais,* No. 38,[32] catches the semi-pastoral, semi-mythological atmosphere of the poem but misses Shelley's clear rhetorical phrases. Thus it does not render the ending forcefully enough.

The double volume 49-50 is an anthology of the *Poetas ingleses "metafísicos."*[33] The little-known translators, Mauricio Molho and Blanca G. Escandon, do not seem to have fully understood the more difficult passages in the original. For instance, "Get with child a mandrake root" is given as "Y en tu preñez arranca la mandrágora" (and, in your pregnancy, tear out the mandrake). The translator of this line seems to be unaware of the old English superstitions which made of the mandrake an almost human and rather sinister plant. Possibly, too, the Anglo-Saxon directness of the phrase disturbed him. Molho's preface says that Donne and Herbert showed a rebellious spirit in their religious poetry. Crashaw, we are told, was too preoccupied with the ornate in religion.

José Luis Cano in No. 65[34] presents Rupert Brooke as a belated Romantic, both in his preface and in the translation. At last, No. 79 brings us a really contemporary English poet, Kathleen Raine.[35] It is very fitting that the translator should be Manent. This Catalan poet is the best-informed person in Spain about contemporary English poetry. This was obvious in his Catalan *Notes sobre literatura estrangera,* published more than twenty years ago. It was again obvious in his three-volume anthology—in Castilian, this time—of *La poesía inglesa:* vol. I, *De los primitivos a los neoclásicos,* vol. II, *Románticos y victorianos,* vol. III, *Modernos.*[36] Manent's method is to translate into loose lines of what may at times turn out to be free verse. Perhaps this method suits him, as he is primarily a Catalan writer, and certainly his own Catalan lyrics keep to careful traditional forms much as Valéry did in French.

But we should be wrong if we assumed he could not be successful with traditional meters in Castilian, as his excellent translations of the poems in Lewis Carroll's *Alice* books can show.[37] The poets included in Manent's volume of *Modernos* are a representative selection down to the time of Dylan Thomas and Vernon Watkins. His *Adonais* selection from Kathleen Raine suffers particularly from the loss of verse-forms tenuously adhered to in the original, but necessary to the light grace of this poetry. For the first time in *Adonais,* the original is given on the opposite page.

Vicente Gaos is the translator of Eliot's *Four Quartets,* Nos. 76-77.[38] Though Gaos has been very painstaking, especially in reading the works referred to in the preface and in the notes, he is not so successful as Muñoz Rojas was with "East Coker" in the *Adonais* selection of Eliot.

The fact that the translations are by Valverde gives added interest to the *Twenty Poems* of Thomas Merton, No. 96.[39] The translation is solid, efficient, and prosaic. Neither in his original poems nor his translations has Valverde recaptured the soar of his first book, when he was a very young poet whom everyone expected to die soon.

We cannot deny that Elizabeth Barrett Browning's *Sonnets from the Portuguese*[40] is as unexpected in this series as Longfellow was. The translation by Julieta Gómez Paz is more successful than that of the previous English nineteenth-century poets in *Adonais,* and two or three of the sonnets capture the tenderness of the original. The title is unsatisfactorily translated as *Sonetos del portugués;* since the original play on words must necessarily be lost, *Sonetos de la portuguesa* would have been far better.

Esteban Pujals' selection from Dylan Thomas, No. 124,[41] is probably the most successful translation from English in the *Adonais* booklets. We can feel the joyful surge and rush of Thomas' poetry. Certain alliterations and the rough force of a word or two here and there may have to have been sacrificed, but that is probably inevitable in transferring any poet from English into Spanish. Jaime Ferrán has been less successful with Yeats, No. 140.[42] The nimble use of singsong meters, which is such a charm with Yeats, is of course quite lost in a free-verse translation. Things are much improved when the translator keeps to something like the original form—adding a rhyme in assonances—as in "Crazy Jane on the Mountain."[43] Following the example of Kathleen Raine's book, the English is given on the opposite page.

Aquilino Duque made a competent selection and translation of poems by Roy Campbell, No. 157.[44] His translation has a pleasant flow, though it may miss something of Campbell's ruggedness. Rather injudiciously, Campbell's political poems, though so favorable to the present politics of Spain, have been quite omitted. As they represent the author's deep convictions, this is surely a mistake.

The most interesting of all the books of translated poetry in *Adonais* and the most ably performed is Ezra Pound's *Los cantos pisanos,* No. 179.[45] The translator, Jesús Pardo (1927-   ), has hitherto only published a very few poems in poetry reviews. He writes a more involved type of poetry than is usual in Spain. He has chosen to select this volume of Pound because he genuinely finds the American poet one of the greatest, if not the greatest, of our age. The lines of Pound are almost more rhythmical in Spanish than in the original. One would not have believed that Pound's bitter refrain in these cantos could be so well rendered in another language. The extensive introduction and notes make this book an important commentary on Pound, apart from its poetic excellencies.

Though German political influence has at times been all too strong in Spain, it never brought with it an interest in German literature. One poet is certainly frequently mentioned—as we can see from the questionnaire in the next chapter—and that is Rilke. Poems by him appear from time to time in reviews, but they are uninspiring in Spanish, missing the rhythmic force of the original German. The best translations from Rilke are from the French and made by Gerardo Diego;[46] the music of the original loses nothing by being transmitted by such a master.

The first German poet in *Adonais,* No. 54, is Trakl.[47] Jaime Bofill y Ferro, another Catalan poet, has given him a vividness which is lacking to most of the translations we have been commenting on. The unlikeness of German to Spanish is perhaps an advantage, when, as in the present case, the translator has made an effort to recreate the poems fully in their new form. This is even truer of Bofill's anthology of German poetry, which is in well-knit and forceful lines corresponding to the original ones. The rhymes are usually in assonance. Relatively few poets are included, the latest being Goethe and Schiller, who fill, between them, more than half the anthology.

This standard of translation is by no means attained to by García Yebra in his selection from Gertrud Von le Fort, No. 56,[48] or by Valverde in *Twelve Poems from Hölderlin,* No. 61,[49] which are both weakly phrased and dull to read.

Carmen Bravo-Villasante's selection from Goethe, No. 98,[50] shows rather less sense of rhythm than Bofill's translations. She has made up an interesting and readable little book, though she could have chosen better poems.

Peregrinajes (Pilgrimages) by Stefan George, No. 105,[51] translated by Alfonso Pintó and Jaime Balet, gives us a shadow of Rubén Darío and French Symbolism. This helps us to form a far-off idea of this German Symbolist.

Nos. 112-113 are the Orpheus sonnets of Rilke,[52] translated by Carlos Barral. These certainly make better reading than the longer poems of Rilke to be found in books translated by Gonzalo Torrente Ballester and Valverde.[53] Rilke's blank verse and even his free verse is so much more rhythmical than these translations and so much more natural in its diction that we cannot help wondering once more why so many Spanish poets who do not read German say they admire Rilke, unless it really is for his prose.

Once we have finished speaking of these French, English and German poets, few foreign poets remain in *Adonais.* Portuguese is a language very like Spanish and the poems chosen from Serpa, No. 36,[54] Casais Monteiro, No. 103,[55] Miguel Torga, No. 89,[56] Fernando Pessoa, No. 147,[57] and the Brazilian Drummond de Andrade, No. 73,[58] remain much as the authors wrote them, allowing for the difference of sounds in the two Iberian languages. It might have been another matter if a poet who uses rhyme and complicated verse-forms, such as José Régio, had been attempted. Angel Crespo's *Antología de la nueva poesía portuguesa,* Nos. 183-184,[59] is an interesting new venture which shows, among other things, how the young Portuguese writers have used Surrealism to help them create their own individual styles. Indeed the only Spanish poet who has a style like any of theirs is Crespo himself, so that he is a very suitable translator. On the other hand, many Portuguese writers are acutely sensual and others are painfully insistent on left-wing politics, but these two aspects are not obvious from this anthology.

The Belgian poet, Edmond Vandercammen, No. 103,[60] known to poets in Spain because of his attendance at the Spanish Poetry congresses, has been translated by Dictinio del Castillo-Elejabeytia into a strong rhythm very like that of the translator's own original poems.

A more unusual book is a selection of poems by the Lebanese writer Mija'il Nu'ayma, No. 132,[61] translated by an Arabic scholar, Leonor Martínez, with the help of a young Moroccan poet, Mohammad Sabbag, who contributed the preface. Nu'ayma's style, apparently, was considered very novel, unconventional, and experimental by critics in his own country when he was young. What strikes us nowadays, reading him in a Spanish translation, is how similar his style is to that of the poets of Moorish Spain, as rendered by García Gómez. The great difference, indeed, is that Nu'ayma loves building up sets of parallel images. In a way this is very like that practiced by Spanish poets in the past and present, as Dámaso Alonso has shown in his essay on *plurimembres*[62]—though these can also be frequently found in other European literatures, so that altogether these Lebanese poems are not so strange in their Spanish clothing as Mohammad Sabbag seems to think.

A Turk with an excellent command of Spanish, Soliman Salom, has collected and translated an anthology of contemporary Turkish poets,[63] who seem much more Western than Nu'ayma, though recognizably oriental as well. This anthology is more interesting than the one of Dutch poetry, No. 155,[64] by Francisco Carrasquer, which seems to miss the essential flavor, for all the translator's enthusiasm. He tells us that he wanted to print the original Dutch on the opposite page, but the publishers thought that too few people knew the language in Spain. Yet, however little a reader of translated poetry may understand of the original, its presence can often add something to his appreciation.

There are no Russian poets in the *Adonais* series as yet, but six recent poems by Boris Pasternak have appeared in a number of *Poesía española*.[65] These poems also appeared in an English translation in 1960.[66] Generally, when Russian works are published in Spain, people say they have been translated from the French. In the case of these poems, there seems to be no doubt that they are a direct translation, and indeed they follow the flow of the original more closely than the English rendering. Yet, insofar as Pasternak is a poet known for his forceful use of colloquial language, the English translation has made more of an effort to imitate that aspect of him.

Neither the Spanish nor the English version attempts to give us the formal meter and the precise use of uncomplicated words which is probably the key to the greatness of Pasternak's original poetry.

We must not forget the translations from Catalan, in the *Adonais* booklets, which consist of an anthology of contemporary poets, Nos. 83-84,[67] and books by Carles Riba, No. 93,[68] and Salvador Espriu, Nos. 136-137.[69] These hardly need comment, since Catalan is sufficiently near Spanish, and the authors, being bilingual, are sure to have revised the translations. There is also an anthology of Galician poetry, Nos. 161-162,[70] which surprises us by containing some poets already known for their work in Castilian.

This list does not of course exhaust all the poets who have been translated into Spanish since 1939, but it does at least give an idea of what is considered interesting by the people who supply the public with poetry. Perhaps the omissions are more remarkable than the inclusions. Why are the Italians so overlooked, even Ungaretti, though he was invited to the Salamanca Poetry Congress in 1953? Again, it is a strange fact that Roy Campbell, the champion of Nationalist Spain in England, was only included in *Adonais* a year after his death in 1957. This was despite his having visited Spain several times between 1948 and 1957, giving a number of lectures and attending two poetry congresses. The fact is that Spanish poetry stands on its own among its own people, so far as any literary phenomenon can.

NOTES TO CHAPTER 10

1. See Chapter 6, note 10.
2. *Poetas españoles contemporáneos* (Madrid, 1952), p. 188.
3. *Ibid.*, p. 326.
4. See Chapter 2, note 62.
5. *El cementerio marino* (Madrid, Paris, Buenos Aires, 1930).
6. See Chapter 7, note 36.
7. Leopoldo Rodríguez Alcalde, *Antología de la poesía francesa religiosa* (Madrid, 1947).
8. *Quince poemas* (Guadalajara, 1954).
9. *Poesías* (Madrid, 1943).
10. *El reino del silencio* (Madrid, 1944).
11. *Fiestas galantes Romanzas sin palabras* (Madrid, 1944), p. 62.
12. *Poesías* (Madrid, 1946).
13. See note 7.
14. *Antología de la poesía francesa religiosa*, p. 114.
15. See Chapter 8, note 18.
16. *Poemas* (Madrid, 1948).

17. *Poemas y estancias* (Madrid, 1950).
18. *Cinco grandes odas* (Madrid, 1955).
19. *Anabasis* (Madrid, 1957).
20. *La serpiente y la parca joven* (Madrid, 1956).
21. *La canción del mal amado y otros poemas* (Madrid, 1960).
22. *Cancionero* (Madrid, 1956).
23. In *Entregas de poesía* (Barcelona) 10, (October, 1944) translated by Ester de Andréis. Nos. 13-14 give a prose essay by Spender, "Crisis de símbolos." No. 17 prints a translation of W. H. Auden's "Victor," by Diego Navarro.
24. (Barcelona, 1948). A free verse translation of this poem by Magariños had previously appeared in *Entregas de poesía* (Barcelona) 3, (March, 1944).
25. *Poetas españoles contemporáneos*, pp. 418-422.
26. *Cantando a la primavera* (Madrid, 1945).
27. *Poemas líricos* (Madrid, 1945).
28. *Aureos instantes* (Madrid, 1945).
29. *Poemas* (Madrid, 1946).
30. *Estudios sobre la palabra poética* (Madrid, 1952), p. 129 ["T. S. Eliot desde la poesía americana"].
31. *Poesías* (Madrid, 1946).
32. *Adonais* (Madrid, 1947).
33. *Poetas ingleses "metafísicos" (siglo XVII)* (Madrid, 1948).
34. *Poemas* (Madrid, 1950).
35. *Poemas* (Madrid, 1951).
36. The *Notes* were published in Barcelona in 1934. The Anthologies appeared in Barcelona from 1945-1948.
37. (Barcelona, 1945).
38. *Cuatro cuartetos* (Madrid, 1951).
39. *Veinte poemas* (Madrid, 1953).
40. *Sonetos del portugués* (Madrid, 1954).
41. *Poemas* (Madrid, 1955).
42. *Poemas* (Madrid, 1957).
43. *Ibid.*, p. 89.
44. *Poemas* (Madrid, 1958).
45. (Madrid, 1960).
46. *Las ventanas* (Barcelona, n.d. [1957]).
47. *Poemas* (Madrid, 1949).
48. *Himnos a la Iglesia* (Madrid, 1949).
49. *Doce poemas* (Madrid, 1949).
50. *Poesías* (Madrid, 1953).
51. (Madrid, 1954).
52. *Sonetos a Orfeo* (Madrid, 1954).
53. *Requiem. Las elegías de Duino* (Madrid, 1946) and *Cincuenta poemas* (Madrid, 1957).
54. *Poemas de Oporto* (Madrid, 1947).
55. *Antología* (Madrid, 1954).
56. *Antología poética* (Madrid, 1952).
57. *Poemas de Alberto Caeiro* (Madrid, 1957).
58. *Poemas* (Madrid, 1951).
59. (Madrid, 1961).
60. *Arcilla de mi carne* (Madrid, 1954).
61. *El rumor de los párpados* (Madrid, 1956).
62. See *Clavileño* (Madrid) 7, (January-February, 1951) ["Teoría de los conjuntos semejantes"].
63. *Poetas turcos contemporáneos* (Madrid, 1959).
64. *Antología de poetas holandeses contemporáneos* (Madrid, 1958). Much the same is true of the anthology of modern Swedish poetry, *Poetas suecos contemporáneos* by Greta Engberg and Vicente Ramos (Madrid, 1961).
65. (Madrid) 91, (July, 1960), pp. 2-5.
66. *Poems 1955-1959* (London, 1960).

67. *Antología de poetas catalanes contemporáneos* (Madrid, 1952).
68. *Elegías de Bierville* (Madrid, 1953).
69. *Antología lírica* (Madrid, 1956).
70. *Antología de la poesía gallega contemporánea* (Madrid, 1959).

11

The Poets Give Their Own Opinions

In 1932, the best-known poets of the day contributed their ideas on poetry to Gerardo Diego's famous anthology. Therein Unamuno says that poets are natural heretics, by which he must mean that he considers poetry as a state of revolt.

Manuel Machado avoids answering in four lines.[2]

Antonio Machado insists, yet again, that poetry is "la palabra esencial en el tiempo" (the essential word in time). He goes on to say that modern poetry begins with Edgar Allan Poe. He disapproves of the "poetas del día" (poets of the present day).

> Ellos propenden a una destemporalización de la lírica, no sólo por el desuso de los artificios del ritmo, sino, sobre todo, por el empleo de las imágenes en función más conceptual que emotiva.[3]

> They tend towards a distemporalization of the lyric, not only because they set aside the artifice of rhythm, but above all, because they use images in a more conceptual than emotive way.

We suspect that Machado was thinking of the poets influenced mainly by Juan Ramón Jiménez. At that time Jiménez had a much higher standing among the young than Machado. The influence of Machado was to increase later (as we have perhaps shown, though in an incidental manner, throughout the course of this book). Machado himself felt that the future was on his side, for he goes on to say that he will print an anthology of his own "poetas futuros."[4] The anthology, of course, never actually appeared. But surely Machado's "future poets" did. So that we may say that his anthology now exists symbolically.

Juan Ramón Jiménez spoke of the influence of certain poets on him—the *Romancero,* Góngora, Bécquer, and Rubén Darío. Later on in this chapter, when we give the answers to our questionnaire presented to certain contemporary Spanish poets, we shall notice these names appearing again and again. Jiménez declared his "Odio profundo a los ismos y a los trucos." (Deep hate for isms and tricks.) He also thought the influence of French poetry on the decline.[5]

Moreno Villa gives a list of poets; Andalusian *coplas,* Heine, Goethe, Schiller, Novalis, Hölderlin, Stefan George, Mombert, Baudelaire, Verlaine, Darío, Unamuno, the Machados, Juan Ramón, Catullus, and Tibullus. He says that yesterday only such things as the pearl, the ruby, the dawn, and the rose were considered poetical, but that now documents, facts, and details make up a part of the poet's material.[6]

Salinas says that poetry cannot be defined. He mentions Walter Savage Landor, Góngora, Mallarmé, Saint John of the Cross, Goethe, and Juan Ramón Jiménez.[7]

We have already commented on and quoted Guillén's critical contribution to Diego's anthology.[8]

Dámaso Alonso tells us that poetry is "Un fervor, un deseo íntimo y fuerte de unión con la gran entraña del mundo y su causa primera." (A fervor, a strong, intimate desire for union with the great inner workings of the world and its first cause.) Between brackets, he attacks the Surrealists: "(El automatismo no ha sido practicado ni aun por sus mismos definidores)."[9] (Automatic writing has not been practiced, even by the very people who defined it.)

Larrea says that literature is a passion.[10] We have already quoted from Diego's contribution.[11]

Lorca's piece was taken down by Diego *viva voce.* He finishes: "si es verdad que soy poeta por la gracia de Dios—o del demonio—también lo es que lo soy por la gracia de la técnica y del esfuerzo y de darme cuenta en absoluto de lo que es un poema."[12] (If it is true that I am a poet by the grace of God—or of the devil—I am also one by the grace of technique and effort and an absolute realization of what a poem is.)

Alberti did not send in a reply. No doubt this was because, at this time, he was wavering about accepting or not accepting the Marxist view of literature. By 1934, when the second edition of Diego's Anthology appeared, he had become a complete Communist.

Aleixandre says that "como dato primero sólo pondré que he nacido en Sevilla y que mi infancia toda es andaluza." (As a fact of primary importance, I can only set down that I was born in Seville and that all my childhood was Andalusian.)[13]

Cernuda sent in a brief note showing his distaste for everything in general. Many people are irritated by these lines, which are nevertheless by now the most famous in the prose section of Diego's book. Their literary quality is evident, though they cannot represent Cernuda's considered and final opinion on life and poetry.

No valía la pena de ir poco a poco olvidando la realidad para que ahora fuese a recordarla, y ante qué gentes. La detesto como detesto todo lo que a ella pertenece: mis amigos, mi familia, mi país.

No sé nada, no quiero nada, no espero nada. Y si aún pudiera esperar algo, sólo sería morir allí donde no hubiese penetrado aún esta grotesca civilización que envanece a los hombres.[14]

It was not worthwhile to go on little by little forgetting about reality in order to remember it now, and in the presence of what people! I detest it as I detest everything belonging to it: my friends, my family, my country.

I know nothing, I want nothing, I hope for nothing. And, if I could still hope for anything, it would only be to die somewhere as yet unreached by this grotesque civilization which makes men so vain.

Altolaguirre refuses to say more than that his favorite poets are Garcilaso de la Vega, Saint John of the Cross, and Juan Ramón Jiménez.[15]

These opinions have been much commented on and quoted. As the aim of this present book has largely been to continue the history of Spanish poetry since the appearance of that anthology, we prepared a list of questions. These were submitted to all the poets who have received special attention in this present book. Only one poet failed to reply. While most of the answers were in writing, some gave theirs viva voce. These were Bousoño, Celaya, García Nieto, Molina, Montesinos, Prado, and Suárez Carreño.

We will make no further comment. The poets must speak for themselves.

The questions were:

(1) What are your ideas on poetry? And the influences acting on you?

(2) What are you trying to do in your poetry?

(3) Whom do you consider important among Spanish classical, Romantic, and early 20th century poets?

(4) What foreign poets do you consider important?

(5) Which are your best poems?

And these are the answers (first in Spanish and then in English):

Germán Bleiberg

(1) Las posibles influencias de toda clase de lecturas no las considero "meras influencias," sino más bien como vivencia o experiencia vital, que se confunde con lo realmente vivido por el poeta.

(2) Con mi poesía no he pretendido nunca nada determinado: expresar un estado de ánimo o aliviarme de una inquietud espiritual, intelectual o sentimental.

(3) Garcilaso, San Juan de la Cruz, Quevedo, Bécquer, Machado, Juan Ramón Jiménez y la mayor parte de los poetas de la "Antología" de Gerardo Diego.

(4) Shakespeare, Novalis, Hölderlin, Shelley, Keats, los franceses de fin de siglo y de principios del XX, Rilke, Eliot.

(5) Creo que están en mi libro *Más allá de las ruinas*.

> (1) I do not consider the possible influence of all kinds of reading as something merely casual. It is more properly a part of living or a vital experience, which mingles with what the poet has really lived through.
>
> (2) I have never tried to do anything definite in my poetry, only to express a state of mind or purge myself of spiritual, intellectual, or sentimental uneasiness.
>
> (3) Garcilaso, Saint John of the Cross, Quevedo, Bécquer, Machado, Juan Ramón Jiménez and the greater part of the poets in Gerardo Diego's *Anthology*.
>
> (4) Shakespeare, Novalis, Hölderlin, Shelley, Keats, the French poets of the end of the last century and the beginning of this one, Rilke, Eliot.
>
> (5) I believe they are to be found in my book *Más allá de las ruinas*.

Carlos Bousoño

(1) Yo creo que todas las poéticas de todos los poetas son verdaderas para ellos, pero objetivamente suelen carecer de valor. Es decir, tienen una validez histórica. Un poeta sólo ve aquella zona del arte que asemeje a lo que hace, ha hecho o hará y por esto,

conociendo los gustos de un artista joven, puede de cierto modo deducirse la línea de su desarrollo futuro. Creo que la poesía es comunicación de un contenido anímico por medio de palabras, lo cual quiere decir que la poesía está en las palabras en cuanto éstas transmiten un estado de alma y que no está en los hechos. No podemos decir que la primavera es poética y no el invierno, la rosa y no la ortiga.

Es muy difícil que el propio poeta señale sus influencias, pero puedo dar una idea—Quevedo, Antonio Machado, Vicente Aleixandre—y luego, el influjo difuso de la propia generación que todo poeta tiene. No se pueden señalar nombres, porque se trata de un ámbito general. Shelley. Verlaine.

(2) Pretendo comunicar mi alma, revelar a mí mismo y a los demás mi propio espíritu. Creo que todo verdadero artista escribe por necesidad, sin fin práctico. La nombradía es agradable, pero no necesaria. Sospecho que ningún artista de verdad escribe para hacerse un nombre.

(3) San Juan, Lope, Quevedo, Góngora, Espronceda, Bécquer, Antonio Machado, Unamuno, Juan Ramón Jiménez, Lorca, Guillén, Aleixandre, Cernuda, Rubén Dario, Neruda.

(4) Verlaine, Baudelaire, Leopardi, Keats, Shelley, Poe, Rilke.

(5) "Cristo adolescente." "La tarde de la Ascensión del Señor." "Tres poemas sobre la Muerte." "Odas celestes."

(1) I believe that all the poets' poetical systems are true for them, but they usually lack objective value. That is to say that they have an historical value. The only zone of art a poet sees is what is similar to what he is doing, has done, or will do. So that, if we know the tastes of a young artist, we can deduce the course of his future development to a certain extent. I believe that poetry is the communication of a state of mind through words, which means that the poetry is in the words insofar as they transmit a spiritual situation and not in the facts themselves. We cannot say that Spring is poetic and not Winter, that the rose is poetic but not the nettle.

It is very difficult for the poet himself to point to what has influenced him. But I can give an idea—Quevedo, Antonio Machado, Vicente Aleixandre—and then the broad influence of his own generation which every poet has. I can't quote names. It's a matter of general atmosphere. Shelley. Verlaine.

(2) I wish to communicate my soul, reveal to myself and others what my own spirit is like. I believe that every true artist writes because he needs to, without a practical objective. Renown is pleasant, but not necessary. I suspect that no true artist writes to make a name for himself.

(3, 4, 5) (See original Spanish above.)

Gabriel Celaya

(1) Mis ideas sobre la poesía en esencial están en la *Antología consultada.*

En la juventud, el Surrealismo francés y, de los españoles, San Juan de la Cruz y Lope. Y después, tantos . . .

(2) Dar testimonio de mi época. Crear conciencia.

(3) Hoy día me interesan los románticos, e incluso los del XVIII (especialmente Quintana), Machado, y los más recientes, Aleixandre.

(4) En realidad, sólo conozco la francesa. Éluard, incluso en su postura posterior al surrealismo. Neruda, Aragon.

(5) El mejor creo que es *Lo demás es silencio,* y los mejores poemas están en los *Cantos iberos.*

(1) My ideas about poetry are, in all essentials, to be found in the *Antología consultada.*

In youth, French Surrealism and, among the Spaniards, Saint John of the Cross and Lope de Vega. And then, so many others . . . .

(2) To bear witness to my epoch. To create a conscience.

(3) Today the Romantics interest me and even the poets of the eighteenth century—especially Quintana—Machado, and others after him. Aleixandre.

(4) I really only know French poetry. Éluard, including his post-Surrealist phase. Neruda. Aragon.

(5) I think my best poem is *Lo demás es silencio* and my best poems are in *Cantos iberos.*

Victoriano Crémer

(1) ¿Realmente le es necesaria una estética al poeta? De mí sé decir que lo único cierto es que cuando escribo procuro abrir bien los ojos y el corazón, a fin de que por ellos se me entre la verdad y la belleza del mundo que me rodea.

Todos ejercen influencia sobre mí. Principalmente aquellos de los que puede desprenderse una lección de lealtad y de verdad.

(2) Comunicarme con los hombres.

(3) San Juan de la Cruz.

(4) Considero insuficiente mi información para decidir.

(5) Algunos de los incluídos en el libro *Nuevos cantos de vida y esperanza,* y ese poema que se nos va quemando dentro, con la vida, y que quizá nunca podremos hacer.

> (1) Does a poet really need an aesthetic system? For my part, I can say that the only certain thing is that when I write I try to open my eyes and my heart wide, so as to let in the truth and beauty of the world around me.
>
> Everyone influences me. Principally those from whom a lesson of loyalty and truth can be drawn.
>
> (2) Communicate with men.
>
> (3) Saint John of the Cross.
>
> (4) I consider I am too scantily informed to decide.
>
> (5) Some of those included in *Nuevos cantos de vida y esperanza,* and the poem which burns within us throughout life and which perhaps we can never write.

Vicente Gaos

(1) Poesía, en sentido amplio, equivale a *literatura;* en sentido estricto, es una manifestación *única,* no confundible con ninguna otra, a pesar de su parentesco con varias, o de lo que éstas le prestan como colaboradoras: la poesía tiene mucho que ver con la filosofía (pero no es filosofía), con las artes plásticas, con la música (pero tampoco es música, ni pintura, etc.). Acaso sea la poesía la *última* (pero no la única última) decantación de todas las formas de expresión humanas.

Unamuno (influencia apuntada por Dámaso Alonso) me parece cierta. Desde luego, debe de haber muchas otras, aunque difusas y combinadas. Creo que mi poesía no tiene un eco claro de ningún autor determinado; lo que no quiere decir que sea muy personal. Probablemente soy un poeta—en materia de originalidad de voz — más bien neutro, opaco.

(2) Expresarme sobre (o ante) el mundo y la vida. Todos los géneros literarios—todas las artes—son eso, expresiones. También comunicar, comunicarme con los hombres. Pero, a la hora

de escribir, el estímulo, o deseo, o necesidad de expresión es superior—o, al menos es más consciente—que el de comunicación. Y es muy probable que haga mal. Yo querría hacer una poesía que hablara de todo y para todos, pero que fuera poética : no por la inocente manía de hacer poesía pura, sino en el sentido de que la expresión poética fuera la única adecuada. Me parecen muy justas las palabras de T. S. Eliot: "Lo que puede decirse igual en prosa que en verso, se dice mejor en prosa."

(3) Esta pregunta y la siguiente me parece mejor que se formularan al revés : qué poetas *no* le parecen importantes a uno. Que a uno *no* le interese, por ejemplo, Whitman es mucho más significativo que que le interese. Las coincidencias en señalar los grandes poetas casi no dicen nada. Pero, en fin, nombres: Jorge Manrique (si "clásico" no se refiere sólo a los Siglos de Oro),—Fray Luis de León,—San Juan,—Lope, Espronceda, Bécquer, Unamuno, A. Machado, J. R. Jiménez. (¿No son estos poetas importantes para cualquiera?)

(4) Virgilio (el mayor poeta de la antigüedad y tal vez del mundo en todos los tiempos), Shakespeare, Donne, Dryden, Wordsworth, Shelley, Milton, Byron, Tennyson, T. S. Eliot, Whitman, Villon, Rimbaud, Baudelaire, Péguy, Dante, Rilke, Goethe, Heine, Hölderlin, V. Hugo, Verlaine, etc., etc.

(5) "La noche," "Vals apasionado," "Cuando contemplo el cielo," "Armonía del mundo," de *Arcángel de mi noche;* "El corazón," "Adolescencia," "Luzbel," "Sobre la tierra," "La encina," "La tristeza" de *Sobre la tierra;* "Raíz del hombre," "Revelación," "En destierro," "Nostalgia" de *Luz desde el sueño;* "¿Qué misterioso deseo nos lleva a convertir la vida en palabras . . .?" "Después de la belleza," "Así," "Cabeza," "No, corazón, te hundas . . ." "No, no te apresures más . . ." "He visto morir a mucho hombre joven . . ." de *Profecía del recuerdo;* "El balcón" publicado en *Papeles de Son Armadans* del libro inédito, *Cantos solemnes.*

(1) *Poetry,* in the wide sense, is the same thing as literature. In the strict sense, it is a *unique* manifestation, not to be confused with any other, in spite of its relatedness to many others or to that part of them that can act in collaboration with poetry. Poetry is very much connected with philosophy (but it is not philosophy), and with the plastic arts and with music (but it is not music, nor painting, etc., either). Perhaps poetry is the last (but not the only last) decanting of all human modes of expression.

Unamuno (influence pointed out by Dámaso Alonso) certainly, I should say. There must of course be many others, though spread out and mingled. I think that my poetry does not give back a clear echo of any particular author. This does not mean to say it is very personal. Probably I am, more properly speaking, a neutral, opaque poet, so far as originality of tone goes.

(2) Express myself about (or in face of) the world and life. All literary *genres*, all the arts are just that—expression. Also, communication. I wish to communicate with my fellow-men. But, at the time of writing, the stimulus, or desire, or need for expression is greater—or, at least, more conscious —than the need for communication. And very probably that's wrong of me. I should like to create a poetry that spoke of everything to everyone but was poetic—not out of an innocent mania for creating pure poetry, but in the sense that poetic expression would be the only adequate one. T. S. Eliot's opinion that what can be said just as well in prose as in verse should be said in prose, seems to me a just one.

(3) I should prefer this question and the next the other way round: What poets do *not* seem interesting to you? If some-one does *not* like Whitman, for instance, that's much more significant than if he is interested in him. That people are in agreement when they single out great poets is almost meaningless. However, here are names: Jorge Manrique (if "classical" does not only refer to the Golden Age), Friar Luis de León, Saint John of the Cross, Lope de Vega, Espronceda, Bécquer, Unamuno, A. Machado and J. R. Jiménez. (Would not these poets be important for any-body?)

(4) Virgil (the greatest poet of antiquity and perhaps of all the ages of the world). Shakespeare, Donne, Dryden, Words-worth, Shelley, Milton, Byron, Tennyson, T. S. Eliot, Whit-man, Villon, Rimbaud, Baudelaire, Péguy, Dante, Rilke, Goethe, Heine, Hölderlin, V. Hugo, Verlaine, etc., etc.

(5) (See original Spanish above.)

José García Nieto

(1) Creo que una de las normas más claras para la realización del hombre como tal es el camino de la poesía. Aunque no creo, ni mucho menos, en mi destino de elegido para este menester, sí sé que a través de una obra poética se hace vivo lo mejor de mí. No puede haber, por lo tanto, propósito en ninguna poética, sino a lo más asombro o conformidad con el resultado.

He citado con frecuencia los nombres de San Juan de la Cruz, Garcilaso, y Antonio Machado. Me gustaría ahora añadir a Juan Ramón Jiménez, cuya sutil corriente de perennidad lírica alimenta, queramos o no, la mayor parte de la actual poesía española.

(2) Está contestado.

(3) Está contestado.

(4) Shelley, Eliot, cuya presencia en la poesía me ha hecho sentir por primera vez la urgente necesidad de conocer perfectamente sus formas expresivas.

(5) Cuando releo mi obra poética me parece que está toda hecha sobre un taller de aprendizaje y casi podría afirmar que cada poema sea un avance sobre lo anterior. Entonces *Tregua* es el libro que prefiero y tengo una particularísima devoción a los *Versos de un huésped de Luisa Esteban*.

(1) I believe that one of the clearest means for a man to fulfill himself as such is that of poetry. Though I in no way believe that I have been chosen by destiny for this special task, I do know that the best in me comes alive through the medium of a poem. Thus there can be no purpose in any poetic system, only, at most, surprise or agreement with the result.

I have often quoted the names of Saint John of the Cross, Garcilaso, and Antonio Machado. I should now like to add Juan Ramón Jiménez, whose subtle current of lyric continuity feeds the greater part of present-day Spanish poetry, whether we like it or not.

(2) Answered above.

(3) Answered above.

(4) Shelley, Eliot, whose poetical presence has made me feel, for the first time, an urgent need of knowing perfectly his way of expressing himself.

(5) When I re-read my poetical work it seems to me to have all been done in an apprentice's workshop. I might almost say that each poem had gained something since the last one. So that *Tregua* is the book I prefer and I have a special fondness for the *Versos de un huésped de Luisa Esteban*.

Ramón de Garciasol

(1) Para mí no hay poesía hasta que no llega al poema y en él se historifica y nace. La poesía es fruto real de un árbol de misterio.

También me parece aclaratorio decir que es la explicación del sentido. (Y dicho de modo poético: con ritmo, despliegue metafórico, belleza, esencialidad . . .) Por tanto, hasta que la abstracta y vaga poesía no está aquí, en el mundo de los hombres y en el poema, mientras no se hace criatura espiritual, no cabe hablar sino de prejuicios o de hipótesis que esperan documentación, existencia. Mi poética nace de mis poemas, no mis poemas de mi poética, aunque es cierto que son la consecuencia de mi posición en el mundo, de mi tiempo, de mi ser previamente dado. No creo que la poesía sea un juego estético—ni deje de serlo, pero por añadidura—sino una manera de salvación; al menos, una justificación del hombre concreto e irrepetible. Desde ese hombre concreto canto, con las raíces nutridas de una tierra y tradición que se me imponen—sin nacionalismos antagónicos— que no es oposición, sino personalidad en la variedad que hace uno al mundo. (Para mayor claridad, véase mi ensayo *Una pregunta mal hecha: ¿Qué es la poesía?.* (Madrid, Escalamo, 1954).)

(2) Lo que no puedo lograr para mi paz, seguridad, y entendimiento por el mero camino racional y lógico. Si me bastase la filosofía o la ciencia para calmar la inquietud radical—¿no será también vivir estar inquieto?—se me haría innecesaria la poesía. La poesía empieza por serenarme y consolarme a mí. Sobrevolando la razón hay una necesidad de expresarse: satisfacer esa necesidad y, si es posible, la de los demás hombres, es lo que intento cuando pienso sobre ello y no hacer poesía. Puesto a escribir, no pienso, exclusivamente, porque canto con todo lo que soy en cuerpo y alma, cada vez más inseparables. Procuro hacer tranquilidad, conciencia, amor, que consigan el hombre verdaderamente libre, en sí, además de en las leyes positivas. Saber es libertad—y responsabilidad—; sentir es consentir, hacer comunidad; vivir empieza por ser convivir. En la medida conveniente, la poesía también hace humanidad, a más de ser una forma noble de humanismo: libertad en comunidad, o es un juego inmoral, indigno del hombre.

(3) (Aquí contesto a la segunda parte de la primera pregunta.) Berceo, que pone en marcha el ser profundo y emocional del castellano—y le da conciencia—a pesar de la mayor antigüedad de las "jarchas"; el Arcipreste de Hita, salud, alegría, inteligencia, y seguridad en el vivir; el pueblo español, heroico y anónimo, del *Romancero;* Jorge Manrique, que representa el sosiego y el señorío castellanos, la dignidad en el dolor; Quevedo, raíz encendida de España y patetismo consciente de la limitación tragicómica del hombre; Lope, el ala de la gracia y espontaneidad popular española; San Juan de la Cruz, que saliendo de la noche oscura le dió a la caza alcance; Fray Luis de León, de pasión

muy ibérica, metida en orden y andadura nobles; Bécquer, instaurador de la sensibilidad moderna en la poesía española; Unamuno, Antonio Machado, Juan Ramón Jiménez, los tres grandes del comienzo de siglo, de problemática y estética complementarias, de cuya unidad saldrá el futuro poeta español perfecto. No me olvido de Góngora, Bocángel, Villamediana y dos docenas más con los que siento y consiento.

(4) Habría que razonar los nombres españoles y extranjeros, y la respuesta se haría más extensa de lo conveniente. La coetaneidad suele deformar.

(5) Para mí, los últimos que escribo. ¿Quién se atreve a decir que ha escrito "algo" mejor? Por ahora, los de mi libro *Tierras de España* (Adonais, 1955). Los que más me satisfacen están en los libros: *La madre, Del amor de cada día, Hombre de la tierra* y *Sangre de par en par.* Las diversas antologías han coincidido en alguno: "Arenga a las rosas y a los hombres" de *Palabras mayores,* más por actualidad que por su categoría poética, creo yo. Mejor representado, hasta este momento, me encuentro en las antologías de Sáinz de Robles y de Rafael Millán.

(1) For me there is no such thing as poetry until we come to the poem. Then it acquires a history and is born. Poetry is the real fruit of a tree of mystery. Also I think it would make things clearer to say that it is the explanation of the meaning (said in a poetical manner with rhythm, development of metaphors, beauty and essentiality). Therefore, until vague, abstract poetry comes here to the world of men and to the poem, until it becomes a spiritual creature, until then the only things to speak about are preconceived notions or hypotheses which as yet have no definite identity, which as yet do not exist. My poetic system is born of my poems and not my poems of my poetic system, though it is true that they are the consequence of my position in the world, of my age, and of my previously given being. I do not think poetry is an aesthetic game—it could be one, but that would be just by the way—but rather a way of salvation, at least a justification of concrete man, man never to be repeated. I sing from the position of that concrete man, with my roots nourished by a soil and tradition which are imposed on me —without antagonistic nationalism—, which is not an opposition, but a personalization in the variety which makes one up in the world. (For further light on the matter, see my essay *A Badly Expressed Question—What is Poetry?* [Madrid, Escalamo, 1954].)

(2) What I cannot achieve in order to win peace, security, and understanding by mere rational and logical means. If phi-

losophy or science were enough to quiet my radical restlessness—is not to be restless the same thing as being alive?—poetry would not be necessary to me. Poetry begins by calming and consoling me personally. Soaring to heights above reason, there is a need for expressing oneself. To satisfy this need and, if possible, that of other men, is what I try to do when I think about it and not to write poetry. When I start writing I am not just thinking. I am singing with all there is in my body and soul—which have become more inseparable than ever. I try to create tranquillity, conscience, and love, that they may attain to a man really free in himself—not merely in positive laws. Knowledge is liberty—and responsibility. Feeling is consenting, forming a community. Living is, in the first place, living with. In its fitting measure, poetry too makes up humanity, besides being a noble form of humanism, liberty within the community. Otherwise it is an immoral game, unworthy of man.

(3) (Here I answer the second part of the first question.) Berceo, who sets the deep, emotional being of the Castilian moving, and gives it consciousness, in spite of the greater antiquity of the *jarchas;* the Archpriest of Hita, health, joy, intelligence, and sureness in living; the Spanish people, heroic and anonymous in the *romancero;* Jorge Manrique, who represents Castilian serenity and worth, dignity in grief; Quevedo, the burning root of Spain and deep feeling conscious of the tragi-comical limits of man; Lope, with his airy, spontaneous, popular Spanish spirit; Saint John of the Cross, who coming out of a dark night in the end seized his quarry; Friar Luis de León, very Iberian in his feelings, controlled by his noble orderliness and stately pace; Bécquer, who brought modern sensibility to Spanish poetry; Unamuno, Antonio Machado, and Juan Ramón Jiménez, the three great men of the beginning of the century, whose philosophical and aesthetic ideas complement each other, so that, when these ideas are united, the future perfect Spanish poet will appear. I do not forget Góngora, Bocángel, Villamediana and two dozen more whom I feel and agree with.

(4) We should have to reason about the relative value of the Spanish and foreign writers and the reply would be longer than is convenient. Being a contemporary usually deforms things.

(5) For me, the last I have written. Who would dare to say that he has written "something" better? Just now, those in my book, *Tierras de España* (Madrid, Adonais, 1955).

Those which satisfy me most are in *La madre, Del amor de cada día, Hombre de la tierra* and *Sangre de par en par.* Different anthologies have agreed about one of them, "Arenga a las rosas y los hombres" in *Palabras mayores,* more because of its up-to-dateness than its poetic worth, I think. I am best represented, up to the present, in the anthologies of Sáinz de Robles and Rafael Millán.

José Hierro

(1) Aquí convendría citar un trozo de la *Antología consultada.*

Las influencias directas son: Rubén Darío, Juan Ramón Jiménez y Gerardo Diego. Y, difusa, toda la poesía anterior.

(2) Dar testimonio del hombre de mi tiempo.

(3) Los predilectos: Jorge Manrique. Lope. Quevedo. Bécquer, Rubén. Juan Ramón. Machado.

(4) Baudelaire. Rimbaud. Supervielle.

(5) No me atrevo a contestar.

(1) The best thing would be to quote a passage from the *Antología consultada.*

Direct influences: Rubén Darío. Juan Ramón Jiménez and Gerardo Diego. And scattered influences; all former poetry.

(2) To bear witness to mankind in my time.

(3) My favorites: Jorge Manrique. Lope de Vega. Quevedo. Bécquer. Rubén Darío. Juan Ramón Jiménez. Machado.

(4) Baudelaire. Rimbaud. Supervielle.

(5) I haven't the face to answer this one.

Ricardo Molina

(1, 2) No he pensado nunca en estética, ni en general ni en particular.

La primera influencia fué Lamartine. Las más profundas Claudel, Gide, y Luis Cernuda.

(3) Góngora. San Juan de la Cruz. Ningún romántico. Juan Ramón Jiménez. Gabriel Miró. Aleixandre. Cernuda.

(4) Tan importante para mí como la española. Dante.

(5) No tengo idea.

(1, 2) I have never thought about aesthetic systems, either in general or in particular.

The first influence was Lamartine; the deepest Claudel, Gide, and Luis Cernuda.

(3) Góngora, Saint John of the Cross. None of the Romantics. Juan Ramón Jiménez. Gabriel Miró. Aleixandre. Cernuda.

(4) As important for me as Spanish poetry. Dante.

(5) I have no idea.

Rafael Montesinos

(1) Ya lo he dicho una vez: no creo en poéticas hechas por poetas. Todo eso es música celestial.

¿Influencias o herencias? En poesía, como en todo, bueno es tener padre reconocido. Estas son mis primeras influencias, es decir, mis poetas preferidos: el primero de todos, el pueblo andaluz, después, los poetas medievales españoles, anónimos y conocidos, Lope de Vega, ese maravilloso poema titulado "Epístola moral a Fabio," todo Antonio Machado, Rafael Alberti, y eso que queda de Bécquer cuando se olvidan sus *Rimas*.

(2) Cumplir un destino al cual yo soy ajeno.

(3) Contestado en el apartado 1. Lo que más estimo es lo que más me gusta.

(4) Rubén Darío.

(5) Los que todavía no he escrito.

(1) I have already said that I don't believe in poetic systems made up by poets. That's all moonshine.

Influences or heritages received? In poetry, as in everything else, it's a good thing to have a recognized father. My earliest influences, or rather, my favorite poets are, first of all, the Andalusian people, then, the Spanish medieval poets, both the anonymous ones and the ones we know the names of, Lope de Vega, the marvellous poem called the "Epístola moral a Fabio," all Antonio Machado, Rafael Alberti and what is left of Bécquer when his *Rimas* are forgotten.

(2) To fulfill a destiny which is alien to me.

(3) Answered under No. 1. What I think most highly of is what I like most.

(4) Rubén Darío.

(5) The ones I have not yet written.

Rafael Morales

(1) No creo en el arte por el arte, es decir, en la poesía por la poesía. Tampoco creo en la poesía por lo social, moda de nuestro tiempo. Creo en la poesía por el sentimiento. Y esa es la mía. Esto quiere decir que si un tema social me emociona yo lo canto; pero igual puede ocurrirme con un animal, con la rueda de un carro, o con un paisaje. No tengo ningún prejuicio formal ni temático. En ellos puede estar oculta la muerte de un poeta. Un ejemplo concreto es Pablo Neruda. Cuando canta los ríos de América—por no citar otros temas suyos—alcanza una altura lírica muy elogiable; cuando escribe lleno de odio no pasa de ser un panfletario que hasta me hace reir. Su prejuicio literario de que hay que hacer *obligatoriamente* una poesía de lucha de clases, le convierte en un prosista vulgar, en un politiquillo de arenga a las masas, o en un ridículo articulista.

(2) Todo poeta legítimo la primera vez que escribe un poema creo yo que no pretende otra cosa que dar salida a una emoción, a un sentimiento. No hablo—claro es—de los poetas que elaboran sus poemas como si fueran obras de artesanía. Estos son como el ebanista que hace un mueble para el despacho, otro para el hall, etc. El poeta es una fuerza centrífuga: va desde su corazón al de los demás. Por eso, yo no pretendo nada con mi poesía. Me alegra mucho, muchísimo, eso sí, que el sentimiento cristiano de mi poesía pueda hacer un bien, pueda hacer mejor a la gente. Pero no pienso en ello cuando voy a escribir.

(3) Lope, Quevedo, Góngora, San Juan de la Cruz, Fray Luis de León. Éstos son, entre los clásicos, los que me interesan en grado sumo, aunque considero interesantes a muchísimos más. Románticos interesantes: Espronceda y Bécquer. Otros del XIX: si se pudiera considerar a Rubén Darío como español, sería el único que me parecería sumamente interesante. Interesantes del siglo XX, excluyendo los actuales: excluyendo los vivos, que es lo que en este caso entiendo por actuales, creo interesantes en alto grado a Antonio Machado, Federico García Lorca y Miguel Hernández.

(4) Los que a mí más me interesan, sin decir con esto que no los haya tan buenos como ellos fuera de mi lista, son los siguientes: ingleses: Byron, Shelley y Keats; franceses: Baudelaire, Mallarmé y Rimbaud; italianos: Leopardi y Carducci; alemanes:

Rilke; portugueses: Gil Vicente y Antero de Quental; hispano-americanos: Rubén Darío. Con referencia a poetas de otras lenguas, no puedo juzgar.

(5) "Choto," y "Agonía del toro" de *Poemas del toro;* "Un potro muerto en una noche de luna," y "A un esqueleto de muchacha," de *El corazón y la tierra;* "Los tristes," y "Los idiotas," de *Los desterrados.*

(1) I do not believe in art for art's sake, that is to say, poetry for poetry's sake. Neither do I believe in poetry for social ends, the fashion of our age. I believe in poetry for feeling's sake. Which is what mine is. What I mean to say is that if a social theme moves me, I sing of it. But the same may happen because of an animal, the wheel of a cart, or a countryside. I have no preconceived notions about form or subject. A poet's death may be hidden within them. A concrete example is Pablo Neruda. When he sings of the rivers of America—not to quote other themes of his—he reaches a very high and very praiseworthy poetic level. When he writes full of hatred, he is no more than a pamphleteer who even makes me laugh. His literary prejudice that one should *obligatorily* write a poetry of class war makes him into a writer of mere vulgar prose, a minor politician who harangues the masses, or a ridiculous journalist.

(2) The first time any true poet writes a poem, I think he does not aim at anything more than freeing an emotion, a feeling. I am not, of course, speaking of poets who elaborate their poems as if they were handicraft. They are like the carpenter making a piece of furniture for the study, another for the hall, etc. The poet is a centrifugal force; his heart goes out towards that of others. For that reason, I am not trying to do anything with my poetry. I am glad, very glad indeed, if the Christian feeling in my poetry can do good and make people better. But I do not think about it when I am going to write.

(3) Lope de Vega, Quevedo, Góngora, Saint John of the Cross, Friar Luis de León. These are, among the classics, the ones that interest me supremely, though I consider very many others interesting. Interesting Romantics: Espronceda, and Bécquer. Others in the 19th century: If Rubén Darío could be considered a Spaniard, he would be the only one who would seem supremely interesting to me. Interesting poets in the 20th century, excluding present-day ones: excluding living poets, which is what I understand in this case by present-day ones, I believe Antonio Machado, Federico García Lorca and Miguel Hernández are highly interesting.

(4) Those who interest me most are the following, though this does not mean that there are not others as good as those on my list: English: Byron, Shelley and Keats; French: Baudelaire, Mallarmé and Rimbaud; Italian: Leopardi and Carducci; German: Rilke; Portuguese: Gil Vicente and Antero de Quental; Spanish American: Rubén Darío. With reference to poets in other languages, I cannot judge.

(5) (See original Spanish above.)

Eugenio de Nora

(1) Sobre estética o poética, véase lo que escribí para la *Antología consultada*. Es bastante extenso, por eso no me atrevo a reescribirlo. Hay, además, cosas sueltas que puedes ver en *Espadaña* con mi nombre o el de "Juan Martínez," que bordean el tema.

La influencia mayor, la vida misma, los hechos. Y entre las personas, sucesivamente, casi todos mis amigos en algún sentido: Don A. G. de Lama, Leopoldo Panero, Dámaso, etc. Y las obras, creo que de todo lo leído queda algo como sugestión, y como formación del espíritu selectivo, también. Pon a Juan Ramón Jiménez, Unamuno, Machado, Miguel Hernández y Neruda, en la técnica unas veces, en el espíritu otras, junto a los anteriores.

(2) Yo trato de hacer poesía, simplemente, pero creo en la transcendencia humana, social y hasta política de la poesía, y no me opongo, en principio, a "utilizarla" con fines exteriores, como arma incluso, a veces. La pretendida "poesía pura" es poesía, en general, rosa y desvitalizada. Lo "patético" abarca todo lo humano, expresado por la palabra poética.

(3, 4) Coincido, en general, con extraña objetividad, en apreciar la grandeza de los clásicos, de los grandes románticos, de algunos modernos. ¿Nombres? Nuestros Garcilaso, Fray Luis, Lope, Góngora, Quevedo, Espronceda y Bécquer, Rubén Darío y los citados en la pregunta 1. ¿De fuera? Especialmente Dante y Leopardi; Shakespeare, Byron y Shelley; Victor Hugo, Baudelaire y Rimbaud; Goethe y Schiller (no Rilke, en absoluto), Puskin, Walt Whitman. . . .

(5) Casi siempre son mis mejores poemas los que coinciden, por el tema, con aspectos profundos, con sentimientos o visiones muy enraizadas en el alma humana. (Hay poetas "superficiales" excelentes, pero eso no es mi fuerte, creo.) Hay tres o cuatro poemas que estimo en *Amor prometido,* casi todos los *Cantos al destino* y los de *España* y *Siempre;* la mitad, aproximadamente (entre ellos los tres finales), de *Contemplación.*

(1) As to my aesthetic or poetical ideas, see what I wrote for the *Antología consultada*. It is rather long, so I do not want to re-write it. There are, besides, odd things you can find in *Espadaña* with my name to them or that of "Juan Martínez," which touch on the matter.

The greatest influence is life itself, facts. As to people, successively almost all my friends in some sense or other— Don A. G. de Lama, Leopoldo Panero, Dámaso Alonso, etc. And as to works, I believe that something of a suggestion is left from everything one has read, and this is also like an education of the spirit of selection. Add Juan Ramón Jiménez, Unamuno, Machado, Miguel Hernández and Neruda to the above, sometimes for their technique and sometimes for the spirit of their writings.

(2) I simply try to make poetry, but I believe in the human, social and even political importance of poetry and I am not opposed on principle to "using" it for outer aims, even sometimes as a weapon. What claims to be "pure poetry" is generally rose-colored, devitalized poetry. "Feeling" embraces everything human, expressed in poetic speech.

(3, 4) In general I agree, with strange objectivity, in valuing the greatness of the classics, the great Romantics and some moderns. Names? Our Garcilaso, Friar Luis de León, Lope de Vega, Góngora, Quevedo, Espronceda and Bécquer, Rubén Darío and those quoted in the first question. In other countries? Especially Dante and Leopardi; Shakespeare, Byron and Shelley; Victor Hugo, Baudelaire and Rimbaud; Goethe and Schiller (not Rilke, by any means), Pushkin, Walt Whitman.

(5) Almost always my best poems are those which are at one, in their subject-matter, with deep aspects and feelings or visions very rooted in the human soul. (There are excellent "superficial" poets, but that is not my forte, I think.) There are three or four poems I think well of in *Amor prometido,* almost all the *Cantos al destino* and the poems of *España* and *Siempre;* half, approximately (among them, the three last ones) of *Contemplación.*

Blas de Otero

(1) Influencias: D'Annunzio, Gide y Schopenhauer, en los que encontré partes "expresadas" de mi "yo."

(2) Conforme.

(3) a) Sin preferencias: los que pusieron verdad con la cabeza y el corazón.

b) Baudelaire, Rimbaud.

c) Péguy.

(4) Eliot, Kipling.

(5) "Río," "Sierra," "Morir."

(1) Influences: D'Annunzio, Gide and Schopenhauer, in whom I found parts of my ego "expressed."

(2) That depends.

(3) a) No preferences; those who used head and heart for truth.

b) Baudelaire, Rimbaud.

c) Péguy.

(4) Eliot, Kipling.

(5) "Río," "Sierra," "Morir."

Leopoldo Panero

(1) Poética. No creo demasiado en las definiciones ni en los programas poéticos; en cuanto más simples, mejores, y en este sentido me atengo al enunciado de la poesía dado por don Antonio Machado como "la palabra del hombre en el tiempo." Creo, efectivamente, que la poesía está hecha desde la temporalidad y en lucha con ella y aspira a alzar la realidad, creando una realidad más alta, intensa y pura. Incidentalmente, puedo decirle a Vd. que de quien más he aprendido en este sentido, es decir, en cuanto a meditación sobre la poesía y reflexión sobre sus problemas es, probablemente, de Keats, a través de su epistolario.

Las primeras influencias formativas en el orden del tiempo fueron para mí las que pueden deducirse de la lectura, repetida muchas veces entre los dieciocho y los veintitantos años, de la primera antología de Gerardo Diego. Después la lectura más amplia, minuciosa y amorosa de las obras poéticas de don Miguel de Unamuno y de don Antonio Machado. También de la obra de Juan Ramón Jiménez, aunque creo que por su carácter ha tenido menos influencia en mí. Más tarde, mi primer contacto iluminado con la poesía inglesa, y dentro de la poesía inglesa muy fundamentalmente con la poesía de Keats y más que nada con la poesía de Wordsworth. Creo, sinceramente, que en Wordsworth he aprendido y convivido la poesía más que en ningún otro poeta. En esa época me sirvieron también de mucho los ensayos críticos sobre ese período de Matthew Arnold y, desde luego, la poesía de los contemporáneos, sobre todo la de Eliot, aunque hoy en día no esté de acuerdo con su sentido de la poesía hasta *Los cuatro Cuartetos.*

(2) Para mí la poesía es, como diría Arnold, "a criticism of life," o sea, una interpretación moral de la vida; no moral, claro es, en un sentido externo, sino en un sentido íntimo viviente. Pretendo, pues, con mi poesía hablar a los demás hombres, acompañarles y sentirme acompañado por ellos.

(3) Me han interesado de un modo constante el Romancero español, el Arcipreste de Hita, Jorge Manrique, Fray Luis de León y Lope de Vega. He aprendido, y continúo siempre aprendiendo, poesía en la obra de Shakespeare, que es, para mi modo de ver, el poeta más grande, dominador y vivo de los tiempos modernos. Entre los románticos prefiero, aparte de los ingleses que ya he mencionado más arriba, a Leopardi y a Baudelaire. La poesía alemana sólo la conozco a través de traducciones.

(4) Ya queda dicho más arriba los que más de cerca han influído en mí, pero tendría que mencionar a muchísimos más. Por ejemplo, dentro de la poesía hispanoamericana, han influído en mí y los considero interesantísimos desde el punto de vista de la evolución poética de habla española, Rubén Darío, César Vallejo y Pablo Neruda. Entre los más contemporáneos ingleses, Edith Sitwell. Entre los franceses, Éluard.

(5) No sé si los mejores, pero al menos el que yo prefiero es "La estancia vacía," todavía no recogido en libro, pero del que publiqué una larga entrega de más de mil versos en la revista "Escorial," hace más de diez años.

(1) Poetic system. I do not believe too much in poetic definitions or programs. The simpler, the better. In this sense, I support Don Antonio Machado's statement that poetry is "man's word in time." I believe, in fact, that poetry is created within time and in conflict with it and that it aspires towards enhancing reality by creating a higher, intenser, purer reality. Incidentally, I can tell you that the person I have learned most from in this matter of meditating on poetry and reflecting about its problems is probably Keats, in his letters.

The first formative influences in order of time were, for me, those that could be drawn from the reading, many times repeated, between eighteen and my early twenties, of Gerardo Diego's first anthology. Then a wider, more detailed and loving reading of the poetical works of Don Miguel de Unamuno and Don Antonio Machado. Also the work of

Juan Ramón Jiménez, though I believe that, because of its nature, it has had less influence on me. Later there was my first glowing contact with English poetry and, very fundamentally in English poetry, with the poetry of Keats, and more than anything, with Wordsworth's poetry. I believe sincerely that I learned more from Wordsworth and lived his poetry more than that of any other poet. At that time of my life, I found Matthew Arnold's essays on that period very useful and, of course, the poetry of contemporaries, above all that of Eliot, though nowadays I do not agree with the course of his poetry up to *Four Quartets.*

(2) For me poetry is, as Arnold would say, "a criticism of life" or rather, a moral interpretation of life. Not moral, of course, in an outer sense, but in a lively inner sense. I am therefore trying in my poetry to speak to other men, to accompany them and to feel myself accompanied by them.

(3) I have felt a constant interest in the Spanish Romancero, the Archpriest of Hita, Jorge Manrique, Friar Luis de León and Lope de Vega. I have learned, and still continue to learn, poetry from the work of Shakespeare who is, to my manner of seeing, the greatest, most dominating and living poet of modern times. Among the Romantics I prefer, apart from the English ones whom I have mentioned above, Leopardi and Baudelaire. I only know German poetry in translation.

(4) I have spoken above of those who have influenced me most fully, but I ought to mention a great many more. For instance, speaking of Spanish American poetry, I have felt the influence of the following poets, whom I consider most important from the point of view of the development of poetry in the Spanish language: Rubén Darío, César Vallejo and Pablo Neruda. Speaking of the latest English contemporaries, there is Edith Sitwell. Speaking of French ones, there is Éluard.

(5) I don't know if it is my best, but at any rate I prefer "La estancia vacía," which has not appeared in book form, but of which I published a long passage of more than a thousand lines in the review *Escorial,* more than ten years ago.

Salvador Pérez Valiente

(1) No me gustaría pedantizar con el bonito juego de la palabra, como en tantas oportunidades al uso. Sin fidelidad a la ocasión de la Historia o la vida no puede escribirse ni una mala línea que valga la pena. Yo trato de servir con mi poesía este mismo

instante de hoy, consoladoramente o no, pues lo de menos en el arte es la presupuesta moraleja. En cuanto a los procedimientos válidos de expresión, parecen justificarse todos, aún los más manifiestamente impuros, siempre que en el definitivo resultado aliente la sinceridad y la pasión, sin las cuales todo poema resulta malabarismo y cada "virtuoso" un pequeño traidor.

Influencias son: en primer lugar, la ya duradera de Rafael Alberti, a quien considero el más grande poeta de la contemporaneidad hispánica. Luego, esa gran lección viva de don Antonio Machado y acaso un poco, y muy ocasionalmente, la del malogrado levantino Miguel Hernández.

(2) Decir lo más desnudamente posible la pequeña historia de cada día; no pararse ante ninguna de las supuestas impurezas, temáticas y expresivas, servir un poco, desde la más insobornable intimidad, al consuelo y la gloria de mis ocasionales lectores. Servir, servir siempre desde lo hondo, con la misma vocación artesana del que labra la tierra y se recuesta en sus raíces. Si el poeta nos resulta sólo un encastillado celeste, de poco consuelo valdría su pobre gloria a largo plazo.

(3) No me va demasiado el sonoro badajo del romanticismo historicista, aunque mi poesía, en el arranque al menos, sea de clara filiación postromántica. Me va mejor la clara fuente de los Cancioneros populares de la Edad Media española y los poetas que, como Gil Vicente y Berceo, manan desde un profundo chorro. La serenidad clásica también de un Fray Luis de León, terso espejo de consolación y de hombría, de belleza y de varonil amor.

(4) No conozco demasiado bien la poesía europea contemporánea. Sólo un poeta extranjero, aunque de lengua castellana, León Felipe, influenció mis primeros pasos en la poesía. Su derramada vena cordial y sus característicos procedimientos tiñen todavía hoy algunos de mis poemas de agridulce humor.

(5) Si un poema es en esencia la desnudez y el cuero vivo, el puro llamear sin halagos y la aleccionadora experiencia de un instante de historia íntima, yo prefiero, entre los míos, el titulado "Letanía del abandono."

(1) I should not like to play the pedant by making fine plays upon words, as on so many current occasions. Without being faithful to the facts of History or life, not even a bad line of poetry could be written, or at least it would not be worth writing. I try to be useful to this present moment today in my poetry, whether what I write is consoling or not, since the least important thing in art is the preconceived moral. As to valid processes of expression, they all seem to

me to be justified, even the most obviously impure ones, so long as the positive result is instinct with sincerity and passion, without which all poems are mere juggling and all "virtuosos" little traitors.

As to influences; first of all, the lasting one of Rafael Alberti, whom I consider the greatest contemporary poet in Spanish. Then there is the great living lesson of Don Antonio Machado and perhaps a little, and very much by chance, that of the late poet from Murcia, Miguel Hernández.

(2) To tell the small tale of everyday as nakedly as possible; not to be held back because of any supposed impurities of subject-matter and expression; to be of some little use, however stubbornly personal I am, by giving consolation and glory to my casual readers. To be useful, always be useful in the deepest way, with the same artisan's vocation the man has who ploughs the earth and reclines on its roots. If the poet only turns out to be a haughty Olympian, his poor long-term glory would be little consolation.

(3) I am not too keen on the noisy clapper of historical Romanticism, though my poetry, in its beginnings at least, is obviously in a Post-Romantic tradition. I am more at my ease with the clear stream of the popular song-books of the Spanish Middle Ages and poets, such as Gil Vicente and Berceo, whose poetry gushes out from the depths. There is, besides, the classical serenity of Friar Luis de León, a limpid mirror of consolation, manliness, beauty and spirited love.

(4) I do not know contemporary European poetry well enough. Only one foreign poet, though in the Spanish language, León Felipe, influenced my first steps in poetry. His broad and cordial manner and his characteristic method still tinges some of my poems with bitter-sweet humor.

(5) If a poem is essentially nakedness and bareness, a pure, unflattering flame, the instructive experience of a moment of one's inner history, the poem of mine I prefer is the one called "Letanía del abandono."

José Luis Prado

(1) Si yo fuera capaz de criticar mi propia obra, mi obra sería perfecta o nula. En mi poesía predomina la ausencia casi completa de la imagen. Es una poesía directa y discursiva. Ausencia del tema mujer. Y creo que de toda ella fluye una nota fundamental de la esperanza.

Ningunas. Acaso, afluencias. La influencia es selecta y voluntaria. La afluencia se produce a pesar de uno.

(2) Un deporte. Una satisfacción íntima.

(3) Lope. Bécquer. Machado.

(4) Me gusta en traducción Goethe, el más traducible de todos. Quizá, Rilke.

(5) "Canto del Paraíso."

> (1) If I were capable of criticizing my own work, my work would be perfect or null and void. An almost complete lack of images dominates my poetry. It is direct and thoughtful poetry. Absence of woman as a theme. And I believe that a fundamental note of hope flows through it all.
>
> No influences. A flow of affluents, perhaps. Influences are selective and voluntary. Affluents are in spite of one.
>
> (2) A game. Inward satisfaction.
>
> (3) Lope de Vega. Bécquer. Machado.
>
> (4) I like Goethe in translation; he is the most translatable of them all. Perhaps, Rilke.
>
> (5) "Canto del Paraíso."

Luis Rosales

(1) No tengo ideas sobre la poesía.

Las influencias actuales sobre mí son: Unamuno, Antonio Machado, después, la Generación de la Dictadura y, naturalmente, la de los poetas de mi generación.

(2) Quiero conocerme a mí mismo—conocer al hombre y a mí mismo —a través de este vehículo de conocimiento que es la poesía.

(3) Los de siempre. Jorge Manrique. Garcilaso. Camões. Lope. Conde de Villamediana. Bécquer. Los demás ya los he dicho.

(4) La nómina sería infinita. Wordsworth. Antero de Quental. Rilke. Baudelaire.

(5) Los que deseo hacer.

> (1) I have no ideas about poetry.
>
> The present influences on me are Unamuno and Antonio Machado, then the *Generación de la Dictadura* and, naturally, the poets of my own generation.

(2) I want to know myself, to know mankind and myself, through the vehicle of knowledge known as poetry.

(3) The usual ones. Jorge Manrique. Garcilaso. Camões. Lope de Vega. Count of Villamediana. Bécquer. I have already spoken of the others.

(4) The list would be interminable. I should say Wordsworth. Antero de Quental. Rilke and Baudelaire.

(5) The ones I want to write.

José Suárez Carreño

(1) La poesía, para mí, como la literatura, es en último término testimonio. Creo que el estado de poesía psicológicamente hablando, es un estado de necesidad. En cuanto a técnica y preocupación por los problemas formales en la poesía, me parecen una etapa necesaria en la que el poeta no se logra pero se prepara para lo que yo considero etapa final de todo creador, la sencillez. Si hubiera que resumir la poesía de alguna manera, yo lo haría en esta frase: poder de evidencia. La poesía, por serlo, hace iluminadamente evidente lo que el razonamiento demuestra o la simple literatura pretende describir y explicar.

Creo que todo poeta tiene dos tipos de influencia: una, la de la rama o linaje de poetas que le precedieron y guardan con él una irremediable afinidad; y otra, la de los contemporáneos inmediatamente anteriores que le dan el gusto y la manera para que su poesía sea actual. Mi rama puede ser: Jorge Manrique, Quevedo, Antonio Machado, Miguel de Unamuno y, en lo de ahora, Vicente Aleixandre y Miguel Hernández. Influencias o como quiera llamarse, de contemporáneos que se leen y contagian de alguna manera con sus menudos poéticos, creo que entre otros pueden ser: Jorge Guillén, Cernuda, Neruda.

(2) Empecé a hacer poesía bajo el efecto de un libro: *Espadas como labios,* de Vicente Aleixandre. Lo curioso es que empecé a hacerlo porque este libro me hizo creer en la posibilidad de una poesía que no siéndolo cerradamente en su formal limitación, podía servir para expresarme. Así, en los comienzos, la poesía fué para mí un intento ciego y alocado de mi propia expresión. Hoy es algo más, es entendimiento. Entender las cosas a través de la simplicidad en el fondo más que racional de la imagen.

(3) Jorge Manrique, Arcipreste, Berceo, Fray Luis de León, San Juan de la Cruz, Quevedo, Herrera, Lope, Bécquer, Espronceda, Antonio Machado, Unamuno, Juan Ramón Jiménez, Jorge Guillén, Federico García Lorca, Alberti, Vicente Aleixandre, Luis Cernuda, Manuel Altolaguirre, Larrea, Gerardo Diego, Miguel Hernández, José Luis Hidalgo.

(5) "El soldado y su muerte," "Recuerdo de los muertos," "El padrón de piedra," "El enlace."

(1) Poetry, for me, like literature, is, in the last resort, a testimony. I believe that the state of poetry, psychologically speaking, is a state of need. As to technique and a care for the formal problems of poetry, they seem to be a necessary stage in which the poet does not succeed but gets ready for what I consider the final stage of every creator—simplicity. If poetry had to be summarized in any way, I should summarize it in the words, "power of evidence." Poetry, being what it is, makes luminously clear what reason demonstrates or ordinary literature tries to write and explain.

I believe that every poet has two kinds of influences: first, the branch or line of poets who preceded him and have an inescapable affinity with him; secondly, that of the contemporaries immediately prior to him from whom he obtains the taste and manner which make his poetry of the present day. My branch might be Jorge Manrique, Quevedo, Antonio Machado, Miguel de Unamuno and, in the present, Vicente Aleixandre and Miguel Hernández. As to the influence or whatever it may be called of contemporaries the reading of whom infects one in some way with poetic mannerisms, I think that among others, this may have happened with Jorge Guillén, Cernuda and Neruda.

(2) I began to write poetry because of the effect of a book, *Espadas como labios,* by Vicente Aleixandre. The curious thing is that I began because this book made me believe in the possibility of a poetry which was not poetry in the narrow sense of limitations of form, and was thus able to be of use to me in helping me to express myself. So that, at the beginning, poetry was for me a blind, mad attempt to find my own means of expression. Today it is something further—understanding, understanding things by means of simplicity in the more than rational depths of imagery.

(3, 4, 5) (See original Spanish above.)

José María Valverde

(1) En algún sitio he dicho que la primera obligación de una poesía es la de ser inconsecuente con el ideario poético de su autor, pero que este ideario es muy conveniente como estímulo, como cauce de la fruición en la forma pura, del regodeo en el crear. ¿Cuál sería entonces mi ideario? Naturalmente, un ideario de impureza estética, de amplitud y de enriquecimiento. La poesía debe parecerse a las artes no-lingüísticas en la belleza autónoma,

suficiente, de sus productos. Por ser de palabra, debe siempre cumplir su responsabilidad de entrañar la totalidad del hombre y su destino, pero no como la filosofía y la ciencia, pretendiendo saber cosas y dar respuestas, sino, más modestamente, narrando, describiendo, echando un poco de luz encima de las cosas, dando un testimonio directo de nuestra vida. Cada época tiene sus problemas poéticos, "los defectos de sus virtudes"; la nuestra, falta de visión de la realidad y, claro está, ausencia de imaginación.

¿Mis influencias formativas? Ante todo mi educación católica, fielmente conservada en lo que un católico debe conservar mientras lo es. Luego, aparte de las lecturas poéticas, mi doctorado en Filosofía, de que no he salido ileso.

(3, 4) Los poetas que me gustan más son, entre otros muchos, Homero, El Romancero, Jorge Manrique, Fray Luis, Baudelaire, Unamuno, Antonio Machado, Wordsworth y Rilke.

(5) Hasta ahora, si hubiera de quedarme con cuatro poemas míos, elegiría: "Despedida ante el tiempo," de *La espera;* "Más allá del umbral," *Cuadernos hispanoamericanos;* "Donde Dios se complace," *Alcalá, 1;* "Montes de azul" en *Cuadernos hispano-americanos.*

(1) Somewhere I have written that the first duty of poetry is to be in disagreement with the poetic ideas of its author, but that these ideas are very convenient as a stimulus, as a channel for the fruition of pure form, for a delight in creation. What are my own poetic ideas, then? Naturally, they imply aesthetic impurity, breadth and enrichment. Poetry should be like the non-linguistic arts in the autonomous, satisfying beauty of its production. Being in words, it should always fulfill its duty of containing the whole of man and his destiny, but not, like philosophy and science, seek to know things and give answers. No, it must be more modest than they. It must relate, describe and throw a little light on things, giving a direct testimony about our existence. Each age has its poetical problems, "the defects of its virtues." The defects of ours are a lack of vision about reality and, naturally, an absence of imagination.

My formative influences? Before all, my Catholic education, faithfully conserved in what a Catholic should keep to, so long as he is one. Then, apart from my own reading of poetry, there was my doctorate in Philosophy, which has not left me unscathed.

(3, 4) The poets I like most are, among many others, Homer, the Romancero, Jorge Manrique, Friar Luis de León, Baudelaire, Unamuno, Antonio Machado, Wordsworth and Rilke.

(5) Up to the present, if I had to choose only four poems of mine, I should select: "Despedida ante el tiempo," from *La espera;* "Más allá del umbral," *Cuadernos hispanoameri- canos;* "Donde Dios se complace," *Alcalá,* 1; "Montes de azul" in *Cuadernos hispanoamericanos.*

Luis Felipe Vivanco

(1) Mis ideas sobre la poesía en general, aunque aplicadas a algunos poetas españoles contemporáneos, las expongo en mi libro: *In- troducción a la poesía española contemporánea.* Creo que debe haber bastantes de esas ideas dentro del libro (no me he dedicado a comprobarlo). Sin embargo, entresaco unas cuantas:
"En vez de la evasión o ensoñación de los románticos yo creo que la poesía consiste en estar más cerca siempre, más cerca de una realidad, haciéndola, a fuerza de imaginación o de palabra concreta imaginativa, más real de lo que era." (pag. 9)
"El libro de poesía que interrumpe—y que nos deja interrumpidos o en suspenso—señala el momento de la constitución de un nuevo y auténtico poeta en su palabra." (pag. 10)
"La poesía, no sólo no es un sueño: es lo más real; no sólo no es un monólogo: es un diálogo esencial y constitutivo del hombre en su ser temporal o histórico." (pag. 15)
"La poesía es un modo de ser hombre en la palabra y *contando con ella.*" (pag. 15)
"Gracias al lenguaje como habla y a sus intenciones propias, el poeta, al asumir la realidad radical de su propia existencia, asume también la realidad existencial de los demás. Y además, al añadir las intenciones de su *decir* a las del habla como materia, le va a dar a la existencia de los demás una realidad que no tenía en su lenguaje convencional y disminuído." (pag. 17)
"El poema es el que mide las demás realidades a través de la realidad radical humana y, por tanto, a través de la libertad y por eso mismo, es el que mide la historia con medidor o metro de intrahistoria." (pag. 30)
Todas estas citas son entresacadas del prólogo o primer capítulo, titulado: "Poesía lírica e intrahistoria." Debe haber muchas más a través de las 660 páginas del libro.

La influencia más importante de mi vocación poética ha sido, desde niño, la del paisaje castellano (y, en general, la geografía de España). Hay en mí desproporción grande entre lo que me emociona la geografía—con emoción religiosa—y lo poco o nada que me emociona la historia. Después del paisaje, los místicos, también castellanos, y a través de ellos—y en castellano—la Biblia. La manera de contar de la Biblia: en el Génesis y el

Exodo, en los Jueces, en los I y II de los Reyes, en los Evangelios, y los Salmos, tan dividuos y antiacadémicos. Y los Profetas, que volvían todo poéticamente para utilizarlo como maldición o anatema. Otra influencia poética importante ha sido la de *La isla misteriosa,* de Julio Verne, que leí antes que el Robinsón, y en general sus mejores novelas de viajes, las más épicas, aquellas en que se inventa la epopeya del cientificismo. El Quijote y las novelas de Cervantes me han influído mucho después. Y presidida por esta influencia, la que yo llamaría novela de humanidad y de aventura humana. O la gran novela rusa del XIX (en la que el sentido de humanidad llega a predominar sobre el de aventura), y la inglesa (en que el sentido de aventura potencia el de humanidad). También he recibido influencia de los presocráticos griegos, y de los pintores del Renacimiento y de algunos filósofos modernos: Bergson y Max Scheler, Ortega y Heidegger. (A Unamuno, incluso como filósofo, lo cuento siempre entre los poetas, lo mismo que a Antonio Machado.) Mi formación plástica de arquitecto ha debido influir en mi poesía. Y atrás de ella toda la plástica moderna, desde Altamira hasta Miró y los abstractos. Por encima de las otras está la de algunos muertos y vivos del 98: Unamuno, Machado (Antonio y Manuel), Azorín y Baroja.

(2) La poesía es exigencia de más realidad (existencial y cósmica). Con mi poesía procuro el mejoramiento del mundo, pero a través del mejoramiento del alma. Sin éste, el primero no es mejoramiento humano sino, a la larga, inhumano. (Durante el XIX, los "malditos" franceses son los que más han hecho por el mejoramiento del alma: Baudelaire, Rimbaud, Laforgue, Verlaine, Victor Francis Jammes, que no es "maldito" del todo pero merecía serlo.)

(3) Voy a citar algunas preferencias: poetas de lengua española (de España y América), gallegos y catalanes: *Cantar de Mío Cid,* canciones galaicas, romances viejos, cancionero tradicional-popular, "Coplas" de Manrique, Berceo, Santillana, Juan Ruiz, Gil Vicente, Garcilaso, Camões, Aldana, Fray Luis, Espinosa, San Juan de la Cruz, Rioja, Caro, anónimo de la "Epístola moral," Lope, Villamediana, Quevedo, Góngora, Espronceda, Zorrilla, Gutiérrez Nájera, Bécquer, Verdaguer, Martí, Rosalía Castro, Machado (Antonio y Manuel), Rubén Darío, Unamuno, Maragall, Gabriela Mistral. Y los poetas incluídos en mi "Introducción."

Miles de poetas contemporáneos que se me imponían desde el primer momento: *Cántico,* de Guillén; *Sobre los ángeles,* de Alberti; *Romancero gitano,* de García Lorca; *Trilce,* de Vallejo; el poema *Residencia en la tierra,* de Neruda; *La destrucción o el amor,* de Aleixandre; *El rayo que no cesa,* de Miguel Hernández; *Abril,* de Luis Rosales; *Alondra de verdad,* de Gerardo

Diego; *La estancia vacía,* de Leopoldo Panero; *Hijos de la ira,* de Dámaso Alonso; *Sombra del paraíso,* de Vicente Aleixandre; *Poeta en Nueva York,* de Federico García Lorca; *La casa encendida,* de Luis Rosales; *Retornos de lo vivo lejano,* de Rafael Alberti.

(4) Péguy, Claudel, Rilke, Apollinaire, Milosz, Ungaretti, Montale, Fernando Pessoa, Éluard, Trakl. No conozco bien los poetas en lengua inglesa. No me gustan traducidos, ni Yeats, ni Eliot, sí en cambio D. H. Lawrence.

(5) Poesía en *El descampado* y *Continuación de la vida.*

(1) In my book *Introduction to Contemporary Spanish Poetry,* I explain my ideas about poetry in general, even though I apply them to certain contemporary Spanish poets. I believe there are a number of these ideas in the book, though I have not set myself the task of finding this out. All the same, I will choose a few of them:

"Instead of the evasions or dreams of the Romantics, I believe that poetry consists of drawing nearer and nearer to a reality, making it more real than it was before, by dint of the imagination and concretely imaginative words." (page 9)

"The book of poems which is interrupted—and leaves us interrupted and wondering—marks a moment in which a new, authentic poet is constituted by his words." (page 10)

"Poetry is not only not a dream. It is the most real of things. It is not only not a monologue. It is an essential and constitutive dialogue of man in his temporal or historical being." (page 15)

"Poetry is a way of being a man in words and *counting on them.*" (page 15)

"Thanks to language as speech and his own intentions, the poet, when he assumes the radical reality of his own existence, also assumes the existential reality of that of others. Besides, he adds the intentions hidden within his *speaking* to those of material speech. Thus he gives the existence of others a reality that was not there before in their conventional and diminished language." (page 17)

"The poem is what measures other realities against radical human realities and, therefore, against liberty. For that very reason, it is what measures history with the measure of interhistory." (page 30)

All these quotations have been drawn from the foreword or first chapter entitled "Lyrical and Interhistorical Poetry." There are sure to be many more throughout the book's 660 pages.

The most important influence which has led me to write poetry has been, from childhood, the Castilian countryside (and, in general, the geography of Spain). There is a wide lack of proportion within me between my geographical emotion—which is religious emotion—and my small or non-existent historical emotion. After the countryside come the mystics, who are also Castilian. Through them—and in Castilian—the Bible. The way things are told in the Bible, in Genesis and Exodus, in Judges, in the First and Second Books of Kings, in the Gospels. And the Psalms, so individual and anti-academic. And the Prophets, who turned everything round poetically, so as to use it for curses or anathema. Another important influence was that of *The Mysterious Island* by Jules Verne, which I read before *Robinson Crusoe*. And, in general, his best travel novels, the most epic ones, in which he invented the scientific epic. *Don Quixote* and the exemplary novels of Cervantes influenced me a long time afterwards. Under this influence, I turned to what I should call the novel of mankind and the human adventure. Or the great Russian novels of the 19th century (in which the sense of brotherhood manages to predominate over the sense of adventure) and the English novels (in which the sense of adventure is more powerful than that of brotherhood). I have also received an influence from the pre-Socratic Greeks and the painters of the Renaissance and one or two modern philosophers such as Bergson, Max Scheler, Ortega and Heidegger. (I consider Unamuno as being among the poets even as a philosopher, just like Antonio Machado.) My training in the plastic arts as an architect must have influenced my poetry, and what lies behind my training, all the modern plastic arts from Altamira to Miró and the abstract painters. More than others, there is that of some of the dead and living writers of the 1898 generation—Unamuno, Machado (Antonio and Manuel), Azorín and Baroja.

(2) Poetry is a demand for more reality (existential and cosmic). I attempt to better the world with my poetry, but through the betterment of the soul. Without that, the former is not human betterment but, at long last, inhuman. (During the 19th century the "poètes maudits" were the ones to do the most for the betterment of the soul—Baudelaire, Rimbaud, Laforgue, Verlaine and Victor Francis Jammes. This last poet was not altogether "maudit," but he deserved to be so.)

(3) I am going to mention some of my preferences. Poets in the Spanish language (Spain and America), Galicians and Catalans. The *Song of Mío Cid,* Galician songs, old ballads,

traditional popular song-books, the "Coplas" of Manrique, Berceo, Santillana, Juan Ruiz, Gil Vicente, Garcilaso, Camões, Aldana, Friar Luis de León, Espinosa, Saint John of the Cross, Rioja, Caro, the anonymous writer of the "Epístola moral," Lope de Vega, Villamediana, Quevedo, Góngora, Espronceda, Zorrilla, Gutiérrez Nájera, Bécquer, Verdaguer, Martí, Rosalía de Castro, Machado (Antonio and Manuel), Rubén Darío, Unamuno, Maragall, Gabriela Mistral. And the poets included in my "Introduction."

Thousands of contemporary poets have made an impression on me from the first moment: Guillén's *Cántico, Sobre los ángeles* by Alberti, the *Romancero gitano* by García Lorca, *Trilce* by Vallejo, Neruda's *Residencia en la tierra, La destrucción o el amor* by Aleixandre, *El rayo que no cesa* by Miguel Hernández, *Abril* by Luis Rosales, *Alondra de verdad* by Gerardo Diego, *La estancia vacía* by Leopoldo Panero, *Hijos de la ira* by Dámaso Alonso, *Sombra del Paraíso* by Vicente Aleixandre, *Poeta en Nueva York* by Federico García Lorca, *La casa encendida* by Luis Rosales, *Retornos de lo vivo lejano* by Rafael Alberti.

(4) Péguy, Claudel, Rilke, Apollinaire, Milosz, Ungaretti, Montale, Fernando Pessoa, Éluard, Trakl. I don't know the English poets properly. I don't care for the translations either of Yeats or Eliot, but I do for those of D. H. Lawrence.

(5) In my opinion they are in *El descampado* and *Continuación de la vida.*

NOTES TO CHAPTER 11

1. *Poesía española antología 1919-1931* (Madrid, 1932), p. 19. We thank all the poets whose answers appear in these pages. We also thank several others who replied to the same questions and who were originally included in an earlier and much longer unpublished draft of this book. This version unfortunately had to be laid aside as too unwieldy, and their answers with it, though with many regrets.
2. *Ibid.*, p. 56.
3. *Ibid.*, p. 77.
4. *Ibid.*
5. *Ibid.*, p. 109.
6. *Ibid.*, pp. 149-150.
7. *Ibid.*, pp. 169-170.
8. See Chapter 2, Note 4.
9. *Poesía española antología 1919-1931*, pp. 218-219.
10. *Ibid.*, p. 236.
11. See Chapter 2, Note 6.

12. *Poesía española antología 1919-1931*, p. 298.
13. *Ibid.*, p. 402.
14. *Ibid.*, p. 423.
15. *Ibid.*, p. 447.

The Position of the Poet in Modern Spain.
The Censorship

The social and economic position of the poet was made a central theme of discussion at the First Poetry Congress in Segovia in 1952, but no very satisfactory light was thrown on the matter. It was agreed that the poet was an indigent member of society, both in Spain and outside it, and that he could not subsist on his poetry. Someone even referred to poets as the proletarians of literature.

Obviously, however, the writing of poetry has acquired increasing prestige in Spain throughout the century. The régime prides itself on having produced poets in great quantity; an excessive number of their writings have been printed, for instance, in the government-subsidized review *Poesía española*. The relative freedom of expression allowed to poets is perhaps due to a desire to encourage them to publish.

Poets have the entrée to a limited number of social gatherings on the strength of their writings. It is not unusual to hear them introduced as So-and-So the poet, though a few dislike this. They are more highly thought of in other spheres of life because of their poetry. For instance, the "Neoclassical" poet Jesús Juan Garcés (1917-   ) (first known through *Garcilaso*) found that they liked him the better at his naval officers' training college because he was a poet.

One of the reasons for the great insistence on poetry in modern Spain is the lesser brilliance of writing in other fields since the Civil War. And one of its results is that the writing of poetry now extends to classes in which it was formerly very rare indeed. We have seen examples of this in the chapter on revolutionary poetry. Another remarkable poet, Manuel Pilares (1928-   ), started life as an Asturian miner. Postmen, waiters in cafés, shoeblacks, or coach conductors may unexpectedly recite or refer to poems they have written.

As a more disputable corollary to this, we find that far more poetry which could be described as "domestic" is now being written. We have already noticed how many poets, upon marrying, have begun to write about their family life. This may seem the natural thing for them to do, but it would probably not have been thought so in earlier centuries. Even in the last century Coventry Patmore was thought of as exceptional in this. It is probably a characteristic of poetry everywhere today to choose much of its subject-matter from the world immediately surrounding it. But María Elvira Lacaci, who was awarded the *Adonais* Prize for 1956, carries this to extremes. She constantly writes, in very prosaic language, about how uncomfortable life is in her boarding-house. Other poems are entitled "En el autobús" (In the Bus), "En el tranvía" (In the Tram), and "Cine de barrio" (Suburban Cinema). She compares her desire to express her feelings in words with putting litter in the dustbin, which other people will afterwards scratch about in to see if there is anything worth having. But, at times, she is even less poetic:

> ayer tarde,
> en el andén del "Metro,"
> escuché a mis espaldas: "Don Ramón,
> ¿también usted con corbata de plástico?"
> "Pues verá . . . entro pronto al trabajo, el café
> me lo bebo de pie . . . ¡se tarda tanto en hacer el nudo!
> y con esto, se coloca y ya está."
> Me volví,
> un vejete simpático,
> pobremente vestido. Sonriente. Expansivo,
> le explicaba a su amigo—a modo de disculpa—
> la adopción voluntaria
> del novísimo invento. "A mis años . . ." decía.[1]

> Yesterday afternoon
> On the underground platform,
> I heard behind me; "Don Ramón,
> So you've got a tie made of plastics too?"
> "Well, you see . . . I have to go to work early. I drink
> My coffee standing . . . It takes such a time to tie the knot!
> With this one, you just put it on and that's all."
> I turned round.
> A nice old fellow
> Poorly dressed. Smiling. Expansively
> Explaining like that to his friend—so as to excuse himself—
> Why he had voluntarily adopted
> This very new invention. "At my age," he said.

And María Beneyto, who had a special mention in the *Adonais* Prize for 1955, writes a poem called *En el mercado* (At the Market) which describes the things she is buying for her kitchen: "Aún quiero aceitunas. Y naranjas. / Y un cadáver de ave."[2] (I want, besides, olives. And oranges. / And the corpse of a bird.)

The writing of poetry is certainly not profitable in Spain. Poetry reviews generally do not pay. *Poesía española* is an exception, and the 150 pesetas a poet receives for a page of poetry in that paper is regarded as the highest possible remuneration. But other benefits may be obtained. There are many more literary prizes in Spain than in most countries. These are of varying sums, and books of poetry may be awarded a prize up to 25,000 pesetas.[3]

Juegos florales (Floral Games, that is to say, poetry competitions ending in a public recitation and prize-giving) are also held all over Spain. Any Spanish poet, even though he does not belong to the locality, can send in his contribution on the set subject. The winner receives a money award.

There have been many poetry collections which publish books of poems by single authors; the majority of the copies are sent to subscribers. If these collections pay at all, it is not usually more than 300 to 350 pesetas. A few books of poetry are published by the official Editora Nacional, which pays some ten times more.

Until recently, many poets paid for the printing of their own books; rising costs are now making this increasingly more difficult to do. Three hundred copies is quite a usual number for a publication of this sort. The cost for a fairly short book of poems (25 to 30 pages of verse) would have been 1,500 pesetas in 1941, 5,000 in 1951 and about 10,000 in 1961.

Besides literary reviews, of which there have been a great number (either subsidized or paid for by private individuals), poetry is popularized in modern Spain by public recitations. There was a great vogue for these in the early 1950's, started in 1948 by Conrado Blanco, the owner and manager of the Teatro de Lara, Madrid. He would hold recitations, called *Alforjas para la poesía* (Saddle-bags for Poetry) in his theater every Sunday morning. (The names of the poets were taken, one by one, out of an ornamental saddle-bag hung over a chair on the stage.) These *Alforjas* became social events, but the audiences showed no discrimination, for they would boo interesting poets such as Panero and Valverde and applaud flamboyant poetasters.

In 1952, Spain held the first of three Poetry Congresses. It was supposed to be international but, as we have already seen,[4] only Roy Campbell, Vandercammen (and Serpa) came specially from abroad for the occasion. At the second Congress in Salamanca, 1953, Ungaretti was present. Flowers were placed on Unamuno's tomb, with a speech by Ridruejo, who also gave the closing address of the Congress, declaring that the exiled poets and those in Spain were all one in the sight of Poetry. The last Congress was held in Santiago de Compostela, in 1954.

Since the Civil War, poets are less often than before men of university standing. Let us take the poets specially commented on in this present work. Of these we find that, in the *generación de la Dictadura,* Salinas, Guillén, Alonso, and Cernuda all worked in important universities abroad. Among the considerably greater number of poets after 1939, however, only Gaos, Bleiberg, and Nora have achieved this distinction, in the United States and Switzerland respectively. Bousoño lectures at the Faculty of Letters, Madrid, Valverde is at the University of Barcelona. Morales and Pérez Valiente were students in Madrid. Among the youngest poets of today, Claudio Rodríguez and Carlos Sahagún are now (1962) readers at Cambridge and Exeter Universities respectively.

Writers in contemporary Spain tend to derive from slightly poorer families than before. Some people have thought that the increasing lack of an academic background has led to a lower standard of poetry-writing. Yet no one would deny the poetic excellence (especially as a deeply well-informed technician of verse) of Miguel Hernández, who received only the bare minimum of formal education.

The Censorship

All books printed in Spain are required to be submitted to censorship (even when they are intended only for sale abroad). The exact effect of this on the writers is very difficult to assess. The object of the censorship is to examine books to see whether they attack religion, the state, morals, and so on. A book is usually read by a single censor, who answers a questionnaire stating whether it does in fact contain such attacks or not. The questionnaire does not, however, inquire what the author defends. That is to say, the authorities are not concerned with directing what he writes, but merely with preventing him from expressing views of which they particularly disapprove. In some of the books written in Mussolini's Italy and many of those published in modern Russia, the course of a work of literature or scholarship will suddenly be held up by unexpected, fulsome, and unconvincing eulogies of the government and what it is supposed to stand for. Nothing of the sort occurs in Spanish books.

We may assume, then, that their statements are more or less spontaneous, though there may be reticences. Or a writer may say something in a less direct manner than he would do in a country enjoying complete freedom of expression. He may acquire skill in this and, in the end, feel very little hampered in his writing. This is obviously what many great authors did in past ages, and we do not think less of them for that. Indeed, a very intelligent Spanish novelist, who worked for a time in the censorship, defended himself by saying that a writer's artistry was improved by the discipline of having to impose restrictions on himself because of a censorship. This may be true in Spain, but it would not apply to all censorships. And, even in Spain, certain interesting works have been prevented from appearing for no very valid reason.

NOTES TO CHAPTER 12

1. *Humana voz* (Madrid, 1957), p. 67 ["El invento"].
2. *Tierra viva* (Madrid, 1956), p. 14 ["El mercado"].
3. *National Prize,* 25,000 pesetas, awarded to Adriano del Valle, Ginés de Albareda, Valverde, Rosales, Ridruejo, Hierro, Morales, Maruri, Diego, Montesinos, José Luis Prado and Luis López Anglada. One year it was not awarded, but would in the ordinary course of events have gone to García Nieto; he was, however, declared, after considerable discussion, to be ineligible because he had, on a previous occasion, received a similar award (the Garcilaso Prize), specially created for his benefit. *Adonais Prize,* 5,000 pesetas, founded 1943, awarded to Suárez Carreño, Hierro, Molina, Alfonso Moreno, Gaos, Lorenzo Gomis, Juana García Noreña (see Chapter 3), Claudio Rodríguez, Fernández Spencer, José Angel Valente, Javier de Bengoechea, María Elvira Lacaci, Carlos Sahagún, Rafael Soto, Francisco Brines, Mariano Roldán and Luis Feria. *Boscán Prize,* 5,000 pesetas, founded 1951, awarded to Alfonso Costafreda, Blas de Otero, Crémer, Nora, Gómez Nisa, Medina, Concha Zardoya, Goytisolo, Lizano, Caballero Bonald and Santos Torroella. Other prizes exist, especially in the provinces.
4. See Chapter 10.

13

Looking Back

No book of this length could hope even to mention the names of all the writers who have published poetry in modern Spain. Our claim is to have drawn attention to representative figures and to give an idea of the different kinds of poetry which have been written since 1939. By the very nature of things, there must be many omissions, some perhaps of real poetic quality. All we can say is that up to the present moment (1962), no new style or movement has appeared in Spanish poetry written in Spain which is not somehow accounted for in these pages.

Having said this, there is little left to do but to recapitulate, in a much briefer form, what we have already said in the course of this book.

In the early years of the present century, first Rubén Darío and then the Machados, Unamuno, and Juan Ramón Jiménez reacted against the rhetoric of late nineteenth-century poetry. This reaction is nowadays known as *Modernismo.* The movement owed much to French poetry of the Parnassian and Symbolist schools, and introduced the use of *correspondances,* in Baudelaire's sense, and of what we have here called "allusive imagery." New, less rarefied subject-matter was sometimes chosen. For instance, Antonio Machado and Unamuno expressed their feelings and thoughts by describing the things around them—countrysides and even the objects in a room.

A younger generation followed. Some paid great attention to perfection of form, as Juan Ramón Jiménez had done; the foremost of these was probably Gerardo Diego. Others, such as Cernuda, wrote of their inner thoughts and feelings in language which would have seemed prosaic to an earlier generation. Others, such as Lorca and the early Alberti, adapted popular Spanish (and particularly Andalusian) verse-forms to a modern style which owed something to Surrealism. Vicente Aleixandre at one time wrote prose poems under the acknowledged influence of Freud; later, his work became more

237

explicit. He had, however, learned from Freud and the Surrealists to use poetic imagery more for what it suggested than for what it said logically. The *correspondances* and allusive imagery of other poets had also been tending the same way.

This new generation of poets, writing in the years immediately before the Civil War, wished to revive interest in those Spanish poets of the past who, they felt, had been neglected. The Góngora Centenary in 1927 was a special occasion, Góngora meaning to Spanish poets much what Donne meant to English poets in the same years. Dámaso Alonso published his anthology of medieval poetry. But it was Miguel Hernández and Germán Bleiberg, two poets politically of the Left, who wrote in the style of certain other sixteenth-century Spanish poets, such as Garcilaso.

Partly the example of these two poets, partly a traditionalist reaction following the Civil War, caused the poets of 1939 and afterwards to express themselves in a Neo-Renaissance form known in contemporary Spain as "Neoclassicism." The ideas underlying this movement are to be found in Ernesto Giménez Caballero's *Arte y estado*. Religious and political issues were no longer thought of as problems. Even the beloved became a Petrarchan abstraction, as she had done in Germán Bleiberg's *Sonetos amorosos* (1936). Ridruejo, García Nieto, and other poets cultivated the sonnet and other severely regular verse-forms, besides restricting their imagery. Special words, such as *voz, costado, río,* and *temprano* were used by Hernández, Bleiberg, Ridruejo, García Nieto, and others with great frequency, and were intentionally made to cover a wide variety of meanings.

Since most of the older poets had emigrated as a result of the Civil War and were officially disapproved of inside Spain, there was an opportunity in 1939 and the years following for minor poets to present themselves to the public as important figures. Ridruejo on the other hand wrote an energetic preface to Antonio Machado's poems, saying what an important poet he was, in spite of his declared Republican sympathies. The publication of Aleixandre's *Sombra del paraíso* and Dámaso Alonso's *Hijos de la ira* in 1944 made young poets wish to show that they too could write in the styles used by poets just before the Civil War. Thus the fashion for "Neoclassicism" began to decline. The end of the World War, too, had some influence on this development, since poets no longer felt that religious and political issues could be set aside in the "Neoclassical" manner.

Facilities for publishing in reviews and in book form encouraged many young poets to take to print, but much of their work had no definite character. They fitted into groups—the Aleixandre school, with Carlos Bousoño as its poetical theorist, a few "Neo-Romantics," such as Rafael Montesinos and Salvador Pérez Valiente, young Catholic poets, such as José María Valverde, and poets of left-wing sympathies, such as Gabriel Celaya, Eugenio de Nora, and José Hierro. There was also the Cordoba school, led by Ricardo Molina, which mingled its reflections on religion and love with observations of the life going on around them. All these poets followed on in the tradition which had begun with Darío, and the influence of one or another of the older poets was generally predominant in each of them. Thus, work of quite a varied character was produced, but no poet stood out definitely among the others.

As we have seen, many of the contemporary poets of Spain are despondent about the genuine value of their own poetry, and that of their contemporaries. The uncertain state of the modern world is usually offered as a reason for this. Certain people in Spain privately express the opinion that the censorship is to blame. Considering the leniency of that organization in dealing with poetry, however, some deeper cause should be looked for. This may be the lack of continuity for which the Civil War and the exile of many poets was responsible or, again, a general decline in the quality of poetry all over Europe.

Though the age has not been experimental, some Surrealist influence can be detected, to which Aleixandre has contributed. If we turn to the poem of Caballero Bonald in Chapter 9, we can see a possibility of this influence being transformed into something more coherent.

This ends our survey of present-day Spanish poetry. In dealing with contemporaries, innumerable omissions were, as we have already admitted, inevitable. This is, so far as we know, the first attempt in book form at a general picture of Spanish poetry today. We have tried, as far as possible, to avoid being too critical. If we have been unjust in any way, we look forward to seeing others supply this deficiency.

Last of all, we should like to dedicate this book to all living Spanish poets, whether they appear in these pages or not.

APPENDIX A

Notes on leading Poetry Reviews

Cántico.

This review was primarily directed by Ricardo Molina and intended to show the existence of a Cordoba school of modern poetry—consisting mainly of the three editors. Some of the numbers were devoted to single poets, such as Molina himself and Celaya. Local color, of the typical Andalusian kind, which we find in Lorca and Alberti, is avoided by these introspective poets, troubled as they are with religious problems and writing frequently in long free-verse lines. Molina, as principal editor of *Cántico,* kept up a long correspondence with other poets at home and abroad. Poets from all over Spain have published in *Cántico.* Space was given to translations of foreign poets, for instance, to Dylan Thomas after his death. Literary visitors to Cordoba were made much of by the *Cántico* group; Aleixandre was there shortly after his health improved in 1949.

Corcel.

This review, though printed in Valencia, was almost entirely directed from Madrid by its Valencian editor, Ricardo Juan Blasco. Its most interesting number was that devoted to Aleixandre. *Corcel* considered itself something of a rival to *Garcilaso;* indeed they began to appear at practically the same time; *Corcel* attempted to maintain a less "Neoclassical" tone than *Garcilaso.*

Elica.

This was a review of Carmelite poets. The Carmelite Order has a long poetic tradition in Spain; Spaniards of all opinions acknowledge Saint John of the Cross as Spain's greatest poet. Most numbers of this review were arranged in two parts, the first devoted to Carmelite poets of the past, and the second to those of the present. The most remarkable of these is Fray Angel María del Sagrado Corazón, but Fray Augusto de la Inmaculada also has published books of poetry.

241

Entregas de poesía.

This was, in many ways, the most ambitious poetry review to appear in contemporary Spain. The editors were Masoliver and Fernando Gutiérrez. The form chosen was a number of brochures, practically a small book of poetry by each author, enclosed in a folder. While Masoliver was abroad, the semi-Surrealist poets of Barcelona, Segalá and Julio Garcés, helped to edit it. Foreign poets were given in the original and in translation; one of the brochures was devoted to Stephen Spender, in spite of his politics at the time of the Civil War.

Escorial.

Escorial was the big literary review of the forties. Ridruejo, Alfaro, and Mourlane Michelena were successively its editors. It published a single number of a poetry supplement called *El jardín de los frailes,* edited by Demetrio Castro Villacañas. *Escorial* was a Falange review, but the ideas of many of those most intimately connected with it, such as Rosales, Vivanco and Panero, were more or less Liberal. In each number of the paper, which was mostly devoted to general literary matters and written in prose, a particular poet was discussed and new poems of his were published. One of the most successful numbers was that containing poems from Aleixandre's *Sombra del paraíso,* shortly before its publication in book form.

Espadaña.

This review was founded in León by Victoriano Crémer, Eugenio de Nora, and Father Lama. In spite of the left-wing opinions of his friends, Father Lama was an admirer and defender of their way of writing. For a time, Panero, Rosales, Vivanco and Aranguren were part editors, but later the original ones resumed complete control. In articles Father Lama attacked García Nieto and his group, and Cano. An anthology of modern Spanish poetry was printed on loose sheets as an offprint, a sheet with each number of the review. This anthology also included a prose commentary written more objectively than the articles in the body of the review.

Garcilaso.

On April 10th, 1943, the government-subsidized periodical *El español* published an article by Jesús Revuelta entitled *Necesidad de un tempismo literario. Lo poético, lo teórico y lo religioso* (A Need for Bringing Things up to the Present Time in Literature. In the Form of Poetry, in the Form of Theory, and in the Form of Religion). The article was a call for a new heroic and religious literature which would correspond fitly to the new politics of Spain. The next number of *El español* (April 17th, 1943) followed up Revuelta's appeal with a double page of poems under the heading, *Juventud creadora: una ética, una política, un estado* (Creative Youth: a Form of Ethics, a Form of Politics, a State). The idea certainly came from Juan Aparicio, the editor of *El español* and the official Spanish press chief. Pedro de Lorenzo contributed an anonymous introductory note to the double page of poems *La joven poesía en España* (The New, Young Poetry of Spain). He began: "Presentamos, hoy, en bloque, un panorama poético, nacido al calor de la nueva España." (Today we present, as a whole, a poetical panorama, born of the warmth of the new Spain.) He explained that these were representative poems by young men between the ages of 15 and 30, most of them as yet unknown. The leading poets included were, in fact, García Nieto, Garcés, Valverde, Cano, Pérez Valiente, and Rafael Morales. Pedro de Lorenzo skillfully avoided a political note in his introduction, and most of the poems were on the usual personal themes of lyrical poetry, but heroic subjects were chosen by Díaz Hierro, Revuelta, García Nieto, and Garcés, the latter contributing a poem called *División azul* (The Blue Division). After this, *Garcilaso* appeared, initially under the patronage of Aparicio. The founders were Pedro de Lorenzo, Jesús Revuelta, Jesús Juan Garcés, and José García Nieto. By the third number, García Nieto had taken the review over and became sole editor. He was not directly subsidized for this, but received the necessary money in exchange for monthly articles which he wrote for the government press by arrangement with Aparicio. This gave him a certain independence, one clear advantage being that purely political poems could be excluded. The anonymous foreword to the first number, written by Revuelta, does indeed suggest that a political tone worthy of the heroic poet Garcilaso would be given to the paper. By the third number, however, Revuelta had ceased to be intimately connected with the review.

Garcilaso brought such poets as Montesinos and Pérez Valiente first to public notice, and such playwrights and prose writers as Víctor Ruiz Iriarte, Eusebio García Luengo, and Julián Ayesta. Nevertheless, much later, on March 18th, 1953, García Nieto declared, in an interview broadcast by Radio Nacional, "La *Juventud Creadora* era yo, realmente" (The Creative Youth was really I).

The presentation and arrangement of *Garcilaso* were much copied by reviews in the provinces.

Halcón.

Luis López Anglada figured as editor, but the real impetus came from Fernando González (1901-   ), a poet of Republican sympathies, living in semi-retirement in Valladolid. We can see, by reading his critical articles in *Halcón* and by observing which poets are most frequently included in the paper, that Fernando González believed the *Garcilaso* group the most important at that time. *Halcón* also published a series of books of poetry, of which the first was Rafael Montesinos' *El libro de las cosas perdidas* (1946). These books contained a photograph of the poet, and a note about him on the flap, written by Fernando González. Some of the books were by López Anglada, Morales, Nora, Pérez Valiente, Gabriel Celaya, and Crémer. Seventeen in all appeared.

La isla de los ratones.

This review was publised by Manuel Arce. Each number was relatively short, thus throwing into relief the poets it included. Poets from all over Spain contributed, though some preference was given to those of Santander, where it was published.

Poesía española.

In 1952, García Nieto became the editor of this government-subsidized review, the aim of which was to include the maximum number of poets from all over Spain. Columns of criticism run down the margin of some of the pages and numerous prose articles on poetry are printed. The disadvantage of including so many writers is that the review has no real tone of its own. The first and last pages are reserved for the most important poets writing in each number.

Proel.

This was a government-subsidized review published in Santander. Prose was included as well as poetry, and each number was quite long. Authors from all over Spain contributed, but the chief interest of *Proel* was that it contained work by and made a name for several Santander poets, such as José Hierro, Carlos Salomón, José Luis Hidalgo, and Julio Maruri.

Raíz.

This review was published by the Faculty of Philosophy and Letters, Madrid, though it was by no means limited to the contributions of students. Prose and verse were both included and even an unpublished play by Lorca. The editor was Juan Guerrero Zamora.

Poetry Anthologies

In 1946 César González Ruano published the first anthology of twentieth-century Spanish poetry which included the poets who had begun writing since 1939.[1] Nobody of importance in the present century was omitted. Since Ruano was living in Barcelona at the time, many poets from that town who wrote in Castilian were included. The most famous of the exiles were well represented. Ruano himself occupied fourteen pages, as against thirteen for Alberti and ten for Aleixandre.

The selection of poets who became known only after 1939 was not so careful as that of the poets immediately before them. This was excusable, considering that many of them had written little at that time. The omission of Valverde, however, though he was still very young, was a defect, for others still younger were included. The anthology was, besides, very long and contained many poets.

Alfonso Moreno's anthology of *Poesía española actual* was shorter and more selective, though some poets whose reputation was probably only ephemeral were chosen. The material was put together in 1944, but the book did not appear till 1946. The first poet was Unamuno and the second Pío Baroja whose only book of verse, *Canciones del suburbio,*[2] had just appeared. Most of the poets were allotted ten to sixteen pages, though some of the younger ones had less, even only a page or two. Salinas, Guillén, Cernuda, and Alberti were well represented, though Alberti's political poetry was intentionally avoided because, according to the anthologist, it was unSpanish.

The anthology published in successive numbers of *Espadaña* paid more attention to the youngest group of poets than either Ruano or Moreno, no doubt because the compilers felt that they belonged to the same generation. They published a chart of poets, rather like a family tree of which the two main branches were the Neoclassicals and the Aleixandre group. Though Father Lama attacked García

Nieto and the poets of *Garcilaso* in the review itself, they were better treated in the anthology.

Federico Carlos Sáinz de Robles published a very long anthology of Spanish poetry from the earliest times to the present day. Only a few of the younger poets were chosen for the first edition though these were given the same number of pages as established poets of the past. The second edition included even more contemporary poets than Ruano's anthology and naturally even younger ones, since Sáinz de Robles was publishing later than Ruano.[3]

The Anthology of Surrealism and the *Antología consultada* were discussed earlier.

José Luis Cano in his *Antología de los poetas andaluces contemporáneos*[4] speaks of the poetical superiority of Andalusia over the rest of Spain. Cela had said recently that poetry had now passed from the South to the North. Cano explains that Cela "se refiere a este momento de 1952" (refers to this present time, 1952), that is to say, to the social poets such as Celaya and Blas de Otero, or Hierro, or Crémer and Nora.

Cano includes Bécquer as a contemporary in spirit. The influence of Juan Ramón Jiménez on subsequent Andalusian poets is clear on reading this anthology. Cano has chosen more exiled poets—mostly rather secondary—than former anthologies had cared to.

In 1953 *Adonais* published an anthology of the poets who had written books for the series.[5] The poems chosen are from the books already issued by *Adonais* and, except in a few cases, selected by the poets themselves. Foreign writers in the *Adonais* series are not represented. Photographs of the poets are given at the end of the book. The foreword is by Vicente Aleixandre, who makes an indirect claim that he was responsible for the end of "Neoclassicism." A special type of poetry, different from that of the past, is now being written: "a los poetas más jóvenes no les oiréis hablar de 'belleza.' " (You will not hear the youngest poets speak of "beauty.")

One or two anthologies of modern Spanish poetry have appeared in South America. The Chilean writer Roque Esteban Scarpa brought out an anthology entitled *Poesía española contemporánea*,[6] after a visit to Spain during which he came to know many of the Spanish poets personally. On the fly-leaf he speaks of the "fuerza ininterrumpida" (uninterrupted strength) of Spanish poetry, which still persists today. Thirty-three poets are given: the Machados, Juan Ramón Jiménez, Unamuno, García Lorca, Salinas, Guillén, Alberti, León Felipe, Cernuda, Marquina, Pemán, Emilio Prados, Aleixandre, Gerardo Diego, Souvirón, Vivanco, Altolaguirre, Panero, Rosales, Miguel Hernández, Ridruejo, Cano, García Nieto, Suárez Carreño, Molina, Leopoldo de Luis, Morales, Gaos, Montesinos, Bousoño, Nora, and Valverde.

Enrique Azcoaga, who has been living in the Argentine since 1951, published a *Panorama de la poesía moderna española*.[7] The anthology is almost as long as and more comprehensive than Ruano's; poets living in Spain and exiles are both included. A few particularly out-spoken political poems are to be found in this book, since the Spanish censorship did not have to be reckoned with. Well over two hundred poets are represented by three poems each. Alberti, Miguel Hernández, José Luis Gallego, Pío Gómez Nisa, and José Luis Hidalgo have five. (Alberti's poems in this anthology are all taken from what was at that time his latest book, *Retornos de lo vivo lejano*.)[8] Domenchina and Panero have four. Some of the single poems selected from other poets are in several parts, so that there is some inequality in the amount of space occupied by each poet. Paulina Crusat's translations of modern Catalan poets[9] have also been drawn on. Azcoaga, in his foreword, declares that modern poetry has a message of human nobility in the midst of the ruined world of today. He pays homage to the "fabulosos" forerunners of modern Spanish poetry, Unamuno, Antonio Machado, and Juan Ramón Jiménez.

A very complete anthology of present-day Spanish poetry is *Antología de la nueva poesía española* by José Luis Cano.[10] Of the so-called *Generation of 1936* he includes Miguel Hernández, Panero, Rosales, Vivanco, Ridruejo, Carmen Conde, Bleiberg, Gil, Gutiérrez, Crémer, and Muñoz Rojas. There are many more names belonging to the next "generation," that of 1940: Morales, Gaos, Celaya, Angela Figuera, García Nieto, Montesinos, López Anglada, Nora, Valverde, Suárez Carreño, Bousoño, Hierro, Maruri, María Beneyto, José Luis Prado, Pérez Valiente, Concha Zardoya, Ruiz Peña, Hidalgo, Molina, Canales, Leopoldo de Luis, Garciasol, Valls, Bengoechea, Gomis, Angel Crespo, Blas de Otero, García Baena, Santos Torroella, Caballero Bonald, and Susana March. Finally, the "1950 generation" brings us the young poets Jaime Ferrán, José Angel Valente, and Claudio Rodríguez. With such a profusion of names, it is unfortunate

Cano should have omitted two of the more outstanding poets of the "1940 generation." The first is Manuel Pilares, with his mining songs from Asturias and his gay, satiric poems, such as the one in which he phrases a prayer as if it were an official petition. The second is Carlos Edmundo de Ory.

Since 1955, Aguilar, one of Madrid's leading publishing houses, has brought out a yearly anthology of the best poetry published in the past year. Many readers may find these more attractive than Cano's anthology, because they are more selective and less thorough.

José María Castellet's anthology *Veinte años de poesía española (1939-1959)*[11] opens with a 78-page preface in which he justifies the arrangement of the poems under the year in which they first appeared instead of under authors. He wishes to keep the poetry in an historical perspective. Changes in Spain and Spanish ideas have affected poets. This means that he sees poems rather as the product of their times than of individuals. The impression is given both by the preface and the anthology that the nearer we approach the present day the greater is the social awareness of Spain's most representative poets—in fact, the more "socialistic" they are, though the word is not used.

Castellet sees a special development of ideas in poetry, through *Hijos de la ira* and the left-wing poets of the *Antología consultada* to poets of the new generation who "tend towards realistic poetry." Somewhat towards the end of the anthology we find Goytisolo's *Los celestiales* (analyzed in Chapter 9). Altogether Castellet has presented quite a plausible picture by skillfully omitting poets and poems that would not fit in conveniently.

1960 saw the publication, in Italy, of the second edition of Oreste Macrì's anthology, *Poesia spagnola del novecento*.[12] All the main Spanish poets from the beginning of this century are included, even Rubén Darío, whom the anthologist considers Spanish by adoption. The first edition (1952) had already extended to such poets as Bousoño and Valverde and this one adds Blas de Otero and others. There is a long preface with a section on each poet, and the poems are given in Italian and in the original.

Even the very latest group of poets in Spain has its brief anthology, *Nuevos poetas españoles,* chosen and prefaced by Jiménez Martos.[13] Eleven poets are represented. Manuel Alcántara, of Málaga, has something of the same tone as Montesinos. Eladio Cabañero is more personal. Gloria Fuertes is direct and outspoken, with a bitter sense of humor. Claudio Rodríguez could have been a Latinized, classical poet if he had lived at a different period; in any case, his poems are rich in metaphor and in the observation of Nature. Each poet in this book has a force of his or her own, which is well brought out in the selection. Perhaps one cannot see how these poets will eventually develop, but certainly they already have their own ways of writing, especially Carlos Sahagún. There is a future for such poetry.

NOTES TO APPENDIX B

1. *Antología de poetas españoles contemporáneos en lengua castellana* (Barcelona, 1946).
2. (Madrid, 1944).
3. *Historia y antología de la poesía española (en lengua castellana) del siglo XIV al XX* (Madrid, 1st edition, 1948; 2nd edition, 1951).
4. (Madrid, 1952).
5. *Antología de "Adonais"* (Madrid, 1953).
6. (Santiago de Chile, 1953).
7. (Buenos Aires, 1953).
8. (Buenos Aires, 1952).
9. *Antología de poetas catalanes contemporáneos* (Madrid, 1952).
10. (Madrid, 1958).
11. (Barcelona, 1960).
12. (Parma, 1st edition, 1952; 2nd edition, 1960).
13. (Madrid. 1961).

BIBLIOGRAPHY

a) *Poetical works of the poets specially mentioned (in order of reference)*:

CHAPTER 1.

Rubén Darío

    Epístolas y poemas (Managua, 1885)
    Abrojos (Valparaíso, 1887)
    Las rosas andinas (Valparaíso, 1888)
    Azul . . . (Valparaíso, 1888)
    Rimas (Valparaíso, 1889)
    Prosas profanas (Buenos Aires, 1896)
    Cantos de vida y esperanza (Madrid, 1905)
    Ode à Mitre (Paris, 1906)
    El canto errante (Madrid, 1907)
    Poema del otoño (Madrid, 1910)
    Canto a la Argentina y otros poemas (Madrid, 1914)
    Sol de domingo (Madrid, 1914)

Antonio Machado

    Soledades (Madrid, 1903)
    Soledades, galerías y otros poemas (n.p. 1907)
    Campos de Castilla (Madrid, 1912)
    Nuevas canciones (Madrid, 1924)
    Poesías completas (Madrid, 1917, 1928 and 1933)

Juan Ramón Jiménez

    Almas de violeta (Madrid, 1900)
    Ninfeas (Madrid, 1900)
    Rimas (Madrid, 1902)
    Arias tristes (Madrid, 1903)
    Jardines lejanos (Madrid, 1904)
    Elegías puras (Madrid, 1908)
    Elegías intermedias (Madrid, 1909)
    Olvidanzas. Las hojas verdes (Madrid, 1909)
    Elegías lamentables (Madrid, 1910)
    Baladas de primavera (Madrid, 1910)
    La soledad sonora (Madrid, 1911)
    Poemas májicos y dolientes (Madrid, 1911)
    Pastorales (Madrid, 1911)

Melancolía (Madrid, 1912)
Laberinto (Madrid, 1913)
Estío (Madrid, 1915)
Sonetos espirituales (Madrid, 1917)
Poesías escojidas (New York, 1917)
Diario de un poeta recién casado (Madrid, 1917)
Eternidades (Madrid, 1918)
Piedra y cielo (Madrid, 1919)
Segunda antolojía poética (Madrid, 1922)
Poesías escojidas (Mexico, 1923)
Poesía (Madrid, 1923)
Belleza (Madrid, 1923)
Poesías de Juan Ramón Jiménez. Chosen and with a Prologue by P. Henríquez Ureña (Mexico, 1923)
Unidad (Madrid, 1926)
Poesía en prosa y verso. Chosen for children by Zenobia Camprubí (Madrid, 1932)
Canción (Madrid, 1936)
La estación total con Las canciones de la nueva luz (Buenos Aires, 1946)
Romances de Coral Gables (Mexico, 1948)
Animal de fondo (Buenos Aires, 1949)
Antología para niños y adolescentes. Chosen by Norah Borges and Guillermo de Torre (Buenos Aires, 1951)
Libros de Poesía (Madrid, 1957)
Tercera Antolojía poética (1898-1953) (Madrid, 1957)

Jorge Guillén

Cántico. 1st edition (Madrid, 1928)
Cántico. 2nd edition (Madrid, 1935)
Cántico. 3rd edition (Mexico, 1945)
Cántico. 4th edition (Buenos Aires, 1950)
Breve Antología (Valladolid, 1956)
Luzbel desconcertado (Milan, 1956)
Lugar de Lázaro (Málaga, 1957)
Maremágnum (Buenos Aires, 1957)
Viviendo y otros poemas (Barcelona, 1958)

Federico García Lorca

Libro de poemas (Madrid, 1921)
Canciones (Málaga, 1927)
Romancero gitano (Madrid, 1928)
Poema del Cante Jondo (Madrid, 1931)
Llanto por Ignacio Sánchez Mejías (Madrid, 1935)
Primeras canciones (Madrid, 1936)
Seis poemas gallegos (Santiago de Compostela, 1936)

Poeta en Nueva York (Mexico, 1940)
Obras completas (Buenos Aires, 1938-1942)
Crucifixión (Las Palmas de Gran Canaria, 1950)
Obras completas (Madrid, 1955)

Rafael Alberti

Marinero en tierra (Madrid, 1925)
La amante (Málaga, 1926)
El alba del alhelí (Santander, 1927)
Cal y canto (Madrid, 1929)
Sobre los ángeles (Madrid, 1929)
Sermones y moradas (Madrid, 1930)
Dos oraciones a la Virgen (Paris, 1931)
Un fantasma recorre Europa (Madrid, 1933)
Poesía (1924-1930) (Madrid, 1934)
13 bandas y 48 estrellas (Madrid, 1935)
Verte y no verte (Mexico, 1935)
De un momento a otro (Madrid, 1937)
Poesía (1924-1938) (Buenos Aires, 1940)
Entre el clavel y la espada (Buenos Aires, 1941)
¡Eh, los toros! (Buenos Aires, 1942)
Antología poética (Buenos Aires, 1942)
De un momento a otro. Cantata de los héroes y la fraternidad de los pueblos. Vida bilingüe de un refugiado español en Francia (Buenos Aires, 1942)
Pleamar (Buenos Aires, 1944)
Pueblos libres. ¿Y España? (Buenos Aires, 1946)
A la pintura: cantata de la línea y del color (Buenos Aires, 1948)
Retornos de lo vivo lejano (Buenos Aires, 1952)
A la pintura. 2nd edition (Buenos Aires, 1953)
Ora marítima (Buenos Aires, 1953)
Baladas y canciones del Paraná (Buenos Aires, 1954)
Coplas de Juan Panadero (Buenos Aires, 1954)
Sonríe China (Buenos Aires, 1958)

Luis Cernuda

Perfil del aire (Málaga, 1927)
Donde habita el olvido (Madrid, 1934)
El joven marino (Madrid, 1936)
La realidad y el deseo (Madrid, 1936)
La realidad y el deseo. 2nd edition (Mexico, 1940)
Ocnos (London, 1942)
Las nubes (Buenos Aires, 1943)
Como quien espera el alba (Buenos Aires, 1947)
Ocnos. 2nd edition (Madrid, 1949)
La realidad y el deseo 1924-1956. 3rd edition (Mexico, 1958)

CHAPTER 2

Manuel Machado

Alma (Madrid, 1900)
Caprichos (Madrid, 1905)
Alma, Museo y Los cantares. Preface by Unamuno (Madrid, 1907)
El mal poema (Madrid, 1909)
Apolo (Madrid, 1911)
Cante hondo (Madrid, 1912)
Canciones y dedicatorias (Madrid, 1915)
Sevilla y otros poemas (Madrid, 1918)
Ars moriendi (Madrid, 1921)
Poesía. Opera omnia lyrica (Barcelona, 1940)
Cadencias de cadencias (Madrid, 1943)

Gerardo Diego

El romancero de la novia (Madrid, 1920)
Imagen (Madrid, 1922)
Soria (Valladolid, 1923)
Manual de espumas (Madrid, 1924)
Versos humanos (Madrid, 1925)
Viacrucis (Santander, 1931)
Fábula de Equis y Zeda (Mexico, 1932)
Poemas adrede (Mexico, 1932)
Angeles de Compostela (Madrid, 1940)
Romances (Madrid, 1941)
Primera antología de sus versos. (Madrid, 1941)
Alondra de verdad (Madrid, 1941)
Alondra de verdad. 2nd edition (Madrid, 1943)
Poemas adrede. 2nd edition (Madrid, 1943)
El romancero de la novia. Iniciales (Zaragoza, 1944)
La sorpresa (Madrid, 1944)
Soria. 2nd edition (Santander, 1948)
Hasta siempre (Madrid, 1949)
La luna en el desierto y otros poemas (Santander, 1949)
Limbo (Las Palmas de Gran Canaria, 1950)
Los deseos correos (Las Palmas de Gran Canaria, 1952)
Biografía incompleta (Madrid, 1953)
Angeles de Compostela. 2nd edition (Madrid, 1953)
Segundo sueño (Santander, 1953)
Variación (Madrid, 1954)
Amazona (Madrid, 1955)
Paisaje con figuras (Palma de Mallorca, 1957)
Amor solo (Madrid, 1958)
Canciones al volante (Madrid, 1960)
Glosa a Villamediana (Madrid, 1961)
Angeles de Compostela. Complete edition (Madrid, 1961)

Miguel Hernández

Perito en lunas (Murcia, 1933)
El rayo que no cesa (Madrid, 1936)
Viento del pueblo (Valencia, 1937)
Sino sangriento (La Habana, 1940)
Seis poemas inéditos y nueve más (Alicante, 1951)
Obra escogida (Madrid, 1952)

Germán Bleiberg

El cantar de la noche (Madrid, 1935)
Sonetos amorosos (Madrid, 1936)
Más allá de las ruinas (Madrid, 1947)
El poeta ausente (Madrid, 1948)
La mutua primavera (San Sebastián, 1948)

Luis Rosales

Abril (Madrid, 1935)
Retablo sacro del Nacimiento del Señor (Madrid, 1940)
La casa encendida (Madrid, 1949)
Rimas (Madrid, 1951)

Luis Felipe Vivanco

Cantos de primavera (Madrid, 1936)
Tiempo de dolor (Madrid, 1940)
Continuación de la vida (Madrid, 1949)
El descampado (Palma de Mallorca, 1957)
Memoria de la plata (Madrid, 1958)

Leopoldo Panero

Escrito a cada instante (Madrid, 1949)
Canto personal. Carta perdida a Pablo Neruda (Madrid, 1953)

Vicente Aleixandre

Ambito (Málaga, 1928)
Espadas como labios (Madrid, 1932)
Pasión de la tierra (Mexico, 1935)
La destrucción o el amor (Madrid, 1935)
Sombra del paraíso (Madrid, 1944)
En la muerte de Miguel Hernández (Zaragoza, 1948)
Mundo a solas (Madrid, 1950)
Poemas paradisíacos (Málaga, 1950)
Nacimiento último (Madrid, 1953)
A la salida del pueblo (Las Palmas de Gran Canaria, 1953)

> *Historia del corazón* (Madrid, 1954)
> *Mis poemas mejores* (Madrid, 1956)
> *Poesías completas* (Madrid, 1960)

Dámaso Alonso

> *Poemas puros y poemillas de la ciudad* (Madrid, 1921)
> *El viento y el verso* (Madrid, 1925)
> *Oscura noticia* (Madrid, 1944)
> *Hijos de la ira* (Madrid, 1944)
> *Hombre y Dios* (Málaga, 1955)
> *Antología. Creación* (Madrid, 1956)

CHAPTER 3

Dionisio Ridruejo

> *Plural* (Segovia, 1935)
> *Primer libro de amor* (Barcelona, 1939)
> *Poesía en armas* (Madrid, 1940)
> *Fábula de la doncella y el río* (Madrid, 1943)
> *Sonetos a la piedra* (Madrid, 1943)
> *Poesía en armas* (Cuadernos de la campaña de Rusia) (Madrid, 1944)
> *En la soledad del tiempo* (Barcelona, 1944)
> *Elegías* (Madrid, 1948)
> *En once años* (Madrid, 1950)

José García Nieto

> *Víspera hacia ti* (Madrid, 1940)
> *Poesía (1940-1943)* (Madrid, 1944)
> *Versos de un huésped de Luisa Esteban* (Privately printed) (Madrid, 1944)
> *Del campo y soledad* (Madrid, 1946)
> *Juego de los doce espejos* (Santander, 1951)
> *Tregua* (Madrid, 1951)
> *Libro de poemas* (2 vols.) (Madrid, 1951)
> *Sonetos por mi hija* (Privately printed) (Madrid, 1953)
> *La red* (Madrid, 1955)
> *El parque pequeño y Elegía en Covaleda* (Madrid, 1959)
> *Geografía es amor* (Madrid, 1961)

Juana García Noreña

> *Dama de soledad* (Madrid, 1950)

Vicente Gaos

> *Arcángel de mi noche* (Madrid, 1944)

Sobre la tierra (Madrid, 1945)
Luz desde el sueño (Valladolid, 1947)
Profecía del recuerdo (Torrelavega, 1956)
Antología poética (Palma de Mallorca, 1957)
Poesías completas (Madrid, 1959)

CHAPTER 4

José Suárez Carreño

La tierra amenazada (Madrid, 1943)
Edad de hombre (Madrid, 1944)

José Luis Hidalgo

Raíz (Valencia, 1943)
Los animales (Santander, 1944)
Los muertos (Madrid, 1947)

Rafael Morales

Poemas del toro (Madrid, 1943)
El corazón y la tierra (Valladolid, 1946)
Los desterrados (Madrid, 1947)
Poesías completas (Madrid, 1949)
Canción sobre el asfalto (Madrid, 1954)
Antología y pequeña historia de mis versos (Madrid, 1958)

Carlos Bousoño

Subida al amor (Madrid, 1945)
Primavera de la muerte (Madrid, 1946)
Hacia otra luz (Madrid, 1952)
Noche del sentido (Madrid, 1957)
Poesías completas. Primavera de la muerte (Madrid, 1960)

CHAPTER 5

Rafael Montesinos

Resurrección (Madrid, 1942)
Balada del amor primero (Privately printed) (Madrid, 1944)
Canciones perversas para una niña tonta (Madrid, 1946)
El libro de las cosas perdidas (Valladolid, 1946)
Las incredulidades (Madrid, 1948)
También es esperanza (Las Palmas de Gran Canaria, 1952)
Dos sonetos sobre el mismo tema (Sevilla, 1954)
Cuaderno de las últimas nostalgias (Madrid, 1954)

País de la esperanza (Santander, 1955)
La soledad y los días (Antología poética 1944-1956) (Madrid, 1956)
El tiempo en nuestros brazos (Madrid, 1958)

Salvador Pérez Valiente

Cuando ya no hay remedio (Valladolid, 1947)
Por tercera vez (Madrid, 1953)
Lo mismo de siempre (Madrid, 1960)

Ricardo Molina

Tres poemas (San Sebastián, 1948)
Elegías de Sandua (Madrid, Córdoba, 1948)
Corimbo (Madrid, 1949)
Elegía de Medina Azahara (Madrid, 1957)

CHAPTER 7

Rafael Múgica (Gabriel Celaya) (Juan de Leceta)

Marea del silencio (Zarauz, 1935)
La soledad cerrada (San Sebastián, 1947)
Movimientos elementales (San Sebastián, 1947)
Tranquilamente hablando (San Sebastián, 1947)
Objetos poéticos (Valladolid, 1948)
Juguetes (Santander, 1948)
El principio sin fin (Córdoba, 1949)
Se parece al amor (Las Palmas de Gran Canaria, 1949)
Las cosas como son (un decir) (Santander, 1949)
Deriva (Alicante, 1950)
Las cartas boca arriba (Madrid, 1951)
Lo demás es silencio (Barcelona, 1952)
Paz y concierto (Madrid, 1953)
Nana del niño grande (Las Palmas de Gran Canaria, 1953)
Ciento volando (with Amparo Gastón) (Madrid, 1953)
Vía Muerta (Barcelona, 1954)
Cantos iberos (Alicante, 1955)
Coser y cantar (with Amparo Gastón) (Guadalajara, 1955)
De claro en claro (Madrid, 1956)
Pequeña antología poética (Santander, 1957)
Entreacto (Madrid, 1957)
Música celestial (with Amparo Gastón) (Cartagena, 1957)
Las resistencias del diamante (Mexico, 1957)
Cantata en Aleixandre (Madrid, Palma, 1959)
Para vosotros dos (Bilbao, 1960)
Poesía urgente (Buenos Aires, 1960)
El corazón en su sitio (Caracas, 1960)

José Hierro

Tierra sin nosotros (Santander, 1947)
Alegría (Madrid, 1947)
Con las piedras, con el viento (Santander, 1950)
Quinta del 42 (Madrid, 1952)
Antología poética (Santander, 1953)
Estatuas yacentes (Santander, 1955)
Poesía del momento (Madrid, 1957)
Cuanto sé de mí (Madrid, 1957)

Victoriano Crémer

Tendiendo el vuelo (Burgos, 1928)
Tacto sonoro (León, 1944)
Caminos de mi sangre (Madrid, 1947)
La espada y la pared (San Sebastián, 1949)
Las horas perdidas (Valladolid, 1949)
Nuevos cantos de vida y esperanza, 1 (Barcelona, 1952)
Libro de Santiago (León, 1954)
Nuevos cantos de vida y esperanza, 2 (Barcelona, 1955)
Furia y paloma (Barcelona, 1956)

Eugenio de Nora

Cantos al destino (Madrid, 1945)
Amor prometido (Valladolid, 1946)
Contemplación del tiempo (Madrid, 1948)
Siempre (Madrid, 1953)
España, pasión de vida (Barcelona, 1954)

Miguel Alonso (Ramón de Garciasol)

Defensa del hombre (Madrid, 1950)
Canciones (Madrid, 1952)
Palabras mayores (Alicante, 1952)
Tierras de España (Madrid, 1955)
Del amor de cada día (Santander, 1956)
La madre (Madrid, 1958)
Sangre de par en par (Caracas, 1961)
Poemas de andar España (Madrid, 1962)

Blas de Otero

Cántico espiritual (San Sebastián, 1942)
Angel fieramente humano (Madrid, 1950)
Redoble de conciencia (Barcelona, 1951)
Pido la paz y la palabra (Santander, 1955)
Ancia (Barcelona, 1958)
Con la inmensa mayoná (Buenos Aires, 1960)

CHAPTER 8

José María Valverde

Hombre de Dios (Madrid, 1945)
La espera (Madrid, 1949)
Versos del Domingo (Barcelona, 1954)
Poesías reunidas hasta 1960 (Madrid, 1961)

José Luis Prado Nogueira

Testigo de excepción (Madrid, 1953)
Oratorio del Guadarrama (Madrid, 1956)
Respuesta a Carmen (Madrid, 1958)
Miserere en la tumba de R. N. (Sevilla, 1960)

b) *Books in verse referred to or of special interest:*

Albalá, Alfonso. *Umbral de armonía* (Madrid, 1952)
Albareda, Ginés de. *Romancero del Caribe* (Madrid, 1948)
Albi, José. *Poemas del amor de siempre* (Alicante, 1947)
Alfaro, María. *Poemas del recuerdo* (Palma de Mallorca, 1951)
Alonso Alcaide, Manuel. *Hoguera viva* (Valladolid, 1948)
Alonso Gamo, José María. *Paisajes del alma en guerra* (Buenos Aires, 1943)
——————. *Tus rosas frente al espejo* (Valencia, 1952)
Apollinaire, Guillaume. *La canción del mal amado y otros poemas* (Versión y prólogo de Juan Ortega Costa) (Madrid, 1960)
Arce, Manuel. *Sombra de un amor* (Madrid, 1952)
Aumente, Julio. *El aire que no vuelve* (Madrid, 1955)
Azcoaga, Enrique. *El poema de los tres carros* (Madrid, 1947)

Beneyto, María. *Tierra viva* (Madrid, 1956)
Bernier, Juan. *Aquí en la tierra* (Córdoba, 1948)
Browning, Elizabeth Barrett. *Sonetos del portugués* (Versión y prólogo de Julieta Gómez Paz) (Madrid, 1954)
Byron, Lord. *Poemas líricos* (Selección, versión y prólogo de María Alfaro) (Madrid, 1945)

Caballero Bonald, José Manuel. *Las adivinaciones* (Madrid, 1952)
——————. *Memorias de poco tiempo* (Madrid, 1954)
Cabañas, Pablo. *Evocación* (Madrid, 1951)
Cabañero, Eladio. *Una señal de amor* (Madrid, 1958)
Campbell, Roy. *Poemas* (Selección, versión y prólogo de Aquilino Duque) (Madrid, 1958)
Cano, José Luis. *Sonetos a la bahía* (Madrid, 1942)
——————. *Voz de la muerte* (Madrid, 1944)

Casais Monteiro, Adolfo. *Antología* (Selección, versión y prólogo de Rafael Morales) (Madrid, 1954)

Castillo-Elejabeitia, Dictinio del. *La canción de los pinos* (Madrid, 1945)

Cela, Camilo José. *Cancionero de la Alcarria* (San Sebastián, 1948)

——————. *Pisando la dudosa luz del día* (Barcelona, 1945)

Cirlot, Juan Eduardo. *La muerte de Gerión* (Barcelona, 1943)

Claudel, Paul. *Cinco grandes odas* (Prólogo y versión de Enrique Badosa) (Madrid, 1955)

Conde, Carmen. *Ansia de la gracia* (Madrid, 1945)

Crespo, Angel. *Junio feliz* (Madrid, 1959)

Drummond de Andrade, Carlos. *Poemas* (Selección, versión y prólogo de Rafael Santos Torroella) (Madrid, 1951)

Eliot, T[homas] S. *Cuatro cuartetos* (Versión, prólogo y notas de Vicente Gaos) (Madrid, 1951)

——————. *Poemas* (Versiones de Dámaso Alonso, Leopoldo Panero, J. A. Muñoz Rojas, Charles D. Ley y José L. Cano. Prólogo de Charles D. Ley) (Madrid, 1946)

Entrambasaguas, Joaquín de. *Voz de este mundo* (Madrid, 1946)

Figuera, Angela. *El grito inútil* (Alicante, 1952)

Garcés, Jesús Juan. *He venido a esta orilla* (Madrid, 1949)

Garcés, Julio. *Odas* (Barcelona, 1943)

García Baena, Pablo. *Antiguo muchacho* (Madrid, 1950)

García Nieto, José. *Retablo del ángel, el hombre y la pastora* (Madrid, 1945)

George, Stefan. *Peregrinajes* (Traducción de Alfonso Pintó y Jaime Balet. Prólogo de Alfonso Pintó) (Madrid, 1954)

Gil, Ildefonso Manuel. *El tiempo recobrado* (Madrid, 1950)

Goethe, J[ohann] W. *Poesías* (Versión, prólogo y notas de Carmen Bravo-Villasante) (Madrid, 1953)

Goicoechea, Ramón Eugenio de. *El amor eterno* (Barcelona, 1943)

Gomis, Lorenzo. *El caballo* (Madrid, 1951)

González, Fernando. *Ofrendas a la nada* (Valladolid, 1949)

Guerrero Zamora, Juan. *Danza macabra* (Madrid, 1950)

Hernández, Miguel. *El labrador de más aire* (Valencia, 1937)

Hölderlin, Friedrich. *Doce poemas* (Versión y prólogo de José María Valverde) (Madrid, 1949)

Jiménez, Salvador. *La orilla del milagro* (Murcia, 1945)

Keats, John. *Poesías* (Selección, versión y prólogo de Clemencia Miró) (Madrid, 1946)

Labé, Luisa. *Cancionero* (Versión castellana y prólogo de Ester de Andréis) (Madrid, 1956)

Laboreta, Miguel. *Vidente idílico* (Madrid, 1949)

Lacaci, María Elvira. *Humana voz* (Madrid, 1957)
Laffón, Rafael. *Romances y madrigales* (Madrid, 1944)
Landínez, Luis. *Sobre esta tierra nuestra* (Zaragoza, 1952)
Lezcano, Pedro. *Muriendo dos a dos* (Valladolid, 1947)
Lloréns, Bartolomé. *Secreta fuente* (Prólogo de Carlos Bousoño) (Madrid, 1948)
Longfellow, Henry Wadsworth. *Aureos instantes* (Selección, versión y prólogo de Santiago Magariños) (Madrid, 1945)
López Anglada, Luis. *La vida conquistada* (Madrid, 1952)
Luis, Leopoldo de. *Los imposibles pájaros* (Madrid, 1949)

Manrique de Lara, José Gerardo. *Río Esperanza* (Madrid, 1960)
Maruri, Julio. *Los años* (Madrid, 1947)
Mayáns, Francisco José. *Estancias amorosas* (Madrid, 1949)
Merton, Thomas. *Veinte Poemas* (Versión y prólogo de José María Valverde) (Madrid, 1953)
Moréas, Jean. *Poemas y estancias* (Versión y prólogo de Paulina Crusat) (Madrid, 1950)
Moreno, Alfonso. *El vuelo de la carne* (Madrid, 1944)
Mostaza, Bartolomé. *Búsqueda* (Madrid, 1949)
Muñoz Rojas, José Antonio. *Los poemas de Crashaw a Santa Teresa* (Madrid, 1942)

Neruda, Pablo. *Canto general a Chile* (Mexico, 1950)
Núñez, Vicente. *Los días terrestres* (Madrid, 1957)
Nu'ayma, Mija'il. *El rumor de los párpados* (Versión castellana de Leonor Martínez, con la colaboración de Mohammad Sabbag) (Madrid, 1956)

Péguy, Charles. *Poesías* (Selección, traducción y prólogo de Vicente Pola) (Madrid, 1943)
Pérez Clotet, Pedro. *Soledades en vuelo* (Madrid, 1945)
Perse, Saint-John. *Anabasis* (Versión, prólogo y notas de Agustín Larrauri) (Madrid, 1957)
Pessoa, Fernando. *Poemas de Alberto Caeiro* (Selección, versión, prólogo y notas de Angel Crespo) (Madrid, 1957)
Pilares, Manuel. *Poemas mineros* (Oviedo, 1948)
Pound, Ezra. *Los cantos pisanos* (Versión, prólogo y notas de Jesús Pardo) (Madrid, 1960)

Raine, Kathleen. *Poemas* (Selección, versión y prólogo de Mariano Manent) (Madrid, 1951)
Rilke, Ranier María. *Sonetos a Orfeo* (Versión y prólogo de Carlos Barral) (Madrid, 1954)
—————. *Cincuenta poemas* (Traducción de José María Valverde) (Madrid, 1957)
—————. *Requiem. Las elegías de Duino* (Texto original alemán con versión castellana e introducción por Gonzalo Torrente Ballester) (Madrid, 1946)

——————. *Las ventanas* (Les Fenêtres) (Traducción de Gerardo Diego) (Madrid, n.d. [1957])

Rimbaud, Jean Arthur. *Poesías* (Selección, versión y prólogo de Vicente Gaos) (Madrid, 1946)

Rodenbach, Georges. *El reino del silencio* (Selección, traducción y prólogo de Carlos R. de Dampierre) (Madrid, 1944)

Romero Murube, Joaquín. *Kasilda del olvido* (Madrid, 1945)

Ruiz Peña, Juan. *Libro de los recuerdos* (Madrid, 1945)

Sahagún, Carlos. *Profecías del agua* (Madrid, 1958)

Salomón, Carlos. *Firmes alas transparentes* (Santander, 1952)

——————. *La orilla* (Santander, 1951)

——————. *La sed* (Madrid, 1951)

——————. *Región luciente* (Madrid, 1953)

Sánchez, Venancio. *Los patios* (Madrid, 1957)

Segalá, Manuel. *Elegías* (Barcelona, 1944)

Serpa, Alberto de. *Poemas de Oporto* (Selección, versión y prólogo de Charles David Ley y Rafael Morales) (Madrid, 1947)

Shelley, Percy Bysshe. *Adonais* (Versión de Vicente Gaos. Prólogo de Walter Starkie) (Madrid, 1947)

Thomas, Dylan. *Poemas* (Selección, versión y prólogo de Esteban Pujals) (Madrid, 1955)

Trakl, George. *Poesías* (Versión y prólogo de Jaime Bofill y Ferro) (Madrid, 1949)

Valente, José Angel. *A modo de esperanza* (Madrid, 1955)

Valéry, Paul. *La serpiente y la parca joven.* (Versión castellana y prólogo de Juan Ortega Costa) (Madrid, 1956)

Valle, Adriano del. *Arpa fiel* (Madrid, 1941)

Vandercammen, Edmond. *Arcilla de mi carne* (Selección, versión y prólogo de Dictinio del Castillo-Elejabeytia) (Madrid, 1954)

Verlaine, Paul. *Fiestas galantes. Romances sin palabras* (Traducción y prólogo de Luis Guarner) (Madrid, 1944)

Whitman, Walt. *Cantando a la primavera* (Traducción y prólogo de Concha Zardoya) (Madrid, 1945)

Yeats, William Butler. *Poemas* (Selección, versión y prólogo de Jaime Ferrán) (Madrid, 1957)

Zardoya, Concha. *Pájaros del Nuevo Mundo* (Madrid, 1946)

c) *Books referred to or consulted:*

Alarco Llorach, Emilio. "La poesía de Blas de Otero." (Discurso inaugural del año académico, 1955-56, Universidad de Oviedo) (Oviedo, 1955)

Aleixandre, Vicente. *Vida del poeta: el amor y la poesía.* (Discurso leído ante la Real Academia Española el día 22 de enero de 1950) (Madrid, 1950)

——————. *Algunos caracteres de la nueva poesía española* (Madrid, 1955)

Alonso, Dámaso. *Poetas españoles contemporáneos* (Madrid, 1952)

——————. (with Carlos Bousoño) *Seis calas en la expresión literaria española* (Madrid, 1951)

Babín, María Teresa. *El mundo poético de Federico García Lorca* (San Juan de Puerto Rico, 1954)

Bousoño, Carlos. *La poesía de Vicente Aleixandre* (Madrid, 1950)

——————. *Teoría de la expresión poética* (Madrid, 1952)

Bowra, Cecil Maurice. *The Creative Experiment* (London, 1949)

Bremond, Abbé Henri. *La Poésie pure* (Paris, 1926)

Breton, André. *Manifeste du Surréalisme* (Paris, 1924)

Cano, José Luis. *De Machado a Bousoño* (Madrid, 1955)

——————. *Poesía española del siglo XX de Unamuno a Blas de Otero* (Madrid, 1960)

Cernuda, Luis. *Estudios sobre poesía española contemporánea* (Madrid, 1957)

Cirlot, Juan Eduardo. *Introducción al surrealismo* (Madrid, 1953)

Clovard, Henri. *Histoire de la littérature française du Symbolisme à nos jours* (2 vols.) (Paris, 1949)

Croce, Benedetto. *Estética* (Madrid, 1912)

Curtius, Ernst Robert. *European Literature and the Latin Middle Ages* (London, 1953)

Diccionario de literatura española (Madrid, 1949), 2nd edition (Madrid, 1953)

Díaz-Plaja, Guillermo. *La poesía lírica española* (Barcelona, 1937), 2nd edition (Barcelona, 1948)

Flys, Jaroslaw M. *El lenguaje poético de Federico García Lorca* (Madrid, 1955)

Gallego Morell, Antonio. *Vida y poesía de Gerardo Diego* (Barcelona, 1956)

García Gómez, Emilio. *Poemas arábigoandaluces* (Madrid, 1930)

Garciasol, Ramón de. *Una pregunta mal hecha: ¿qué es la poesía?* (Madrid, 1954)

Giménez Caballero, Ernesto. *Arte y estado* (Madrid, 1935)

Gómez de la Serna, Ramón. *Los ismos.* 2nd edition (Buenos Aires, 1943)

Góngora, Luis de. *Las soledades* (Nuevamente publicadas por Dámaso Alonso) (Madrid, 1927)

González Muela, Joaquín. *El Lenguaje poético de la generación Guillén-Lorca* (Madrid, 1955)

Guerrero Zamora, Juan. *Nueva nómina de la poesía contemporánea* (2 entregas) (Madrid, 1948)

——————. *Noticia de Miguel Hernández* (Madrid, 1951)

——————. *Miguel Hernández poeta (1910-1942)* (Madrid, 1955)

Gullón, Ricardo and Blecua, José Manuel. *La poesía de Jorge Guillén* (Zaragoza, 1949)

Hierro, José. *Quince días de vacaciones* (Santander, 1951)
Homenaje a Antonio Machado. Conferencias dadas en los cursos de verano para extranjeros en Segovia, los días 25 a 28 de julio de 1951 (Segovia, 1952)

Lind, George Rudolf. *Jorge Guillens "Cántico"* (Frankfurt am Main, 1955)
Lorenzo, Pedro de. *Fantasía en la plazuela* (Madrid, 1953) (See pp. 179-183 on the *Juventud Creadora*)

Machado, Antonio. *La guerra* (Madrid, 1937)
Moreno Báez, Enrique. *La poesía de Juan Ramón Jiménez*. Conferencia leída el 13 de septiembre de 1947 y publicada en homenaje a Juan Ramón Jiménez por el Ayuntamiento de Moguer. (Moguer, 1948)
Muñoz Rojas, José Antonio. *Sobre los poemas recientes de T. S. Eliot* (Offprint of *Arbor*, 49, [Madrid, 1950])

Nadeau, Maurice. *Histoire du Surréalisme* (Paris, 1945)
Neddermann, Emmy. Die symbolistichen Stilelement im Werke von *Juan Ramón Jiménez*. Hamburger Studien zu Volkstum und Kultur der Romanen. (Hamburg, 1935)

Ortega y Gasset, José. *La deshumanización del arte e ideas sobre la novela* (Madrid, 1925)
Ory, Carlos Edmundo de. *El bosque* (Santander, 1952)
——————. *Nuestro tiempo: Poesía* (with Darío Suro: *Nuestro tiempo: Pintura*) (Madrid, 1951)

Palau, Graciela. *Vida y obra de Juan Ramón Jiménez* (Madrid, 1957)

Río, Angel del. *Vida y obras de Federico García Lorca* (Zaragoza, 1952)
——————. *Antología general de la literatura española* (2 vols.) (Madrid and New York, 1954)
Romancero de la guerra civil (Madrid, 1936)

Salinas, Pedro. *La poesía de Rubén Darío* (Buenos Aires, 1948)
Sarmiento, E[duardo]. *The Religious Sense in Some Contemporary Spanish Poets* (Reprinted from *The Downside Review* [Exeter, 1937])
Serpa, Alberto de. *Poetas . . . Poetas . . .* (Diário do I Congresso de Poesia em Segóvia) (Oporto, 1952)

Trend, John Brande. *Federico García Lorca* (Cambridge, 1951)
——————. *Rubén Darío* (Cambridge, 1953)
——————. *Antonio Machado* (Oxford, 1953)

Valverde, José María. *Estudios sobre la palabra poética* (Madrid, 1952)
Vivanco, Luis Felipe. *Introducción a la poesía española contemporánea* (Madrid, 1957)

Zurbiria, Ramón de. *La poesía de Antonio Machado* (Madrid, 1955)

d) *Anthologies of poetry:*

Aguirre, José Manuel. *Antología de la poesía contemporánea* (Zaragoza, 1961)

Albi, José de and Fuster, Joan. *Antología del surrealismo español* (*Verbo*, 23-25, [Alicante, 1952])

Alonso, Dámaso. *Poesía española. Antología. Poesía de la Edad Media y poesía de tipo tradicional.* Selección, prólogo, notas y vocabulario por Dámaso Alonso) (Madrid, 1935)

Antología consultada de la joven poesía española. (Santander, 1952)

Antología de "Adonais." (Madrid, 1953)

Antología de poesía española 1954-1955. Recopilada por Rafael Millán. (Madrid, 1955)

Antología de poesía española 1955-1956. Recopilada por Rafael Millán. (Madrid, 1956)

Antología de poesía española 1956-1957. Recopilada por Rafael Millán. (Madrid, 1957)

Antología de poesía española 1957-1958. Recopilada por Jiménez Martos. (Madrid, 1958)

Antología de poesía española 1958-1959. Recopilada por Jiménez Martos. (Madrid, 1959)

Antología de poesía española 1959-1960. Recopilada por Jiménez Martos. (Madrid, 1960)

Antología de poesía española 1960-1961. Recopilada por Jiménez Martos. (Madrid, 1961)

Antología parcial de la Poesía Contemporánea. Supplement to *Espadaña* (León, 1944-1945)

Azcoaga, Enrique. *Panorama de la poesía moderna española.* (Buenos Aires, 1953)

Bofill, Jaime and Gutiérrez, Fernando. *La poesía alemana de los primitivos al romanticismo* (Barcelona, 1947)

Cano, José Luis. *Antología de los poetas andaluces contemporáneos* (Madrid, 1952)
—————. *Antología de la nueva poesía española* (Madrid, 1958)

Carrasquer, Francisco. *Antología de poetas holandeses contemporáneos.* (Selección, versión y prólogo de Francisco Carrasquer) (Madrid, 1958)

Castellet, José María. *Veinte años de poesía española 1939-1959* (Barcelona, 1960)

Conde, Carmen. *Poesía femenina española viviente. Antología* (Madrid, 1954)

Crespo, Angel. *Antología de la nueva poesía portuguesa* (Madrid, 1961)
Crusat, Paulina. *Antología de poetas catalanes contemporáneos* (Madrid, 1952)

Diego, Gerardo. *Poesía española. Antología 1915-1931* (Madrid, 1932)
——————. *Poesía española. Antología (contemporáneos).* 2nd edition (Madrid, 1934)

Engberg, Greta and Ramos, Vicente. *Poetas suecos contemporáneos* (Madrid, 1961)

González, Fernando. *Las mil mejores poesías de la literatura universal* (Selección, ordenación y prólogo de Fernando González) (2 vols.) (Valladolid, n.d. [1953])
González Alegre, Ramón. *Antología de la poesía gallega contemporánea* (Introducción, versión y notas de Ramón González Alegre) (Madrid, 1959)
González-Ruano, César. *Antología de poetas españoles en lengua castellana* (Barcelona, 1946)

Manent, M[aría]. *La poesía inglesa* (Translated by M. Manent) (3 vols.) (Barcelona, 1945-1948)
Martos, Jiménez. *Nuevos poetas españoles* (Madrid, 1961)
Molho, Mauricio and Escandon, Blanca G. de. *Poetas ingleses "metafísicos" del siglo XVII* (Madrid, 1945)
Moreno, Alfonso. *Poesía española actual* (Madrid, 1946)

Onís, Federico de. *Antología de la poesía española e hispanoamericana* (Madrid, 1934)

Pemán, José María. *Poesía nueva de Jesuítas* (Madrid, 1948)

Rodríguez Alcalde, Leopoldo. *Antología de la poesía francesa religiosa* (Madrid, 1947)

Sáinz de Robles, Federico Carlos. *Historia y antología de la poesía española (en lengua castellana) del siglo XIV al XX* (Madrid, 1948), 2nd edition (Madrid, 1951)
Salom, Soliman. *Poetas turcos contemporáneos* (Selección, versión, prólogo y notas de Soliman Salom) (Madrid, 1959)
Scarpa, Roque Esteban. *Poesía española contemporánea* (Santiago de Chile, 1953)

e) *Articles and poems of special interest published in periodicals:*

Alonso, Dámaso. "La injusticia social en la literatura española." In *Hora de España,* 2, February, 1947, Valencia.

Bleiberg, Germán. "Juan Ramón Jiménez." In *Diccionario de literatura española.*

——————. "El lírico absoluto: Juan Ramón Jiménez." In *Clavileño*, 10, July-August, 1951, Madrid.

Brennan, Gerald. Article on recent Spanish books in *New York Times*, October 11th, 1953.

Caba, Pedro. "La decadencia de la poesía lírica." In *La estafeta literaria*, 7, June, 1944, Madrid.

Cirlot, Juan Eduardo. "Arbol agónico." In *Fantasía*, 16, June, 1945, Madrid.

Crónica del centenario de Góngora. 1 and 2, 1927, Madrid.

Curtius, Ernst Robert. "La poesía de Jorge Guillén." In *Insula*, January, 1952, Madrid.

Gaos, Vicente. "De Luis Rosales a José García Nieto." In *La estafeta literaria*, 25, 1946, Madrid.

García Baena, Pablo. "Rumor oculto." In *Fantasía*, 38, January, 1946, Madrid.

García Nieto, José. "La poesía joven." In *La estafeta literaria*, 5, March, 1944, Madrid.

——————. " 'Poesía española' es una revista objetiva, amplia e integradora." In *Correo literario*, 43, March, 1952, Madrid.

González Muela, Joaquín. "El aspecto verbal de la poesía moderna española." In *Revista de filología española*, 35, 1951, Madrid.

Hernández, Miguel. "Quien te ha visto y quien te ve." In *Cruz y raya*, July-September, 1934, Madrid.

Huidobro, Vicente. "Arte poética." In *Agora*, 15-16, January-February, 1958, Madrid.

Jiménez, Juan Ramón. "Recuerdo a Ortega y Gasset." In *Clavileño*, 24, November-December, 1953, Madrid.

——————. "Toda la luz nunca vista." Poem first published in *Insula*, 92, August, 1953, Madrid.

——————. "Eco de dama de soledad." In *Poesía española*, 12, December, 1952, Madrid.

"Juventud española: una ética, una política y un estado." In *El español*, April 17th, 1943.

Ley, Charles David. "Some Spanish Poets of Today." In *Bulletin of Hispanic Studies*, 86, 1945, Liverpool.

——————. "The Poetry of Germán Bleiberg." In *Bulletin of Hispanic Studies*, 101, 1949, Liverpool.

——————. "Los poetas de 'Garcilaso.' " In *Garcilaso*, 35-36, March-April, 1946, Madrid.

Luis, Leopoldo de. "La poesía de Carlos Bousoño." In *Papeles de Son Armadans*, February, 1962.

Montesinos, Rafael. "El polvo de los pies." In *Cuadernos hispanoamericanos*, 133, January, 1961, Madrid.

Morales, Rafael. *Mensajes de poesía,* 8, November, 1941, Vigo. (Poetical theories).

Muñoz Rojas, José Antonio. Translation of "The Hound of Heaven." In *Cruz y raya,* 15, June, 1934, Madrid.

Ory, Carlos Edmundo de. "El teléfono en la poesía." In *Fantasía,* 12, September, 1944, Madrid.

"Poesía social" (Questionnaire). In *Correo literario,* February, 1953, Madrid.

Revuelta, Jesús. "Por qué no nos gusta el Quijote." In *El español,* January, 1943, Madrid.
————. "Necesidad de un tempismo literario. Lo poético, lo heroico y lo religioso." In *El español,* October 4th, 1943, Madrid.

Ridruejo, Dionisio. "Cronos y Ceres en Valladolid." In *Arriba,* December, 1945, Madrid.

Sahagún, Carlos. "Nacimiento de Venus." In *Agora,* 15-16, January-February, 1958, Madrid.

Valverde, José María. "Nuevas elegías." In *Fantasía,* 17, July, 1945, Madrid.

Wilson, Professor Edward Meryon. "Guillén and Quevedo on Death." In *Atlante,* Vol. I, No. 1, January, 1953, London.

f) *Other Spanish periodicals and poetry booklets mentioned:*

Caballo verde para la poesía. Madrid, 1935-1936. Editor, Pablo Neruda. Printer, Manuel Altolaguirre.
Carmen. Revista chica de poesía española. Madrid, 1927-1928.
Correo literario. Madrid, 1950- .

El español. 1st period. Madrid, 1942-1947.

Hordino. Collection of books of prose and verse. Santander, 1951-1953. Editor, Carlos Salomón.
Hora de España. Madrid and Valencia, 1937-1939.

Insula. Madrid, 1944- .

La estafeta literaria. Madrid, 1944- .
Lola. Amiga y suplemento de *Carmen.* Madrid, 1927.

Norte. Collection of poetry booklets. San Sebastián, 1947-1950.

Tito hombre. Collection of books of prose and verse. Santander, 1951-1953. Editor, José Hierro.

g) *Reviews primarily devoted to poetry, from 1939 onwards:*

Acanto. Supplement to *Cuadernos de literatura.* Editor, José García Nieto. Madrid, 1947-1948.

Advige. Editor, Diego Sánchez del Real. Córdoba, 1951-1955.

Aglae. Editor, Manuel Alvarez Ortega. Córdoba, 1951-1953.

Agora. Cuadernos de poesía. Editor, Rafael Millán. Madrid, 1951- .

Alba. Hojas de poesía. Editor, Ramón González-Alegre Bálgoma. La Coruña and Vigo, 1951-1952.

Albores del espíritu. Editor, Francisco Adrados Fernández. Tomelloso, 1946.

Alcándara. (Continuation of *Almenara*). Editor, Miguel Fernández. Melilla, 1952.

Aldebarán. Editors, Carlos Romero, Fernando S. Dragó, José Ramón Marra López. Madrid, 1955.

Alfar. Editor, Miguel Fernández. Cádiz, 1949 (typewritten).

Alfoz. Editors, Mariano Roldán Villén, Antonio Gómez Alfaro, Rafael Osma Rodríguez, Carmelo Casaño Salido. Córdoba, 1952-1953.

Alisio. Editor, Pino Ojeda. Las Palmas de Gran Canaria, 1952.

Aljaba. Mensaje poético. Editor, Emilio Ruiz Parra. Jaén, 1951-1953.

Aljibe. Published by the Faculty of Philosophy and Letters, Sevilla, 1951-1954.

Alma. Editors, María Sola, Miguel Angel de Argumosa. Madrid, 1949-1950.

Almenara. Hojas de poesía. Editors, José Manuel Aguirre, Pablo de Antoñana. Zaragoza, 1950-1952.

Al-Motamid. Verso y prosa. Spanish and Arabic. Editor, Trinidad Sánchez Mercader. Larache and Tetuán, 1947-1955.

Alor. Hojas de poesía. Editor, Francisco Rodríguez Pereda. Badajoz, 1950- .

Ambito. Poesía y polémica. Editor, Manuel Pinillos. Gerona, 1951-1952.

Andábata. Editors, L. Gracia Torrecillas, Carmelo P. Masías. Senes de Alcubierre (Huesca), 1952 (typewritten).

Angelus. Editor, R. P. Francisco Juberías, C. M. F. Zafra. 1953- .

Arcilla y pájaro. Cáceres, 1953.

Armonías del Duero. Zamora, 1953.

Arquero. Editors, Julio Mariscal Montes, Mir Jordana, Gala Velasco. Madrid, 1952.

Arquero de poesía. Editor, Manuel Pareja. 1952-1954.

Arte joven. Editors, Vicente Ramos, Adolfo Lizón and others. Alicante, 1940.

Atalaya. Editor, Agustín Luque. Madrid, 1953.

Atica. Poesía, Vida, Crítica. Editor, Pedro Ardoy. Barcelona, 1951-1953.

Aturuxo. Editors, Miguel G. Vidal, Tomás Barros. El Ferrol, 1952- .

Avance de poesía. Supplement to *Santa Cruz.* Valladolid, 1948-1950.

Avellano. Granada, 1945.

Axati. Editor, Juan Cervera-Sanchis. Lora del Río, 1960 (typewritten).

Azarbe. Editors, Salvador Jiménez, Juan García Abellán, Jaime Campmany, José Manuel Díez. Murcia, 1946-1948.
Azemar. Barcelona, 1952.

Baladre. Editors, Eugenio Martínez Pastor, Jesús Hernández. Cartagena and Orihuela, 1956.
Bernia. Editors, Vicente Ramos, Pintor L. Casanova. Alicante, 1951-1953.
Brisa. Editor, E. López. Valencia, 1955 (typewritten).

Caleta. Córdoba, 1953-   .
Cancionero. Pliegos de poesía y arte. Editor, Martín Alonso. Madrid, 1941.
Cántico. Hojas de poesía. Editors, Ricardo Molina, Pablo García Baena, Juan Bernier. Córdoba, 1947-1948, 1954.
Capitel. Editor, Angel García López. Jerez de la Frontera, n.d.
Caracol. Editor, Víctor Catena. Granada, 1950.
Caracola. Editor, José Luis Estrada. Málaga, 1952-   .
Clavero. Salamanca, 1956 (typewritten).
Codal. Supplement to *Berceo.* Logroño, 1950-1952.
Corcel. Pliegos de poesía. Editor, Ricardo Juan Blasco. Valencia, 1942-1946.
Cuadernos de poesía. Editor, Jesús Nieto Pena. Málaga, 1941.
Cumbres. Editor, Emilio Ruiz Parra. Utrera, 1949-1952.

Dabo. Pliegos de poesía. Palma de Mallorca, n.d.
Doña Endrina. Editor, Antonio Fernández Molina. Guadalajara, 1951-   .

El gato verde. Editors, Alejandro Gago, Adolfo Castaño. Santander, 1951-1952.
El gorrión. Editors, Francisco J. Bahone, Antonio Barrientos. Cádiz, 1960.
Elica. Supplement to *El monte Carmelo.* Published by the Discalced Carmelites. Burgos, 1950-1952.
El jardín de los frailes. Supplement to *Escorial.* Editor, Demetrio Castro Villacañas. (Single number.) Madrid, 1950.
El laberinto. Editor, Rafael Millán. Madrid, 1956.
El molino de papel. Editor, Amable Cuenca. Cuenca. 1955-   .
El pájaro de paja. Carta circular de la Poesía. Editor, Gabino-Alejandro Carriedo. Madrid, 1950-   .
El pobre hombre. Editor, Enrique Sordo. Santander, 1948-1949.
El postillón. Editor, Rafael Manzano. Barcelona, 1955-1956.
El sobre literario. Selección de entregas. (Printed in sets in envelope) Editor, Ricardo Orozco. Valencia, 1950-1952.
Entregas de poesía. Revista de poesía y ensayos. Editors, Juan Ramón Masoliver, Fernando Gutiérrez. Barcelona, 1944-1947.
Espadaña. Revista de Poesía y Crítica. Editors, Antonio G. de Lama, Eugenio de Nora, Victoriano Crémer. León, 1944-1950.
Estría. Cuadernos de Poesía que edita el Colegio Español de Roma. Editor, Father José María Javierre. Rome, 1951-   .

Estrofa. Editor, Julián Velasco de Toledo. Burgos, 1953-1956.

Fantasía. Cuadernos poéticos. (Single number.) Editor, Luis Ballester Segura. Valencia, 1951.

Floresta de varia poesía. Cuaderno literario de los anales de la Universidad Hispalense. Editor, Francisco López Estrada. Sevilla, 1951-1953.

Gánigo. Editor, E. Gutiérrez Albela. Santa Cruz de Tenerife, 1953-   .

Garcilaso. Juventud Creadora. Editor, José García Nieto. Madrid, 1943-1946.

Gevora. Badajoz, 1952.

Guadalquivir. Entregas poéticas. Editor, Javier Lasso de la Vega. Sevilla, 1951-1952.

Halcón. Revista de Poesía. Editor, Luis López Anglada. Valladolid, 1945-1949.

Horizontal. Editor, Antonio Manuel Campoy. 1946-1949.

Ifach. Anejo literario del I.S.O. de Alicante. Editors, Vicente Ramos, Manuel Molina. Alicante, 1948.

Intimidad poética, de los jóvenes intelectuales de España. Published by the Grupo de Amigos de la Poesía. Alicante, 1943-1945.

Intus. Revista de poesía y crítica. Editor, Julio García Morejón. Salamanca, 1951-1952.

Isla. Verso y prosa. Editor, Pedro Pérez Clotet. Jerez de la Frontera, 1937-1940.

Ixbiliah. Editor, María de los Reyes Fuentes. Sevilla, 1954-1955.

Jaire. Poesía de Dios. Editada por sacerdotes pacenses. Editors, Juan María Robles, Francisco Horrillo. 1954-1955.

Jinjol. Pliegos de Poesía. Editor, Head of the S.E.U. (Single number.) Murcia, 1952.

Ketama. Suplemento literario de *Tamuda.* Editor, Jacinto López Gorgé. Tetuán, 1953-1957.

La calandria. Editor, Enrique Navarro. Barcelona, 1951-1953.

La caña gris. Editor, Vicente Ventura Beltrán. Valencia, 1960-   .

La isla de los ratones. Hojas de poesía. Editor, Manuel Arce. Santander, 1948-1952.

La luna negra. Editors, José Manuel Cardona, José María Rodríguez Méndez. Barcelona, 1952.

La niña. Editors, Diego J. Figueroa, Pedro Bargueño, Juan Manuel Aguirre. Huelva, 1954.

Loreley. Sevilla, n.d.

Luces y sombras. Las Palmas de Gran Canaria, 1946.

Madrigal. Puerto Real (Cádiz), 1952-   .

Malvarrosa. Editor, Manuel Ostos Gabella. Valencia, 1954-

Manantial. Cuadernos de poesía y crítica. Editors, Jacinto López Gorgé, Pío Gómez Nisa. Melilla, 1949-1952.
Mensaje. (Poesía.) Published by the Círculo de Bellas Artes. Tenerife, 1945-1956.
Mensajes de poesía. Editor, Eduardo Moreiras. Vigo, 1951-1953.
Molino de papel. Editor, Antonio Gallego Morell. Granada, 1954-1955.

Numen. Revista popular de poesía y estudios poéticos. Editor, Julio Sigüerza. Vigo, n.d.

Pajaritas de papel. Editor, Juan Bonet Gelabert. (Single number.) Palma de Mallorca, 1951.
Papel azul. Supplement to *Gibralfaro.* Editors, José A. Muñoz Rojas, Alfonso Canales. Málaga, 1951-1952.
Pilar. Letras y arte. Editor, Antonio de Zubiaurre. Zaragoza, 1945.
Platero. Editor, Fernando Quiñones. Cádiz, 1951-1954.
Pleamar. Editor, Mario Angel Marrodán. 1952- .
Poesía castellana. Editor, J. Enríquez de la Rúa. Zamora, 1955.
Poesía de España. Editors, Gabino-Alejandro Carriedo, Angel Crespo. Madrid, 1960- .
Poesía española. Editor, José García Nieto. Madrid, 1952- .
Posío. Editor, José Luis Varela. Orense, 1945-1946.
Proel. Verso y prosa. Editor, Pedro Gómez Cantolla. Santander, 1944-1950.
Punto. (Continuation of *Indice.*) Editor, Tomás Seral y Casas. Madrid, 1948-1949.

Raíz. Cuadernos literarios de la Facultad de Filosofía y Letras. Editor, Juan Guerrero Zamora. Madrid, 1948-1949.
Rocamador. Edita: El Grupo de Poesía del Círculo Cultural del Movimiento. Palencia, 1955- .

Sazón. Murcia, 1951.
Sigüenza. Editor, Vicente Ramos. (Single number.) Alicante, 1943.

Tabarca. Alicante, 1944.
Thalassia. Cádiz, 1955 (typewritten).
Trilce. Editors, Antonio Leyva Fernández, José Antonio Suárez de Puga. Guadalajara, 1952-1953.

Uriel. Editor, Gerardo Ruiz, C.M.F. Logroño, 1954- .

Verbo. Cuadernos literarios. Editor, José Albi. Alicante, 1949- .
Verde viento. Antología viva de poesía y pensamiento. Editors, José E. Rodríguez Méndez, Miguel de la Villa. Barcelona, 1949-1950.
Versos a media noche. Madrid, 1952.
Vértice. Supplement to *Studium.* Edited by the Colegio de Teología de PP. Capuchinos. Pamplona, 1948- .